Cabinets
Bookcases
& Closets

Cabinets
Bookcases
& Closets

Tom Philbin

CREATIVE HOMEOWNER PRESS®

A DIVISION OF FEDERAL MARKETING CORPORATION,
24 PARK WAY, UPPER SADDLE RIVER, NEW JERSEY 07458

Manufactured in United States of America

Current Printing (last digit)
10 9

Editor: Shirley M. Horowitz
Assistant Editor: Marilyn M. Auer
Art Director: Léone Lewensohn
Additional drawings: Paul Sochacki

We wish to extend our thanks to the many designers, companies, and other contributors who allowed us to use their materials and gave us advice. Their names, addresses, and individual indentifications of their contributions can be found on *page 160*.

LC: 80-69620
ISBN: 0-932944-21-3

CREATIVE HOMEOWNER PRESS®
BOOK SERIES
A DIVISION OF FEDERAL
MARKETING CORPORATION
24 PARK WAY,
UPPER SADDLE RIVER, NJ 07458

FOREWORD

This book recognizes that there are few shortcuts when it comes to building a solid cabinet or bookcase, assuming that the builder wants it to be at least as good as products that are purchased already made. Any high-quality piece of furniture will require time, effort, and knowledge. In light of this, we suggest that you carefully read all of Section I — which covers techniques and materials — before you begin work on any of the projects. Not only will this enable you to do a better job, but a job that will suit your needs exactly. For example: the project may specify a particular material, such as birch plywood; if you cannot find birch plywood in your local lumberyards, you will find other options when you review Chapter 4, "Basic Materials."

A thorough reading of Section I can serve you in another important way: it will give you a basic grasp of cabinetry and bookcase making. You will find principles of cutting, measuring, finishing and other information required for the job. After mastering these principles, the bookcases and cabinets within this book — and variations on them — will be within your reach by applying what you have learned.

There are additional hints and tips sprinkled throughout the chapters in Section I; their application may rescue a difficult situation. For example, a number of the projects in Section II require that duplicate pieces of material be cut. In Chapter 10 you will find information on how to make jigs which will make such cutting jobs easier and faster.

The cabinet and bookcase projects offered in Section II vary in complexity, but we trust that there is something here for everyone — even those who had not, until now, considered building anything.

Tom Philbin

CONTENTS

PROJECTS

1 Storage Plus

This storage/divider unit has access from both sides. Designed from simple construction principles, this divider/cabinet fits into a variety of spaces. Directions for building this unit appear in the Section II Projects.

A storage unit can be designed to meet your specific needs. This unit could also serve as a room divider. It holds books, records, and a hidden stereo system. Because it has been stained to match the wood used elsewhere in the room, the piece blends well. For mobility and versatility, you can put this type of unit on several large casters (see Chapter 6).

The primary reason for building cabinets and bookcases is to expand storage space. However, these units can serve as structural elements and should also enhance decor.

AS STRUCTURAL ELEMENTS

With the cost of housing spiraling upward, many homeowners are trying to get more from their current homes. One answer is to re-evaluate and rearrange the space available, which can be often divided into more usable parcels.

Dividers

A handsome cabinet or bookcase can serve as a divider to visually separate various areas of the home. One such use could be in a children's room. To create a degree of privacy, a simple-floor-to-ceiling divider can divide the one original room into two rooms, giving each youngster the feeling that the area is a personal refuge — a place that is his or her own.

There are many ways such cabinets can be built, depending on the needs of the occupants. For example, if one of the youngsters is a devoted reader, one side of the unit can be built to house books. The other person might be more interested in models or collections, and so the other side of the divider can be built with open cabinets to display these items. Since both young people would have other possessions to store as well, building in drawers on the bottom half of the unit can add storage potential, and free up room space.

Dividers can also be used to segment areas in the attic and basement into rooms. Such units can be built solid to completely isolate each section, just as though the divider were a wall.

One classic use of cabinets and bookshelves as dividers — where privacy is not a factor — is the L-shaped living room/dining area with the dining room in the short leg of the L. Here, a divider works to separate the areas. A large room such as a family room, where the activities are diverse, would also benefit.

For nonprivacy dividers, the unit you build need not be large; a floor-to-ceiling structure that is three to five feet wide will be sufficient to give the impression of separation. Dividers of almost any height can also be positioned to direct foot traffic.

Better Traffic Flow
Cabinets and bookcases can also be located so as to create better traffic flow. For example, if traffic currently feeds into a living room directly from a front entry, thus disrupting the activities of people in the room, judicious placement of a cabinet near the door can reroute traffic into a more efficient pattern.

In the kitchen a freestanding island cabinet can serve as an attractive barrier against cross-traffic that interferes with the activities of the homemaker. This is because an open kitchen invites people to take the shortest distance between two points, which is often right across the work centers in the kitchen. If there is a freestanding cabinet in the middle of the room, the tendency will be for the traffic to go around it. The cabinet will also offer additional counter and storage space. Another useful configuration is a cabinet placed between the kitchen and dining area. This can serve as a bar, eating counter, or room divider.

DECORATIVE ASSETS
Display
Cabinets can also be used for display in the main living areas of the home — and storage need not be sacrificed! For example, a cabinet against the wall can have large drawers below with open shelves above that display valued china, trophies or photos. Illuminated with a couple of track lights, this display center can add a dramatic dimension to the decor.

Bookcases can also be used for display, because the books are attractive and add warmth and character to a room.

Finishes
Many people think of cabinets and bookcases as merely utilitarian, but they can add to the appearance of a room, particularly since there are so many finishes that can be used to harmonize with the home's architectural or design style. There are, of course, regular wood finishes; however, the home craftsperson can choose from a wide variety of other materials to add richness, distinction and color to the newly built pieces. Finishes will be found in Chapters 10 and 11.

The end base cabinet in this kitchen serves as both a storage unit and a room divider. The kitchen area limits are defined by the end cabinet, which also offers additional counter space and storage.

Useful storage shelves can be fitted into many unexpected places. These shelves are sized for specific items. The clear jars allow one to see contents at a glance and make the colors a decorative aspect of the room.

The kitchen island can be made any needed size and provide working and storage areas or a snack table. It will help to separate cooking and eating areas and to direct foot traffic away from food preparation areas.

Paints and Stains. The most basic finishes, as detailed later, leave the wood grain intact by letting it show through the clear wood or colored finish. You can also find products that simulate antique finishes.

Paint, of course, is available in an infinite number of hues. Look over the color chips of manufacturers. The colors can lend a wood grain effect to material such as particleboard or wood that does not have a grain pattern, or can depart from traditional natural tones to create nearly any color you wish.

Cabinets or bookcases which are painted are usually positioned outside formal areas such as living rooms, because most people feel that paint does not afford a fine finished

It is possible to use less expensive lumber if you are planning to paint your shelves. These specially-sized shelves have been painted the same as the kitchen cabinets. The shelves will be easy to maintain with soap and water. The louvered shutters are also painted to match.

This laundry work area is built of unit sections. Part can be installed and in use while another section is being constructed.

This built-in unit was designed and finished to complement the room and meet all storage problems. All shelves adjust so books and magazines may be rearranged. The bottom support is recessed for easy cleaning. Painted to match the walls, the unit suits the room.

look. However, if applied properly paint can offer a beautiful result and, as an additional positive factor, it is washable. The kitchen and bath are prime areas for painted woodwork — wherever items get hard use.

As some of our examples show, paint can be particularly effective for decorative accents. Most often, cabinets and bookcases are painted only one color, but this limitation is being overcome. A two-tone or stripe effect can add personality and interest. Note, for example, the multi-color cabinets in the laundry room in the accompanying photograph. This can be achieved without a great effort, and the results are quite dramatic.

Ceramic Tile. Another good finishing material is ceramic tile, which comes in deep tones and medium shades as well as patterns, and in a range of textures. Sizes and shapes include hexagons, triangles and diamonds, plus the traditional squares and rectangles. The grout, used to fill spaces between tiles, now also can be purchased in various colors. This provides extra design possibilities, and avoids the dirt-collecting white grout so often found in older ceramic tile surfaces.

While primarily used as a surfacing material on countertops, tile is an excellent insert material for cabinet doors. As one of the photos shows, a patterned tile (in this case white and blue) inserted in a door can add contrast and depth to cabinets of simpler design or of plainer wood.

Resilient Flooring. Resilient flooring tiles (12″ x 12″) can be used as an accent material, or as a top surface covering. The only requirement is that the cabinet surface be clean and dry where the tiles will be installed. You can apply the tiles with adhesive, or use the self-adhesive type; both types come with installation instructions.

The Butcher Block Look. In recent years the butcher block look has gained in popularity; it is an easy surface to add to the top of a cabinet.

Butcher block consists of alternating strips of hardwood — usually walnut and maple — which are preassembled into pieces normally 25 inches wide, with lengths up to 12 feet (though longer sections may be bought) and thicknesses of ⅞ inch, 1½ inches and 1¾ inches

There is no mystery involved in applying butcher block. It is cut to the size required using a circular or other type of saw or a router (but you must use a bit that can go through hardwood).

Plastic Laminate. Because plastic laminate is hard, impervious to damage from

Open shelves are practical for items which are used frequently. This single shelf provides easy access and keeps work area clear.

This kitchen combines many materials, but has a unifying tone of earth colors. The wood, the tile and the brick have distinct and different textures, but the dark grout used with the tile and the dark mortar used with the brick, enable the eye to see the whole area rather than the individual units.

The nature of redwood allows its use in baths and other usually damp areas, if the wood is protected by several coats of sealer.

Older cabinets can be rejuvenated with paint and wallpaper. The paper has been applied to cabinet doors and drawers.

most contact, and to cleaning, it is also usually thought of as a counter-surfacing material.

But these virtues make it an excellent covering for an entire cabinet. Its broad range of colors and textures rivals that of tile but, like tile, it is expensive. Thus, it is usually a good idea to restrict its use in full covering jobs to small relatively small pieces.

Wallcoverings. Wallcoverings may also be used to finish cabinets and to visually tie together the overall decorating scheme of a room.

Wallcoverings can be applied to the insides of cabinet doors using the same pattern and color as that on the walls. Many manufacturers also offer curtains in the same design as the wallcovering. If you are going to hang wall coverings on cabinets in the bathroom, then a moisture-proof material such as vinyl or vinyl-clad should be used. One of the newest coverings available for this type of application is a new self-adhesive vinyl from Style Tex. The company says that that gauge is thicker than other self-adhesive vinyls, making it easier to work with.

Design Consistency

Since cabinets and bookcases are part of the decor, it is important that the new furniture pieces harmonize with the existing decorating scheme or furniture finishes. There are a number of considerations when establishing this sort of harmony.

Color. While there are color rules on which hues or shades match or coordinate well, the judgment must be based on your own taste. We suggest that, whenever possible, you obtain a swatch of the color you consider using — paint chip, strip of wood, or piece of fabric — and hold it against other items in the room to see how well it blends with them.

Size. Another consideration is the size of the bookcase or cabinet. If the other furniture in the room is average-sized, you may not want to add a large unit because it will appear disproportionately large and upset the balance of the room.

Style. Finally, the style of the piece should harmonize with the rest of the items in the room. If you have modern furniture, the piece you make should have sleek, modern lines. If your other furniture is Colonial, Italian Provincial, or Mediterranean, then stick to building the same style.

Matching the new cabinet or bookcase to what is in your home already, particularly if

In this kitchen the cabinetmaker has used the wood's natural color and grain as the room's primary decorative focus. This is one case where a clear finish without stain was sufficient.

the style is one of the ornate designs, may seem at first to be extremely difficult. Raised panels on doors, for example, often look as though they require the skill of a master craftsman to duplicate or approximate. But fortunately, such is not the case. For harmonizing you have two excellent means at your disposal. The first is the router, a sometimes ignored tool which can be indispensable. There is a tremendous array of bits available for the tool, ones that will enable you to make cuts and shapes that exist on any piece of furniture you see.

The other means of decor harmonizing — one that is often used in conjunction with the router — is application of moldings. Here we are speaking in the broad sense to include not only standard moldings, but plaques and emblems. These also come in a tremendous variety of designs and colors. By knowing the basics of cutting and assembling the molding, and the finishing options available to you, you can analyze the style you currently have and then come up with suitable "trimmings". Remember that no matter what the style, a cabinet or bookcase is basically a box to which the woodworker — you — adds the stylistic characteristics and design.

Though wood is a hard material and is usually cut at angles, it can be carved and sanded to soft, rounded shapes. The curving corners and edges of the doors and drawers in this kitchen contribute to a flowing, relaxed atmosphere.

Moldings in many styles and sizes are available to woodworkers. Molding can be applied to cabinet doors or drawers.

Because wood may be stained to any number of shades, it allows coordination with many other materials and textures. This detail of rounded cabinetry framing shows use with a contrasting texture of a wood-weave filling.

The most common reason for installing any cabinet or bookcase is to provide storage, and there are three types of structural styles available to achieve it: built-in, built-on and freestanding. In this chapter we present ideas and examples that define and illustrate these styles. We also give some general hints on their advantages and disadvantages, as well as tips on modifying units so they will more closely tie in with your individual storage needs.

STRUCTURAL DIFFERENCES
Built-ins

This refers to any cabinet or bookcase which is completely or partially built into the wall. This involves removing the wall material — usually wallboard or plaster — and mounting the unit in the cavity between the studs.

Built-ins would also include units that appear to be structurally part of the house, even though no wall material has been removed.

In some cases the entire unit is built separately and then mounted between studs, in other situations the backside of the exposed material becomes the back side of the cabinet.

The major advantage to built-ins is that they occupy a minimum of floor space. The unit is recessed the depth of the wall — usually 3⅝ inches and mounted off of the floor. This may not at first seem like much space, but built-ins work well in baths and kitchens where space is usually at a premium. You can, however, use them in any room or area of the house where the wall material can be easily removed.

For most homes, built-ins in the wall and off the floor must be fairly shallow. Their capacity is not extensive, simply because they are mounted only on the studs. For proper support, they must be kept within a certain size. (See "Installing Cabinets", Chapter 12). Built-ins may also be mounted on the floor as well as in the wall. These may be any size you wish, giving the benefit of the extra wall space without worrying about adequate support.

In some cases, cabinets or bookcases can be built into a false wall, or built into a particularly wide wall, utilizing space that otherwise might be wasted. For example, many homes have little — or sometimes large — alcoves that can be filled with a built-in bookcase or china closet. When the unit is finished, it offers a custom look to the wall, and provides a focus. Indeed, it will look as though the house was designed that particular way just to accommodate the unit.

Built-ins which go in the wall are not as practical in masonry walls, or for any wall where removing the material presents structural problems. They also are not for the apartment dweller, since there is usually a prohibition against the tenant damaging the walls in any way.

Built-on

This method calls for completely building the unit and then mounting it on the wall; it sometimes may be assembled on the wall. This configuration does not appear to be part of the house.

A built-on will look good when properly mounted. The unit must be centered on the wall and be in keeping with the overall visual impression of the other items in the room.

The built-on shares with the built-in one attribute not found with the free-standing: if mounted on a wall, the floor space beneath the built-in or built-on is left free. However, a built-on can be removed so you can take it with you if you move, something that is not possible with a built-in mounted inside the wall. After a built-on had been detached you would need to patch the wall, but the overall structure of the wall would be intact.

On the negative side, the built-on must be finished on the front and on one or both sides, something that can be avoided for a built-in which is recessed into an alcove.

Free-standing

As the name implies, this type of cabinet or bookcase stands by itself. It is not connected to the wall or to any other part of the house. These units may be stationary, or mounted on casters. Some examples of free-standing bookcases and cabinets include: room dividers, islands, or serving carts.

Free-standing units are particularly good for apartment-house living. They do not have to be fastened to anything, and therefore can be taken with you when and if you move.

Built-in units must look as if they belong in a room. These combination cabinet/bookcase units fit naturally into the areas flanking the fireplace. The same paneling that covers other walls in the room is used on the backs and sides of the bookcases.

Floor-to-ceiling windows dictated the height of the built-on bookcase/display shelves. For security, the top and bottom of each unit will have been firmly attached to the ceiling and floor. Sides should be toe-nailed to the back and the shelves attached to the sides and back before the unit is screwed onto the wall.

Shelf space should be flexibile and adjust to different needs. In planning shelf and cabinet areas, you should consider your specific situation and not be bound by "manufacturer's standard dimensions" if they are too limiting. Decide what you need and design the layout to fulfill your particular requirements.

Almost every storage problem has an answer. Here, trays are stored vertically for easy access. Dividers prevent excessive leaning and create a logical arrangement.

No matter what your requirements or space availability, storage can be designed to meet your needs. Here, a built-on has uniform-sized doors that hide odd-sized drawers. The unit shown is a commercially constructed one, but the Vertical Bathroom Storage Project in Section II will let the homeowner/cabinetmaker produce a similar piece suited to individual needs.

Structurally, free-standing units are usually more complicated to build than are the other types. This is not inevitable, and later we will give suggestions geared to overcoming this disadvantage.

Modular Units

The modular unit is most often free-standing and, while not a structural style per se, it deserves recognition as a building method.

The big advantage to building modular units is that they can be put together quickly, in assembly-line fashion. For example, in the modular cube project in Section II, all that is needed is the "how-to" for one cube. Then you can build as many as you wish to create the unit. Therefore, you can potentially turn out — as one carpenter put it — "a lot of cabinet" within a relatively short period of time because you can cut all the sides at once, all the backs one after the other, and make all the joints at the same time. When carrying this out, however, extra care must be taken with the measurements. Most carpenters build as they go along because lumber sizes can vary. Measure each piece of lumber and adjust as necessary. A nominal 2x4 can range in actual size from 1½ inch x 3½ inch to 1⅝ inch to 3⅝ inch.

Another advantage to this type of unit is that you can build it in degrees, as your time, budget and storage needs demand. For example, if building a modular bookcase, you might decide to build six cubes now. A year from now, when your storage requirements increased, you could build three additional cubes.

MODIFICATIONS AND ALTERNATIVES

While it is always helpful to look at different storage styles and units and then to choose what appeals to you, when transplanting a basic style you can run into obstacles. Often you simply do not have the space. There are several ways to overcome this problem.

One answer is to make the unit smaller. Rather than building it short and wide, you can make it tall and narrow. If you take this option, however, first determine whether you will retain the same cubic space as in the original design. For example, if there is a storage unit which is currently 3 feet wide and 4 feet high and 2 feet deep, the cubic space is 24 cubic feet. Will the new size give you as much cubic space and fulfill the same needs?

In many cases you will not need to modify an item a great deal. If, for example, you like a particular cabinet or bookcase that is too deep for your available space, cutting it down 6 inches or so in depth might still give you enough storage.

Shelves

You can also gain space by repositioning or adding shelves. Shelving is flexible. In later chapters we will show various shelf hangers — standards and brackets or pilasters — that will enable you to move shelves closer or further apart, depending on your needs. If you have many tall books, you can locate the shelves farther apart; if you have paperbacks, position the shelves correspondingly closer. The point here is to realize that the extra storage is available within the same amount of cubic feet.

PLANNING

Before you start sawing the wood, plan the project carefully and thoroughly. Make sure that the piece you will build is adequate not only for your present needs, but for future requirements. Consider not only what you will be storing in it now, but what will be going into it later. If necessary, build it larger to accommodate those future items.

Pencil, paper and eraser can be invaluable in this regard. Make a rough sketch of the project on plain paper or ½ inch box grid paper (with ½ inch equaling 1 foot in the sketch) to see how it works out.

If your project involves plywood or other large-panel materials, you can save by cutting the maximum number of pieces from each sheet. There are some suggestions on how to cut stock offered in the Chapter 4, "Basic Materials," and Chapter 11, "Time-Saving Techniques".

Any modification you make to plans or ideas presented in this book will probably not involve serious building changes. Once you know the basics of cutting, joinery and fastening, it will be as easy or as difficult as the trim, finishing and size determine. In any

Built-in or free-standing units? It is sometimes hard to tell. These cabinets are separate pieces, but the paint and wallpaper treatment makes them look built-in and a single unit. Note the lock on the door below the sink: this is a very practical addition for any area where you may be storing cleaning materials.

case, a cabinet or bookcase is a box — simple or fancy — with a back, sides, top, bottom and front, whether open or closed or with doors.

Shopping for Materials

Before buying materials and hardware for your chosen project, list the items you will need. The fewer trips to the store, the smoother and faster your progress will be. Since there have been rises in the cost of wood and plywood, it is a good idea to shop around for prices. You can call a series of local lumberyards for prices — be very specific — and also ask friends who have built such projects where they purchased their materials so that you will find the best possible price.

Needed storage was added to this room with built-in bookcases/cabinets. Painted to match the walls, and given a touch of style with simple moldings, these units appear to be a part of the room.

Although this extensive storage unit appears to be part of the original design of this room, it was added using materials which blend with those already part of the structure of the house. By following a style which complements the existing materials and architectural features, these units fit into the space as if the room had been designed for them.

3 Molding and Trim

Whether coordinating new cabinets and bookcases with existing furniture, or just trimming them as you like, a do-it-yourselfer has more limited capacity than does a cabinet shop. The shop has large machines that are capable of taking a solid piece of stock and cutting out deep designs or fancy scrollwork; the tools in the do-it-yourself arsenal do not offer this versatility. This does not mean that the do-it-yourselfer is bereft of the means to enhance newly made pieces. Using molding and a router you can trim out to achieve many of the professional effects.

MOLDING

In essence, molding works by giving the furniture item a cut-from-solid-stock look. All that is involved is to attach the molding to the face of the door, or drawer or cabinet, with brads and glue. If your joints are tight and your nails well hidden, only an extremely close scrutiny would be able to reveal that molding had been used in the three-dimensional design.

Moldings come in many different configurations. The molding may be made of softwood or hardwood; cedar, pine, fir, larch and hemlock are commonly available at lumberyards. As with lumber and plywood, however, availability depends on the particular region you live in.

You can obtain standard, unfinished molding in any length up to 16 feet, with the lengths increasing in 2 feet increments. You may also obtain it in odd-length increments — 3 feet, 5 feet, and so on — if this suits your purposes better.

Molding is available in nominal and actual sizes, similar to board sizing, with the actual size being smaller than the nominal. For example, a nominally 3 inch wide piece of case molding would actually be approximately 2⅝ inches wide. And, as with board, this is something you must keep in mind when planning your projects dimensions.

Techniques for milling molding are not perfect. Molding of the same nominal sizes will have fractional differences in the measurements. It is therefore suggested that you

Simpler even than using molding or a router is the addition of flat pieces of wood around the rim of a door to create a recess in the center. Simple butt joints or miter joints are frequently chosen for this type of construction.

buy all your molding from the same mill lot and that you hold the pieces up, superimposing one upon the others, to make sure that they are all the same size. Fractional differences in sizes can detract from the even appearance and professional-looking effect that you desire.

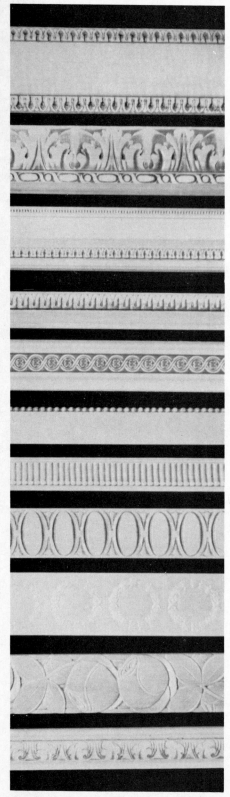

Moldings are available in a variety of fancy scrollwork as well as simpler designs.

Standard Molding

A number of standard molding styles have retained their popularity throughout the years. Following is a lineup of these basic styles. While most of these have been designed for specific uses other than furniture — such as base molding for walls — there is no prohibition against using them on a bookcase or cabinet if the molding fits into the overall design plan.

Base Shoe. This is normally used with base molding, which covers the gap between the base shoe and the floor.

Base Molding. The molding used along the bottom of walls, it is available in many styles.

Quarter Round. In cross-section, this looks like a quarter of a circle. It is most commonly used to finish corners.

Half Round. In cross-section, and in the smaller sizes, this looks like a half a circle. In the larger sizes half round molding has an oval shape.

Casing. This is probably the molding most frequently used around the house. It is used to trim edges of doors and windows, and is a very popular molding for finishing cabinets.

Mullion. This is a fluted molding which is used as vertical trim between windows.

Chair Rail. This molding was originally designed to protect walls from the backs of chairs. But today it is regularly used for decorative purposes, installed horizontally midway up the wall.

Panel Molding. If you cover a piece of cabinetry with paneling, this type of molding can come in handy in hiding the seams and will make the panel edges appear inset.

Corner Guard. This is a decorative molding, available in a V shape, for covering outside corners of pieces. An inside corner guard is also available, but it is unlikely that you would use it.

Astragal. Another decorative molding, it is normally used to divide windows.

Cove. This is the standard molding used to cover ceiling joints, but it is sometimes added to cabinets.

Specialty Moldings. In addition to standard moldings, there is a wide variety of special-use moldings available; they come with cuts made in the surface. Our advice is to visit a few lumberyards and see what is in stock so you can determine if the available moldings will fit into your project. Like other wood moldings, this type will be purchased unfinished.

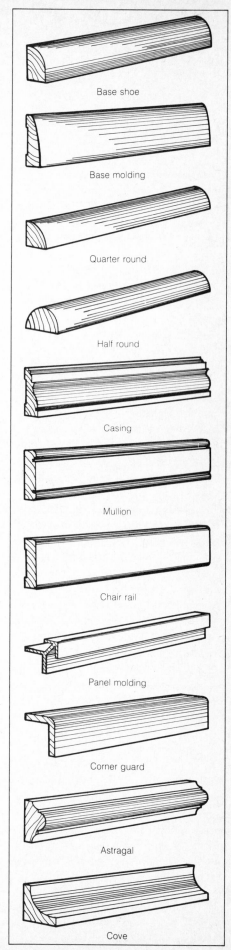

Base shoe

Base molding

Quarter round

Half round

Casing

Mullion

Chair rail

Panel molding

Corner guard

Astragal

Cove

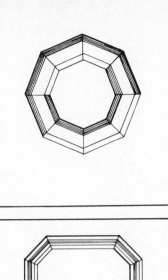

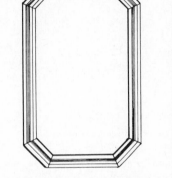
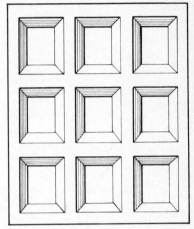
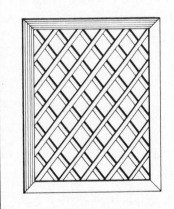
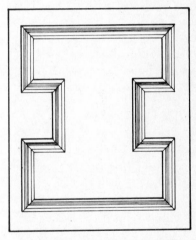
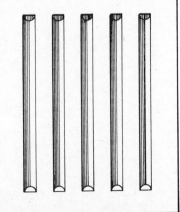

This is an ornate example of applied moldings.

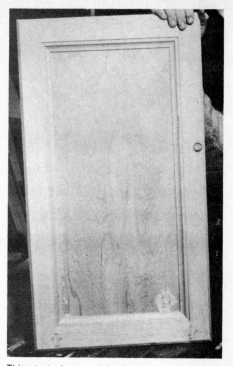

This started as a plain door — a piece of ¼ inch plywood. Then 1 x 2 strips were secured to the edges, moldings were added, and the exterior edges were beveled with the router.

Prefinished

Some moldings come prefinished. There are plastic moldings which come in white, as well as wood ones that have their faces covered with vinyl and imprinted with various wood patterns. There are also moldings designed to be used with paneling; i.e., to cover the top and bottom edges and spaces between panels. Their practicality for most cabinets and bookcases applications, however, is questionable.

Working with Molding

When cutting molding (as noted in Chapter 7) a good backsaw and a miter box are essential to create the miter, which is the most common joint required for joining pieces of molding. Once the molding has been cut you can attach it with brads and glue. Use a minimum amount of glue; that is, just enough so that it will adhere to the material but not so much that it will squeeze out when the piece is pressed in place. Above all, you want to keep the glue off the molding face. Removing the glue can affect the wood in terms of the way it colors the finish you are using.

Use just enough brads to hold the molding in place. As detailed in Chapter 6, you can use a brad driver to push the brads in place. Use a nailset to slightly sink the heads of the nails below the surface; then fill with wood filler and sand smooth.

Sometimes the molding must be sanded to remove minor imperfections. Do this very carefully so that you will not change the shape of the material.

Molding, not so incidentally, can make up for some imperfections if you leave gaps in joints; the molding can be used to cover them neatly.

Molding gives a cabinet or bookcase a cut-from-solid-stock look. Here, panel molding is mitered at the corners and applied at the edges of a rectangle of plastic laminate (such as Formica's Alabaster Slate). The same system will work for nearly any thin inset, such as a contrasting wood or a wicker weave.

THE ROUTER

The versatility of the router is due to its variety of bits. The accompanying chart gives an indication of this. In brief, however, they come in a range of diameters and shapes to help you make just about any cut you need. When the decorative cuts and grooves are combined with molding, then the possibilities for trimming a cabinet or bookcase increase dramatically.

Working with the Router

The easiest way to make cuts or grooves in the face of a cabinet door is to use a jig of your own making with commercially available guides. The guides are just simply rings of metal. They come in various sizes to accommodate various bit sizes, and they screw to the baseplate of the router with the bit projecting through them. The bits, of course, can be raised or lowered to cut to whatever depth you wish.

To use one of the guides, clamp your jig or board — a straightedge or a board cut to whatever shape you need — to the face of the material to be cut. Then run the router along the material with the ring riding against the jig or the board.

Before cutting it is always best to make careful use of the measuring techniques and tools detailed in Chapter 5. If you have to make a fancy cutout on the router, it is a good idea to first make a paper pattern. Divide the piece of paper into one-inch squares — or whatever size is most convenient — then draw the outline you need over on the squares. You can then cut out the pattern and tape it to the wood as a guide, or tape the pattern in place, draw the outline from it, and then remove it.

The router is an extraordinarily versatile tool. Here it is used to bevel a molding glued to the edge of a door.

ROUTER BITS

Straight bits

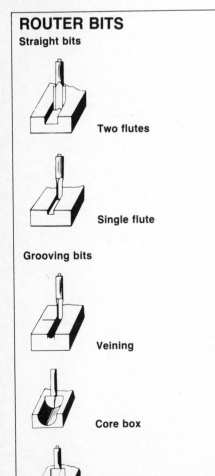

Two flutes

Single flute

Grooving bits

Veining

Core box

"V" grooving

Grooving bits

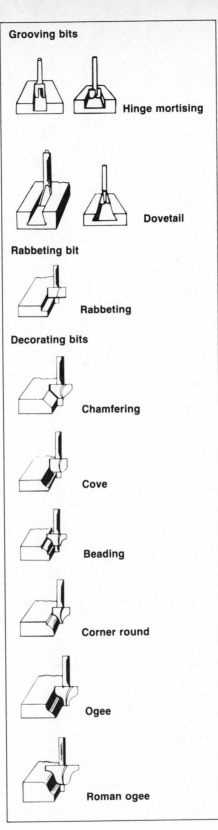

Hinge mortising

Dovetail

Rabbeting bit

Rabbeting

Decorating bits

Chamfering

Cove

Beading

Corner round

Ogee

Roman ogee

Trimming bit

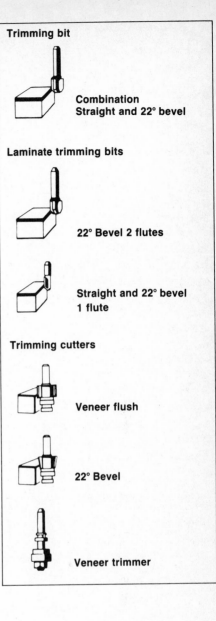

Combination
Straight and 22° bevel

Laminate trimming bits

22° Bevel 2 flutes

Straight and 22° bevel
1 flute

Trimming cutters

Veneer flush

22° Bevel

Veneer trimmer

The most popular material for building cabinets or bookcases is, of course, wood. By "wood" we mean boards — finished lumber normally up to 1 inch thick. But there are a number of other commonly used products, the chief of which is plywood, but also hardboard and particleboard. The latter is a material that has gained greatly in popularity in recent years, probably because it is strong but relatively inexpensive.

SELECTION OF MATERIAL

The most popular board (1 inch or less thickness) stock for building cabinets (or, for that matter, anything with wood) is pine. Usually it is a solid, easily worked and easily finished material that is cheap and plentiful. Availability is an important attribute: many woods are hard to obtain or to match.

You can save money by buying Common lumber instead of Clear and cutting clear, usable sections from it. Even if you buy double (or even triple) the amount you would need using Clear, you are still likely to come out ahead.

Pine Boards

In a sense, to just say "boards are of pine" is not a complete definition because there are different species. Indeed, pine comes in great profusion — twenty or more different species — each identified by the tree that the boards are cut from, such as yellow pine, white pine and sugar pine.

Names really do not matter in this case. The most crucial element is selecting the wood based on the job at hand. In general, white pine is available in 1 inch x 4 inches to 1 inch x 18 inches wide, with sizes in width increasing in two-inch increments (1x2, 1x4, etc.). Yellow pine is normally used as sheathing board and is not a factor in do-it-yourself projects. Sugar pine is generally thicker than 1 inch, but it also may be used.

Dimensions. The named, or nominal, wood sizes — 1x4, 1x6, 1x8 — are not the actual sizes. Dressing the boards at the mill reduces the size somewhat. As the boards increase in nominal width, they lose more and more stock. Nominal length remains the actual length. The accompanying table shows actual and nominal sizes, and it is essential that you be conscious of them when figuring the dimensions of your project.

Grading

Finished pine, like other wood, comes in various grades. The best type is Clear, so called because it does not have knots or blemishes in it. It also is not commonly stocked, and is therefore expensive. One grade down from Clear is Select, which is cheaper and comes in three subdivisions: Numbers 1, 2 and 3. Number 1 is the best of the three, with only a few blemishes on one side of the board and perhaps more on the other. Numbers 2 and 3 will have more blemishes — and will cost less. Usually, lumberyards will carry Numbers 2 and 3 Select but not Number 1, although it is likely you can find what you need using the grades that are available.

The lowest grade, but still a perfectly good wood, is Common; this will have more than a few blemishes and knots. It is often used where a project will be painted or covered in some way. When you need Clear stock, an excellent money-saving trick is to buy Common and cut out only the Clear, unblemished portions you need. You will have a lot of waste but will probably still save money over buying all Clear or all Select. You would have to estimate the percentage of the Common that would be usable, and then buy enough wood to compensate for the wastes. You must also check that the sizes of the pieces you would cut for the sides, back, doors, and so on, could be cut from the individual pieces of Clear wood left after cutting out the blemishes.

Choosing the Best Pine. When selecting pine, always look at each board with the following quality criteria in mind. Ask yourself these questions.

(1) Is the board flat? Does it lie flat on the board beneath it?

(2) Is it straight? Raise the board and sight down it to the other end; any curve will show up right away.

(3) Is the board warped? Look at the end nearest you and sight to see if it is parallel with the end farthest away. To double check, lay it on the floor. The end farthest

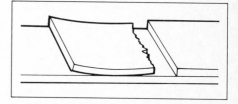

Boards should lie flat. To select boards that are true sight down the length of the edge. A little bit of warpage is allowed as long as it doesn't interfere with the project, but nothing drastic should be tolerated.

Do not buy boards with pith lines — they will warp. Pith lines occur in boards which have been cut from the center of a tree. They appear as brown lines.

away should be flat. You can adjust for a little warpage, but nothing drastic will be usable.

(4) How many knots are there and in what condition are they? Some grades of pine will have knots, but if these are tight the wood is acceptable.

(5) When you cut the board up for your project, can you eliminate the knots? By carefully positioning the pieces to be cut out, you may be able to avoid most of the knots.

(6) Are you finishing the wood with a clear finish or with paint? If with paint, the knots may be unimportant.

(7) Are there pith pockets? Pith is a soft brown exudation on a board that looks like a brown line running lengthwise on the board. Do not buy wood with these pockets. Pith usually causes board to warp.

(8) Does the board have sap pockets? If so, avoid such stock unless you can cut the sap pockets out. Sap can also cause a board to warp.

Estimating Materials. Using your plan, calculate how much lumber or plywood you will need to build your project. For example, assume that your project is to be built with ¾ inch plywood. Determine the exact size of each piece in your project and draw a plan to scale for a cutting layout on a piece of 4 x 8 plywood. If you are planning to paint the completed project, the direction of the grain on the surface (veneer) ply may not be important; you may be able to cut pieces without regard to the resulting directions of the grain. However, if you are going to finish the project with a transparent stain, varnish, lacquer, or oil, you may need to purchase more plywood to allow for matching the grain in a uniform direction and attractive relationship.

This vanity, made of cedar on a 2 x 2 framework, blends well with 1 x 6 cedar planks used on walls. The top is built separately, covered with plastic laminate and attached with screws.

Other Softwoods

Pine is characterized as a softwood, which means that it comes from a cone-bearing tree. The terms "softwood" does not mean that a wood is softer than another wood designated "hardwood". (Indeed, one "hardwood" —balsa — is used in model airplane making; it is so soft that it can be cut with a knife.)

Cedar and redwood are two other softwoods that are frequently specified for cabinets and bookcases; several of the projects in Section II call for these woods. They not only look good, but can be used for exterior projects as well as for interior ones because the wood does not need to be preservative-treated, and holds up well over time.

There are quite a few other softwoods, many of which are shown in color in Chapter 10.

One problem you may face is that of availability of certain softwoods when looking for board or for other forms you need. This will depend upon the lumberyards in your area. For example, a local lumberyard might have cedar — but not in sheathing

form. It might stock redwood — but only in fence post form. It is suggested that you telephone a number of lumberyards to discover what is available. If the wood is not on hand, ask how you may go about getting the stock. The dealer may not be willing to put through a special order to get your boards, but he may know someone else who would.

Hardwoods

With hardwoods (which get their name from the leaf-bearing trees), it is a chancy situation. In general, hardwoods — mahogany, oak, birch, and maple are some examples — come in random lengths from 8 feet to 16 feet and in widths from 4 inches to 12 inches. But what you will be able to find varies from region to region.

The hardwood you buy will be clear; dealers do not bother to stock other grades. Hardwoods are generally better-looking than softwoods — hardwoods have nicer grain and color, and are easier to tool than softwood. You should, however, be warned that you will pay handsomely for it.

The wood you buy, if a softwood, will

This built-on is constructed of 1 x 8 redwood planks nailed together. It has been faced with 1 x 2 boards around the front edges and across the lower shelves to retain magazines.

Lumber may be flat (quarter) sawn (*left*) or vertical (plain) sawn (*right*). Flat sawn boards are tight grained — good for finishing and tooling. Vertical sawn boards are less desirable, but satisfactory. Flat sawn is more expensive.

PLYWOOD GRADES AND USES

Grade	Face	Back	Plies	Uses
A-A EXT.	A	A	C	Outdoors; cost may limit use to projects when both sides show
A-B EXT.	A	B	C	Outdoors when both sides show
A-C EXT.	A	C	D	When only one side will show
C-C EXT.	C	C	C	Best for framing construction
B-B EXT.	B	B	B	Utility plywood; for some concrete forming, walks, and other rough use
A-A INT.	A	A	D	Best panel; for cabinets, built-ins, and other construction where both faces will show
A-B INT.	A	B	D	A little less than A-A
A-C INT.	A	C	D	Good face, fair back; for paneling where one side will show
B-D INT.	B	D	D	Utility grade; for rough projects such as underlayment for flooring
C-D	C	D	D	Sheathing grade
CDX	—	—	—	Sheathing grade; usually for exterior use, panels may be used indoors

Lumber-core plywood is the strongest, although most expensive, plywood available. Lumber core plywood has a solid lumber core to which face veneers are laminated. This material is used for fine cabinets, built-ins and furniture.

Shown are two types of veneer core plywood, which can be recognized by the layers or plies of the core. In the upper picture the plies are made of thin sections of wood cut at different directions to the grain. In the lower picture the plies are made of alternating layers of thin sections of wood and compressed wood chips. The inner plies are thicker than the wood veneer face plies.

come dressed on all four sides. If you buy hardwood, it will come in the rough unless you specify that it be dressed on two or more sides. But this is mill dressing. Before you work with it, ensure that the surfaces are smooth. In almost all cases this requires that you sand imperfections from the top and bottom, and then smooth the edges with a plane and sandpaper.

Grain. The grain pattern of the wood you buy will be dictated by whether the wood has been quarter-sawed or plain-sawed. The accompanying illustration indicates these cuts. The quarter-sawed produces a tighter, parallel grain pattern. The plain-sawed has a loop characteristic. Quarter-sawed is better wood but, again, you can expect to pay for it. The roundup of hardwoods and softwoods in Chapter 10 shows the differences clearly.

MODERN ALTERNATIVES

In addition to lower cost, there are advantages to using plywood, particleboard, and hardboard.

Plywood

Plywood is one of the staples for carpentry projects. It commonly comes in 4 foot x 8 foot sheets ¼ inch, ½ inch, and ¾ inch thick. It consists of two veneers of wood (which can be one of many different types) sandwiched over a core — usually bonded wood chips or lumber. The edges of the plywood with a wood-chip core are more difficult to finish than are the edges of plywood over a lumber core — called, logically enough, "lumber core plywood."

One major distinction between plywood and regular boards or lumber is that for plywood the nominal size is the actual size — a ¾ inch thick panel is really ¾ inch thick.

As with regular stock lumber, plywood is graded. Each plywood side, or face, has a letter designation which indicates its quality. Plywood stamped Grade A should have no blemishes or defects; any blemishes found in this grade will have been patched for a smooth surface. Grade B will have a few patches and defects. Grade C will have small knots and knotholes as well as checks (splits). Grade D is the least attractive grade; large knotholes are allowed. As an example: plywood stamped AC would mean one side is virtually perfect, with the other side blemished to some degree.

In theory, you can buy any combination of letters desired, but in practice the grades you will most often find are: Grade AC interior; AD interior; and, AC exterior plus

CD, which is used for house sheathing. The panels will be marked INT. for interior, or EXT. for exterior.

The only difference between exterior and interior plywood is the glue that is used when the plies are put together. Exterior has glue that is weatherproof; the adhesive on interior plywood is not.

The key money-saving hint when selecting plywood for any job is to buy and use only what is just good enough for the job — do not buy a better grade than is necessary. If you will have one face showing, then all that is required is a panel or panels with one good side. If you are going to paint the plywood, then find something smooth enough to be painted.

Money-Saving Tips. There are a few other ways to save money when buying plywood. One way to check the "cut-up" bin — the place where plywood scraps are placed — to see if you can get enough for your job. If you will be using the pieces for an exterior project, check that you are getting exterior plywood; the EXT. stamp should be on all the pieces. Another recourse is to buy plywood stamped "Shop". This is material which has been damaged (such as edges chipped, or face sanded through), but you can often cut away the bad parts and have enough good material left for your purposes.

The big advantage of Shop material is its price; it runs about one half the cost of a regular plywood panel of the same size, a not inconsiderable point as lumber prices rise.

Plywood Edges. Plywood is a versatile material, but its edges are unsightly. Most projects will look better if you cover the edges in some way. As with most operations in cabinetry and bookcase making, there are several methods that will do a good job.

One way to handle the edges is to plan the project so that any exposed edges will have molding applied over them. An alternative is to tack on strips of thin wood, ripped from the same plywood as the rest of the piece you are building. For an especially good-looking solution, miter the joints of these strips before adding them to the plywood edges. Another simple step is to cover the edges with veneer tape. These are thin wood strips which come in a coil and are applied with contact cement. Installation instructions vary a little from brand to brand, but are always included in (or on) the package.

Particleboard

Particleboard can be found under various names — pressboard, chipboard or flake-

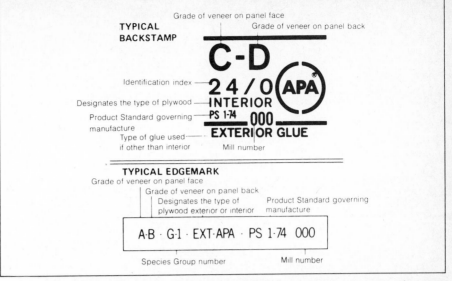

Plywood approved by the American Plywood Association is marked with these types of stamps. This is your assurance that the product meets rigid standards and is what it claims to be.

You can fill the end grain of plywood to be painted, using any of several kinds of wood putty. These come either powdered (to be mixed with water), or prepared (ready to use). Spackling compound will also work. When the putty is thoroughly dry, sand lightly and finish.

A laminated plastic surfacing material can be applied to edges of plywood units using the same contact cement recommended for applying laminate to counter tops. Apply strips to edges first, then to the top surface. A thicker, more massive effect can be gained by first nailing a 1″ or 1¼″ facing strip all around the underneath edge.

Plywood with a core of bonded wood chips is less desirable than lumber core material, but is widely used. Particleboard core plywood has a compacted-sawdust look. The core is actually wood fibers held by a resin binder. The face veneers may be laminated to one or to both sides of the panel — the example shown is laminated to just one side.

Particleboard and chipboard have edges that look like this. They may or may not have laminated wood faces. This material is sometimes used as sheathing applied over a frame.

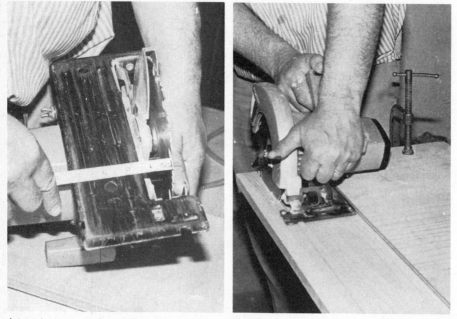

A good way to make straight cuts with a circular saw is to measure the distance from the baseplate to the blade and clamp a straightedged board this distance from where you want to cut. The straightedge will guide the saw.

board. It is made from wood chips and sawdust glued together under high pressure. It is available in thickness ranging from ¼ inch to 1⅞ inch, and comes in 4 x 8 foot panels.

Particleboard has a few disadvantages that you should be aware of, which may counteract its low-cost advantages.

Particleboard is very heavy — much heavier than plywood. If you become involved in a project requiring large sheets of material you can experience difficulty handling the larger pieces. In addition, its edges cannot hold fasteners well, although screws and glue are sometimes used.

Particleboard also is subject to attack from

water. In my own case, for example, particleboard was once installed as a base for a kitchen countertop. Unfortunately, water crept in and swelled the base material, leaving no alternative but to replace the entire countertop.

Finally, particleboard is murderous on saw blades, tending to dull them quickly. If you are cutting it, only a carbide-tipped blade should be used.

You can use particleboard for most of the jobs for which you would use plywood or boards, keeping in mind that you would want to sink the fasteners into the faces of the sheets rather than into the edges.

Hardboard

This is the material that no one ever sees and that no one ever should see. Brown in color, it is designed for use as drawer bottoms, cabinet backs, sliding doors (which are finished in some way) and the like.

Hardboard is composed of wood fibers that are pressed together under heat into sheets. It comes in two basic forms — exterior and interior, also called untempered and tempered. The tempered material is used outdoors, the untempered indoors.

Basic hardboard comes with one smooth side and one side cross-hatched (a useful feature for holding nails when it is used as underlayment). It can be fastened with nails or screws and glue, but it is a good idea not to put any fastener closer to the edge than ¼ inch The nails should be no more than 4 inches apart for snug fastening.

Hardboard can be painted, but it must first be sealed with a thin coat of shellac or an undercoater such as BIN.

CUTTING TECHNIQUES

The projects in this book do not require complicated techniques and cuts. Crosscuts (cutting across the grain), rips (cutting with the grain) and a few bevel cuts will suffice.

There is no great mystery to making accurate cuts. First cut the stock down to a manageable size, assuming you are working with large sheets to begin with. For example, if you are cutting a 4 x 8 sheet of plywood, cut it down (or, the lumberyard will make straight cuts for a nominal price) to half its size, or perhaps into quarters if your project allows this.

If using a radial arm saw or stationary saw, set the fence (as instructed in the booklet provided by the manufacturer) and begin cutting. Be sure, of course, to first make careful marks on the stock. Measure them twice, as mentioned in Chapter 5. Remember to figure in the saw cuts (kerfs as they're called) into your cutting. Cut on the outside of your markings, not on them — the fractions of an inch they add up to can be meaningful. The radial arm saw is found to be useful by many people for this type of work. It is really a circular saw that is attached to an arm which can be slid back and forth to make various cuts. The arm itself is also movable, and the saw can be tilted to make slanted cuts. There are also accessories available for drilling, sanding and shaping but, as with any power tool, it is usually best to stick to a tool specifically designed for a particular job. If you are working with portable tools, follow the same guidelines. Make careful marks — get full use of your measuring tools.

Once you have finished cutting, use your measuring tools to determine that the pieces are the correct size and that they are square or at the angles they are supposed to be.

If you are using a circular saw, you can use a long straightedge to guarantee the accuracy of straight cuts. Just clamp the straightedge — a metal one, or a straight, narrow piece of plywood — to the piece to be cut. The baseplate cut of the saw should ride against the straightedge (next to the factory edge if cutting plywood); then make the cut along the straightedge.

Blades. You can choose among a variety of blades when sawing wood or plywood. As mentioned, a carbide-tipped one works well for particleboard, which is particularly tough. For thin plywood — ¼ inch and ⅛ inch material — use a plywood-cutting blade. For any plywood thicker than this, use a combination blade. This type of blade is good for both ripping (cutting with the grain) and crosscutting. You can also use this saw on board stock.

When using a radial or table saw, keep the good face of the plywood toward the blade. Use a sharp combination blade or a fine-toothed one without much set. The blade should extend beyond the plywood by the depth of the teeth. One person can easily handle large panels with the help of an extension support with a roller. It can be free-standing or clamped to a saw horse.

A sabre saw enables you to cut irregular curves and shapes. By placing the front of the sabre saw platform against the face of the panel, and tilting the blade downward to scratch the panel surface, you can work a saw slot into the panel for interior cuts without having to drill a pilot hole. Use the finest tooth for your blade and apply firm, even pressure on the saw to get a smooth, even cut.

When using a portable power saw, keep the good face of the plywood down.

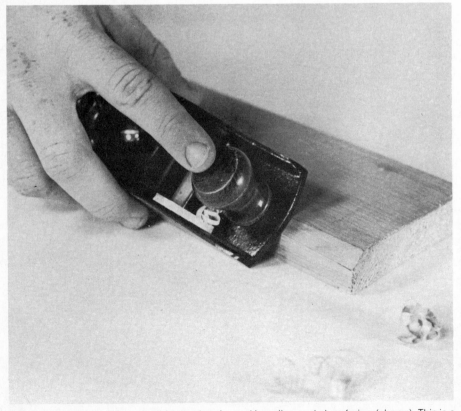

Block planes are used for smoothing end grain, and beveling and chamfering (shown). This is a basic woodworking plane; for general use, buy a jack plane or a block plane. Do not substitute a smoothing tool for a plane.

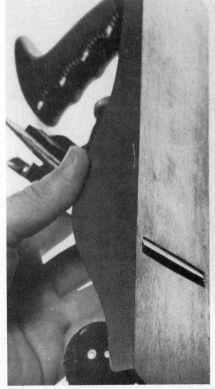

Keep plane blades square with the sole (bottom) of the plane. You can adjust the depth of the blade with the thumbscrew; adjust the angle of the blade with the lever.

5 Measurements

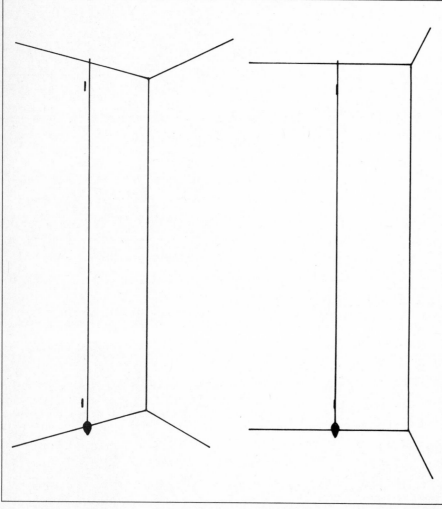

Pencil marks made behind the plumb bob should be obscured when you sight along the string.

One seemingly simple step can often spell the difference between success or failure when building a cabinet or bookcase: correct use of measuring tools. The following is a roundup of the tools and usage techniques you are likely to employ.

ACCURATE MARKINGS

A number of the projects offered later will require that you mount members on the wall. For some installations or guidelines, you must draw straight, vertical lines. To establish the marks for the lines, you will discover the plumb bob.

The Plumb Bob

The plumb bob is a tear-drop-shaped weight attached to a string. To use it, just hang the plumb bob from the ceiling about an inch away from the wall. Make sure the string does not touch the wall, because any surface irregularity, such as a bump, could throw off the string measurement.

Stand in front of the string after it stops swinging, and pencil in two marks: one will be directly behind the string at the ceiling; the other will be behind the string near the bottom of the wall. Move back a few feet and, keeping one eye closed, sight up and down the string. The string should obscure both marks. If it does not, try again. Then snap a chalkline across the two marks for a straight line. You can buy a chalkline, or you can make your own.

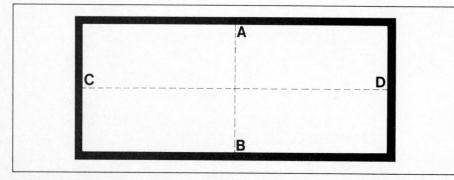

To find the center of a room: use a long, metal tape measure to find the length of each wall or floor area, and mark the centers (ABCD). Cut a length of string about a foot longer than the room width (AB) and rub the string with chalk. Drive a small nail into the floor at A and another at B; tie the chalked string tightly to each in turn, leaving no slack. Pluck the string smartly, snapping it against the floor. Repeat the process at points CD for the two short walls. The intersection of the two chalked lines marks the center of the floor.

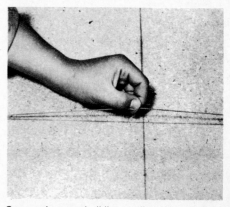

Snap only one chalkline until you are sure of the overall layout. You may need to move the next line slightly.

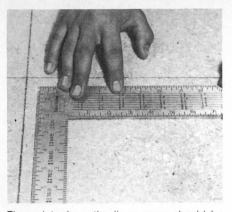

The point where the lines cross should be square. Check it with a framing square. If the lines are not square, re-snap the lines.

Marking Tools

The tools most commonly used to measure and mark lumber include: framing square, tri-square, and adjustable square.

Framing Square. The framing square is nothing more than an L-shaped piece of flat steel, with one leg of the L measuring 16 inches and the other measuring 24 inches. You can lay it across a board with one leg tipped down so that it butts against one edge; then mark the board for crosscutting. Another use is when marking a 45° angle on a board. As shown in the illustration, just lay the square on the board so that the edges of the board bisect the corresponding 45° angle on the square, and mark where the angle has fallen.

Try Square. The try square has a movable metal blade and a wooden handle. It is used for quickly checking the accuracy of 45° and 90° angles. It also works well for checking the ends of boards to see if they have been cut squarely. Just hold the try square against the board. If the fit is snug, it is square; if there is space, it is not square. The try square comes in various lengths, up to 12 inches, which is the most useful size.

You can also use the try square to mark narrow boards to length.

Adjustable Square. Another operation that may be required for your project is marking lines on wood or plywood that are parallel to the edge of the stock. For this, use the adjustable square. The metal part of the tool rides along the edge of the stock while the blade part slides along the surface, with a pencil held against the end to make the mark. This tool can also be used for determining 45° and 90° angles.

Drawing Lines

Many projects will require you to draw straight lines on the wall or floor, or across large sheets of material. This is usually

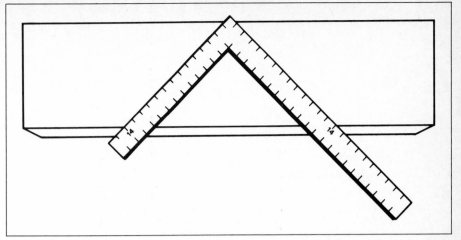

The arms of a framing square are marked in one inch increments. To draw a 45° angle, position the square so that the board's edge intersects the two scales at the same number.

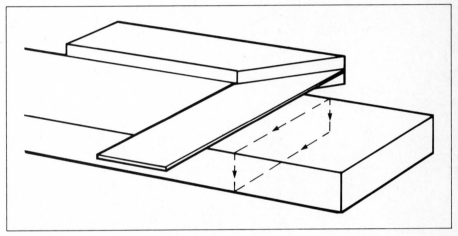

Use a try square to mark the end of a board for a square cut. Mark a long face first, then each of the short sides, finishing with the second long face.

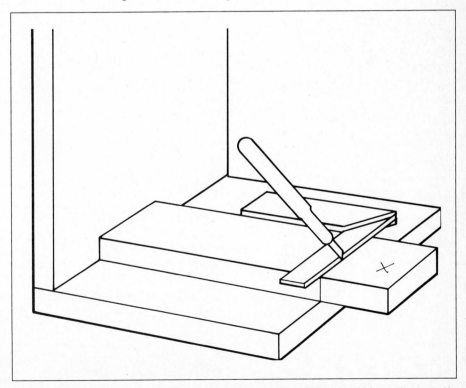

The most accurate way to mark lumber is with a knife or scriber. Where possible, put the board in place and scribe it to fit. Pencil an X on the excess and make your cut on this piece.

When the bubble in a level is between these lines, the work is level. A 3-bubble level is your best investment; the frame can be wood or metal (metal is shown).

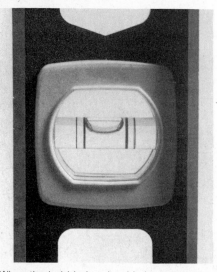

When the bubble in a level is between these lines, the work is plumb or exactly vertical. You also can obtain horizontal and vertical on flat surfaces such as walls; the level need not ride an edge.

accomplished using a chalkline. Previously we gave instructions on how to make your own chalkline. A purchased chalkline consists of a coil of line rolled in a box filled with blue chalk. To use it, set one end of the cord over one of the marks already made, with the other end across another mark. Hold the line taut in this position, then lift at the center and snap the line. A perfectly straight line will result.

Leveling

This is another crucial procedure when building cabinets or bookcases. Get into the habit of checking the various erected components of your piece as you build it. The level can also be used to check the trueness (straightness) of a piece as long as the span does not exceed the length of the level (4 feet).

When using a level (either a wood or a metal level will work satisfactorily) first clean off the surface where the level will be placed, and then wipe off the level itself. Even a speck of foreign matter can throw it out of alignment.

Read the level four ways. That is, place it horizontally on the surface and observe the bubbles. They will float exactly in the center of the level markings. If acceptable, turn the tool end over end, so you have reversed the positions of the ends, and read it horizontally again. Then hold the level on the surface vertically — on end — and read it first one way, then the reverse. The bubble should always be between the two indicator lines.

MEASURING TIPS AND TRICKS

For every measuring operation — and in this we include marking angles and the other measuring-related steps — repeat the sequence of measurements to ensure that you get the same result both times. If they do not agree, recheck, and re-mark if necessary.

Whenever possible, try to avoid measuring — use a precut length or width of material as a guide, or hold the piece of stock to be cut in place against the parts that are completed and then mark and cut it to fit. If you are experienced at cutting all components to size beforehand, by all means do so;

you will save time. For others, however, the cut-to-fit method offers less chance of wasted material.

Another trick is to add up the component sizes for a particular item and then compare it to the overall size. The two should be the same, after deducting overlaps or joints from the sum of the components. For example, if you were installing a series of cabinets, and knew that they should occupy six feet of wall space, the linked-together widths of the cabinets to be installed should also equal six feet.

Rulers. If using a ruler, try to measure without using the first inch of the tool. The metal clip on the tool often makes the rule difficult to read. If you have had the tool for some time, the edges might be damaged and thus slightly inaccurate. It is safest to read the length beginning at the one inch mark, or even at the two inch mark.

If working with someone else on a project, be sure that you both use the same brand of ruler. There are usually fractional differences between ruler brands — 12 feet ends up a different actual dimension for different manufacturers — and this can result in mismatched pieces of precut, expensive materials.

If possible, use increments other than the first inch on rule. Here, a dado is being measured without using rule end, since ruler edges can be slightly off.

6 Fasteners and Other Hardware

FASTENERS

When assembling cabinets and bookcases, you usually can use either nails or screws. Use of screws results in a stronger job, with the added benefit that the unit can be taken down or disassembled later if desired. You may occasionally have need of other fasteners such as bolts, which are discussed here along with the basic screws and nails.

Nail Selection

A brief consideration of how nails are characterized may be useful. First, the length of a nail is indicated by the letter d, which stands for penny, and which goes back to old English times when nails were sold for a penny a pound. Sizes run from 2d, which is 1 inch long, all the way up to 60d, or 6 inches As a nail becomes longer it becomes thicker; i.e., the diameter increases.

Common nails. This is one of the nails most often used by the average do-it-yourselfer. It has a flat head and the top of the shank is grooved to allow a good grip. Its most common application is in general construction work; common nails rarely play an important role in building cabinets or bookcases.

Finishing Nails. This is the nail that will be most useful in building bookcases or cabinets. It is a thin nail with a small head that is designed to be hidden or set below the surface. Once a piece is assembled, these nailheads are hit with a nailset of appropriate size to sink them slightly below the surface. The resulting depressions are then filled with wood putty. After the finish has been applied

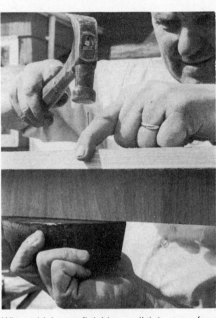

When driving a finishing nail into a surface without much support, have a helper hold a weight under the area, as shown.

it is difficult to determine exactly where the nailheads were placed — and that is just what you want.

Brads. This is just the name given to finishing nails 1½ inch or smaller. This type of nail is used where strength is not the prime factor, as when assembling spice racks or similar nonload-bearing pieces. It is also used for securing molding.

Exterior Use. Nails are generally made of steel, but if you will be using them outdoors — where they will be subject to attack from moisture — choose a galvanized type. Galvanized nails will resist moisture; the hot-dipped type is best. Rust can destroy the appearance of any project.

Dry Wall Nail. This is the best nail to use when securing Sheetrock, a brand name of drywall, also called plasterboard. The nail comes in one size and has either a straight or barbed point, with a large flat head. It is designed to be driven into the Sheetrock until the nail dimples or depresses the paper surface; joint compound is then applied over the head with a large, flexible joint compound knife. Tape and more compound are added to fully hide the nails.

Spiral Nails. This nail has tenacious gripping power. It is used to secure flooring but can also be put to good use securing wood members to framing. It should be driven with a heavy hammer (16 oz. rather than 13 oz.).

Masonry Nail. This nail is used for attaching something to masonry. Some masonry nails have round shanks, while others have square shanks; they can be used interchangeably. These types of nails must be driven with a heavy hammer, and it is wise to wear safety goggles to guard against flying masonry chips. Most craftsmen prefer toggle bolts or expansion anchors to masonry nails when hanging items on masonry, because they are easier to use.

A brad driver enables easy handling of the very small fasteners (brads) used for molding.

Nail Usage

When using nails you must take a number of factors into account.

Length. You can figure out the length of the nail required from the thickness of the piece of material being driven in place; just triple it. For example, if the stock is ¾ inch plywood, then you should use a nail 2¼ inches long. The idea is to use a nail that is long enough so that at least two thirds of it sinks into the second layer of material.

You will usually need finishing nails when assembling cabinets and bookcases.

COMPATIBLE SIZES: PLYWOOD, SCREWS, AND DRILLS

Plywood Thickness	Screw Length	Screw Size	Drill Size for Shank	Drill Size for Root of Thread*
¾"	1½"	#8	¹¹⁄₆₄"	⅛"
⅝"	1¼"			
½"	1¼"	#6	⁹⁄₆₄"	³⁄₃₂"
⅜"	1"			
¼"	1"	#4	⁷⁄₆₄"	¹⁄₁₆"

*If splitting is a problem (as in edges) make hole for threaded portion ¹⁄₆₄" larger (⁹⁄₆₄", ⁷⁄₆₄" respectively).

A tack hammer with a magnetic head helps you start small nails and tacks without mashing your fingers. After you start the nail, reverse the hammer head to drive it in.

Pre-drilling is occasionally called for in careful work where nails must be very close to an edge, particularly in plywood. The drill bit should be just slightly smaller in diameter than the nail to be used.

When pulling nails, insert a block beneath the hammer head to increase the leverage. If the nail does not pull easily, try a pry bar or nail puller.

"Toenailing" means driving a nail at an angle. Straight-in nailing is stronger.

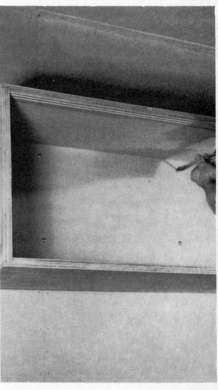

To hang cabinets on frame walls fasten long wood screws to the wall studs through the cabinet backs.

Thin Wood. If the material being secured is thin use two smaller nails instead of two big ones. This lessens the chances of the wood splitting. There is no formula we can give you on this, but you will soon be able to judge when small nails need to be substituted.

Securing Horizontal Members. When fastening a member horizontally, such as cleats for shelves, drive the nails downward. The weight on the cleat tends to drive the nail deeper rather than pulling the nail out, as would occur if the nail were driven horizontally or upwards.

Using a Nailset. To set a nail, use a nailset. First, drive the nail within a ¼ inch of the surface with a hammer, then use a nailset to drive the nail flush and slightly (¼ inch) below the wood surface. Fill the depression with wood putty. If you expect to be setting a lot of nails, buy a nailset with a head

sized to the nail you are using. Otherwise, use any nailset size that will work.

Staggering Nails. If you are securing a board near the end, do not drive nails close to each other in the same line if the nails are parallel to the grain. This could split the wood. Instead, stagger nail locations.

Types of Screws

A screw can come with any of three different head styles: flathead, roundhead and ovalhead.

The flathead type can be driven flush with the surface of the wood, countersunk or counterbored (driven deeply into the wood with the hole above filled with a wood plug).

Roundhead screws are used where appearance is not a prime concern, because their heads remain visible.

Ovalhead screws are a combination of round and flathead screws; the heads are

oval. The heads on these screws are quite handsome and are designed to remain exposed. They are available in plated brass and in pure brass, or chrome plated. Flatheads, in contrast, are commonly available in steel only.

Slots. Screw heads may have straight slots or the Phillips type — criss-cross slots. It is said that the Phillips allows more turning force to be applied to the screws, but in practical terms it does not matter which type is used for cabinetry or for bookcase construction.

Length. Screws come in a variety of lengths, from a tiny ¼ inch to 6 inches long, with the gauges or diameters classified by number ranging from 0 to 24, or ¹⁄₁₆ inch to ⅜ inch. Once past 4 inches long, however, you will find it difficult to drive a screw with a regular screwdriver, and substitution of a bolt is suggested.

Screw Usage

Length. In putting together a cabinet or bookcase the screw used should be ¼ inch less than the combined thicknesses of the pieces being joined. In some cases, such as when screwing into the end grain of wood, this formula does not work. In these instances it is suggested that you use a screw which is twice as long as the top piece of the two materials being secured. The screw diameter should be in proportion to the item being assembled. There is no iron-clad formula, but a glance at the screws specified for particular projects in this book will give you a good idea of proper diameters. (See also Wall Installation, Chapter 12.)

Drilling Pilot Holes. If you are drilling into a hard wood — i.e., wood that is physically hard, not the species category — then pilot holes should be drilled for the screws. The hole should be the diameter of the threaded part of the screw without the threads. In a soft wood, pilot holes are not required. You can tell if a pilot hole is required by driving a test screw. If it goes in easily, no pilot hole is required. If the test screw is difficult to drive and springs back — moves counterclockwise slightly after you lift the screwdriver from it — then the wood is hard enough to need pilot holes.

Countersinking Screws. On some projects you may want to countersink flathead screws. Sink them flush to — not below — the surface. There is a countersinking bit available, which is the simplest method. It is a cone-shaped bit designed to make a countersink as deep as you require; i.e., as deep as and the same diameter as the head of the screw. First drill the pilot hole (if required), then use the countersinking bit to drill the countersink. Remember to allow for the depth of the countersink when calculating how long the screw must be.

Counterboring. Counterboring involves drilling a hole deep enough to recess the head of the screw sufficiently so that it can be covered by wood putty or a plug. To do this, drill a hole equal to the length of the screw plus the depth of the counterbore. If you are just filling the hole with wood putty, a ¼ inch counterbore is sufficient; if installing a plug, make the counterbore depth ½ inch. The hole diameter should be that of the screw without the threads. Use another bit to drill a hole that is the same diameter and length of the shank of the screw used. Finally, use another bit, same size as the screw head diameter, to drill the counterbore.

If you expect to be making a fair number

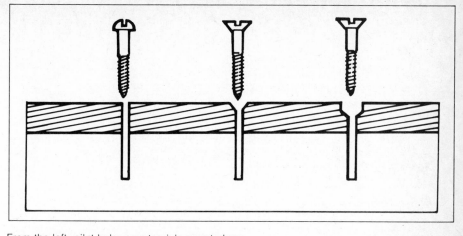

From the left: pilot hole; countersink; counterbore.

The Stanley Tools *Screwmate* device countersinks and counterbores in one operation.

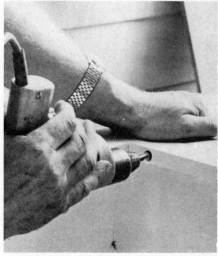

An electric screwdriver makes light work of driving and drawing screws.

of counterbores of a particular size, then it is suggested that you buy a screwmate such as the one put out by Stanley Tools. This bit drills the pilot hole, shank hole and counterbore in one operation. The screwmate comes in various common screw sizes. If, for example, you will be using #10, 1¼ inch screws, then you would buy a screwmate of the same size to drill the counterbores for it.

Using an automatic or manual driver. Driving screws is tedious work, but it can be speeded up with some automatic mechanical assistance. One of the best devices available is an electric screwdriver drill. This electric drill accepts screwdriver bits and drives or removes screws. However, it costs around $100, and may be beyond your budget. A good alternative is the Yankee screwdriver. When you push on the drill bit it turns on and drives the screws. If you are working with very large screws, then use a brace and bit. Incidentally, do not confuse the electric screwdriver drill with a screwdriver bit used in a regular drill; the latter does not work as well.

Covering Screws with Plugs

One way to cover screwheads is with wood plugs. There are various plastic and metal types available, but you can also buy ones made of wood, called "boat plugs", at marine supply stores. These are commonly available in mahogany, teak and oak, in various diameters — ⅜ inch, ½ inch, ⅝ inch and ⁷⁄₁₆. In the cases where the plugs do not match the grain and color of the wood used in a particular project, they can provide an attractive accent.

If you need plugs made from a specific type of wood, then you will have to cut them yourself. This is done with a plug cutter and drill press or drill. Set the cutter so that the plug will be about ⅜ inch to ½ inch thicker (longer) than the counterbore. Then slice the board horizontally to separate plugs from board. Plugs are normally counterbored ½ inch deep.

(1) Dip the plug halfway in white glue.

(2) Stick the plug in the counterbore hole.

(3) Gently tap the plug with a hammer until it is securely in place.

(4) Using a very sharp wood chisel, chip off half — or a little more than half — of the protruding plug.

(5) Use the chisel again to chip off some more of the plug, directing your blows from the high side (this guards against the plug splitting) to within 1/16 inch of the surface of the board.

(6) Use a belt sander to remove the rest of the plug.

When installing any plug that uses the same wood as that used in the furniture, rather than using the plug as an accent, install the plug with the grain running in the same direction as the stock used for the project. The plugs will thus be as unobtrusive as possible; indeed, when installed properly they are nearly invisible.

NUTS AND BOLTS

Nuts and bolts are not often required for cabinet and bookcase projects, but they do offer extra strength and valuable flexibility. In some instances you may find them necessary.

Selection

Lag Screw. Also called a lag bolt, this looks like a wood screw. It is threaded, has a smooth shank, and comes to a point. However, it come in larger sizes and its head has flat or hexagonal sides; it is designed to be turned by a wrench. Most do-it-yourselfers use lag screws in the smaller sizes — around 1 1/2 inches long — because the bigger lag screws are more difficult to turn. They are most often used to mount something to wood, but are also required by the larger-sized expansion shields.

Lag screws may be used for indoor projects, or can be found in a galvanized finish for exterior applications. Nuts are not required for lag screws.

Carriage Bolt. This fastener is used with a nut or, if the wood is soft, with a washer. It

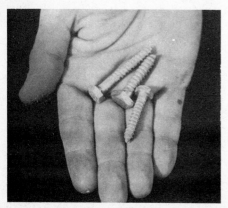
Lag screws come in assorted sizes.

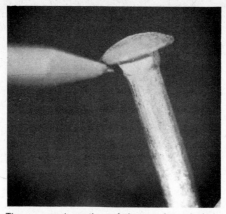
The squared section of the carriage bolt is driven into wood as the bolt is tightened, thus preventing the bolt from turning.

has a partially threaded shank, a square end, and a round head with a square piece beneath it.

Machine Bolt. A machine bolt installs like a carriage bolt through a drilled hole, but it does not have any square component under the head. Machine bolts, as with other types of bolts, come in various sizes. They are particularly useful when assembling purely functional items such as workbenches, where vibration can be an important factor. A machine bolt is used with a nut, or with both a nut and a washer.

When you buy a machine or carriage bolt the necessary washer will come with it. This will be your standard flat washer. However, there are several other kinds of washers and nuts worth considering, and which are described later.

Toggle Bolt. This bolt is used when hanging something on a hollow wall. It can be used in plaster, wood, Sheetrock, or masonry. The toggle bolt consists of a machine screw with a pair of collapsible wings. Once inside the wall, the wings will pop open.

The toggle bolt screws are available in various lengths so that you can buy the size suited to the thickness of the material you are hanging. The screw must be long enough to go through the wall thickness and the item to be hung.

Hollow Wall Anchors. You probably know these by their most popular trade name, Mollys. They, similar to toggle bolts, also are designed for use on hollow wall material. They work like a toggle bolt in the sense that wings on the device expand behind the wall as you tighten the screw, but unlike the toggle bolt the wings are built onto the fastener.

The hollow wall anchor selected for any job should have a shank as thick as the wall material. This may range up to 1 3/4 inch

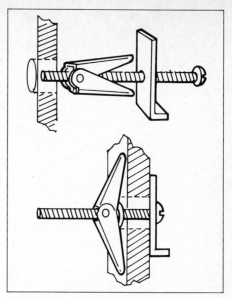
To use a toggle bolt, slip the screw through the item, slip on the "wings" and push the collapsed wings through the hole in the wall. Inside the wall the wings will pop open.

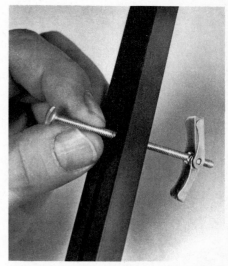
Toggle bolts have spring-loaded flanges that open and hug the back of a hollow or block wall after the unit has been inserted. Molly bolts are similar to toggles.

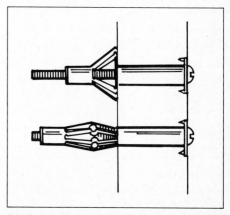
A hollow wall anchor slips through a predrilled hole in the wall. Tightening the screw spreads its wings apart, and pulls them back against wall. The screw is then withdrawn, passed through item, and retightened.

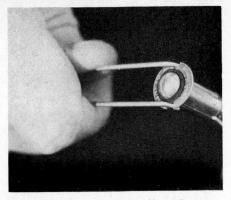

If a hollow wall anchor turns without the screw expanding its wings, this tool will hold it while the screw is being tightened.

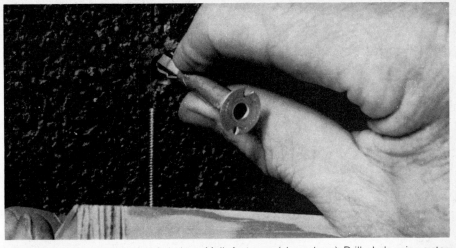

In hollow masonry walls use toggle bolts or Molly fasteners (shown here). Drill a hole using a star drill or carbide-tipped bit, then insert Molly and tighten. Once it is secure you can remove the bolt and use it to hang the cabinet. For gypsumboard walls, where stud fastening is not possible, Molly bolts can be used if loads are light.

thick, but in most homes an anchor with a ⅜ inch or ½ inch shank will be sufficient, because these are the most common wall thicknesses.

Usage and Installation

Hollow Wall Anchors. Drill a hole (do not punch it) that is the exact diameter of the widest part of the shank of the anchor; the package will give the hole size you should drill. Drill another hole, of the same size, in the material to be hung. Slip the anchor, with the screw in place, through the hole in the material to be hung and then into the wall. Tighten the screw. As you do, the wings on the anchor will expand and grip the back side of the wall.

Make sure that the hole you drill is clean, not ragged. The part of the anchor that contacts the wall has small metal teeth which grip the surface of the wall material. If the edges of the hole are ragged these teeth may not be able to bite securely and the entire fastener will turn in the hole — without the necessary wing expansion. If this occurs, you can buy a small metal tool which will hold the anchor in place firmly, but it is best to avoid this problem at the outset by drilling a smooth hole.

Machine screws (they have a flat end and are threaded their entire length) are used with hollow wall anchors. Use one that is long enough to pass through the material on the item to be hung plus the wall thickness, and which penetrates at least a half inch into the anchor sleeve.

When using a hollow wall anchor or toggle bolt on hollow wall material, do not exceed fifty pounds per anchor. If you are hanging something from the ceiling, five pounds is the limit.

Carriage Bolt. To use a carriage bolt, drill a hole that is the same diameter as the shank. Slip the bolt through, then hammer

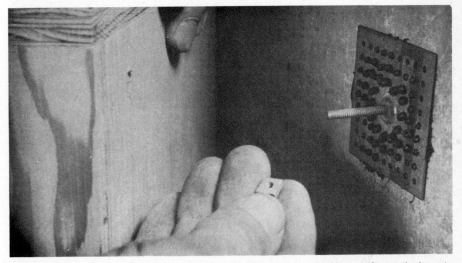

Solid masonry walls or walls of poured concrete, call for anchor bolts. You can fasten the base to the wall with black mastic, letting it squeeze through the holes. Hang your unit once the mastic has set, using washers. Toggle bolts in expansion shields can also be used.

the head down: The squared-off component under the head wedges into the hole and locks the fastener in place. Then add a nut and washer if you wish. A carriage bolt is useful if you are connecting members where quarters are cramped so that you cannot easily turn a nut on the bolt.

Expansion Shield

Expansion shields work similarly to hollow wall anchors, and are most often used in masonry. To use one, drill a hole in the wall that is as wide as the diameter of the sleeve of the device, and as deep as the sleeve length. The sleeve may be lead, fiber or plastic depending on the manufacturer; the lead sleeve is the best. Drill a corresponding hole through the item. Slip the sleeve into the hole drilled in the wall. Slip a screw in the sleeve; the screw should be long enough to go through the back of the item to be hung and

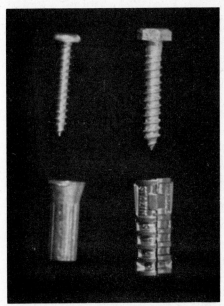

Use expansion bolts in solid material. They take a lag screw (right) or machine screw, depending on the size of the item being hung.

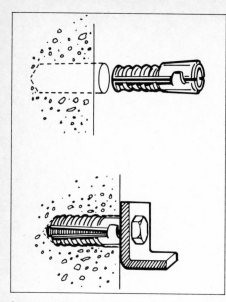

An expansion sleeve is inserted into a hole drilled in masonry. Then the screw is passed through the item and turned. The sleeve expands, locking the fastener in place.

halfway into the sleeve. Then tighten the screw. As you do this the sleeve will expand, locking itself against the sides of the hole by friction and pulling the item against the wall.

Toggle Bolt. Drill a hole in the wall and the item to be hung — for example, a cabinet back — then slip the bolt with the wings collapsed, through both holes. Holes should be just big enough to allow the device to pass through. Inside the wall the wings will pop open. Then, tighten the screw. As you do this the wings gradually pull against the backside of the wall material, locking the back to the wall.

While primarily used on plaster, wood, or wallboard, toggle bolts may also be used on masonry blocks. Blocks have voids in them. Just drill through the block (walls are about an inch thick) into the void, and then use the toggles as you would on any hollow-wall material.

Specialty Washers and Nuts. One such is the cap or acorn nut (so called because it looks like an acorn). It is designed to be used on the end of the bolt, where good looks are important.

Wing Nut. This has wing-shaped projections which can be gripped by the fingers or a tool. It is used for assembling items that you may someday wish to take apart.

Lock Washer. This type of fastener is used to ensure that the bolt does not move. Once installed it locks itself tenaciously in place.

HARDWARE
The hardware used on a cabinet varies from the purely functional, such as pilasters for

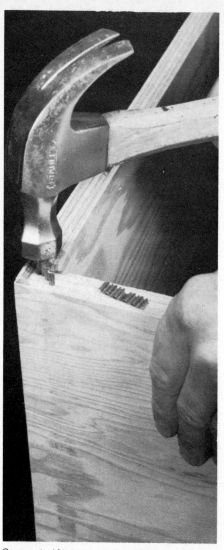

Corrugated fasteners can reinforce miter joints in ¾" plywood.

hanging shelves, to pieces that have both functional and decorative purposes, such as hinges.

Hinges
The hinges used are dictated by the type of door being used: lip, overlay or flush. As with drawers, the lipped door is one in which there is a lip cut all the way around the edge. The overlay door overlaps the door opening. The back of the flush door recesses into the cabinet opening, with its face flush with the edges of the face of the cabinet. (Detailed information on doors will be found in Chapter 8.)

One of the most preferred hinges is the pivot or pin style used for the overlay door. This is a concealed hinge: one hinge mounts on the top of the door and one hinge is on the bottom. The metal has been formed so that one part attaches to the cabinet frame, and the other goes on the top of the door.

A popular hinge for the flush door is the

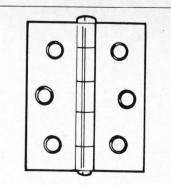

A butt hinge is a plain hinge, but one which is very useful for flush doors.

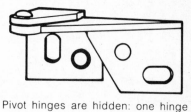

A butterfly hinge is just one of many decorative hinge shapes that are available.

Pivot hinges are hidden: one hinge mounts on the very top of the door; the other on the bottom.

butterfly, in which the metal has been stamped in the shape of a butterfly. Most of these come in brass and add a nice decorative accent.

The butt hinge is also frequently chosen. It is a plain design, and is intended to be mortised into flush doors.

A hinge that is widely used on all three types of doors is the self-closing hinge. A spring inside the hinge automatically and gently swings the cabinet door shut when the spring is released.

Hinge Sizes and Styles
The overall thicknesses and styles of hinges vary greatly, and it is a matter of picking what is best for your door style. In this regard, you might ask to see the hinge catalogue at your local hardware store, or visit a store which specializes in kitchen cabinet hardware.

Hinges are available in various metals and

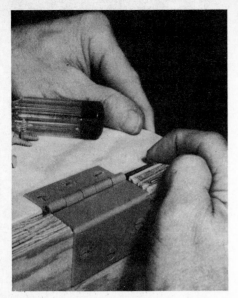

A semi-concealed loose-pin hinge offers the same appearance as ordinary butt hinges once the door is closed, because only the barrel shows. However, they are much better for flush plywood doors because the screws go into flat plywood grain. A variation, called a chest hinge, can be used in the same way.

Semi-concealed hinges can be easily hung in overlapping (lipped) doors. They work well in plywood since the screws go into flat grain. These have ½ inch insert and are made for doors of ¾ inch plywood which have been rabbeted to leave ¼ inch lip.

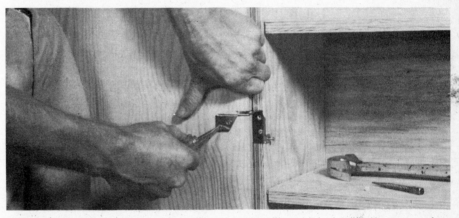

colors. Chrome is the most popular finish, but brass (plated or pure) is also commonly available as well as antique black, copper and other finishes.

You can pick any size hinge that seems in visual proportion to the door. You may assume it is strong enough, because hinges are designed to be far stronger than they need to be (with eight times the necessary support, according to one engineering study). Installation instructions are usually on the package that the hinge comes with. Many manufacturers have a design that enables the consumer to convert the card into a template for proper hinge placement. The easiest type of hinge to install is the offset.

Concealed pin hinges mount directly on the cabinet side. Assembly is simplified because no face frame is needed. Only the pivot is visible from the front when the door is closed. Doors will be easier to hang if at least one side of the hinge mounts from the front, so that you can see what you are doing.

Pulls and Knobs

For style, it is important to select pulls and knobs for doors and drawers that will complement the hinges. Knobs and pulls are bought separately from hinges, but there is such a wide variety available that you shouldn't have any difficulty getting what you need. Many manufacturers sell matching hinges and pulls or knobs. If you wish — and if decor won't be compromised — you can also use knobs and pulls which are different in style but complementary, such as porcelain and crystal. They are commonly available.

Knob/Pull Installation

Knobs (and pulls for drawers) are not difficult to install. In some cases, a screw is built

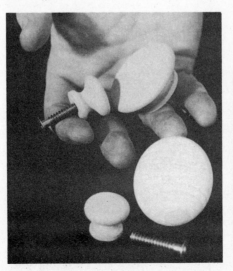

For some knobs and pulls used for doors and drawers a hole is drilled and the knob mounted from the backside. A screw is provided. Some pulls have the screw already built in — you just screw the knob in place.

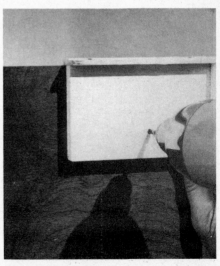

A simple jig is helpful for marking and drilling. Nail a lip of lattice or other thin wood to a rectangle of stock. The jig fits over the corner of the door and guides the drill to the same spot on each door.

into the knob or pull. In this case you just drill a pilot hole and screw the pull onto the door. In other cases holes are drilled in the door and screws (provided) are run through the back side to hold the knob in place.

For symmetry, it is important that knobs or pulls be on at the same point on each drawer or door. For doors there is a simple jig that can be built for marking the holes, as indicated in accompanying photograph.

Catches. You can choose from among several kinds of door catches. The three types most commonly used are: the magnetic, the roller, and the spring or friction type.

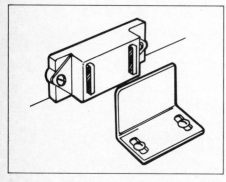

A magnetic catch is one of the easiest types of catches to install.

The best of the three is the magnetic catch. The big advantage is that the catch usually will continue to work even if the door warps, because most magnetic catches have floating, self-adjusting heads. All that is required for the door to stay shut is for any part of the catch to make contact with the piece on the frame.

You only need one magnetic catch on a standard size door. If the door is particularly large, two catches are advisable — one at the top and the other at the bottom. If the door is very heavy you can purchase a heavy-duty catch.

The roller catch has a pair of rollers mounted next to one another. A mechanism attached to the door locks between the pairs of rollers to keep the door closed.

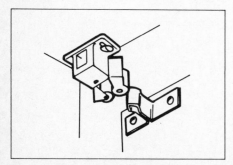

The roller catch piece attached to the door locks in place between a pair of rollers.

If you do not want any pull or knob hardware to show on a lipped door, then use the spring or friction catch. To close, you just push the door closed. To open the door, you pull or tug it again.

Casters and Glides

Casters and glides can benefit many pieces of furniture. Casters make an item easier to move for cleaning or extra use, and glides keep the feet of whatever you have built from digging into and marring the floor covering.

Casters come with many features, many of which relate to the specific use of the furniture being built.

Capacity. Casters are made to support varying amounts of weight, which could be a factor if you are going to be loading, for example, a bookcase that will hold many heavy books. So, before selecting which caster you want, note the caster's capacity, which will be right on the box or card they come in.

Swivel Feature. If you wish, you can buy casters that swivel 360°. This is a desirable feature for cleaning behind furniture, or for three-dimensional displays.

Materials. The material that the wheels are made of may be plastic, or hard or soft rubber. Each is geared to perform best on a specific floor covering. Plastic is a good choice for floors that are carpeted, hard rubber is best on concrete, and soft rubber works well on resilient flooring.

Metal casters are also made. While most are for industrial use, the shiny, ball-shaped decorative caster used on upholstered furniture is good for furniture on carpet or resilient flooring.

It is very likely that the legs on your project will be of solid wood, in which case plate-type casters are recommended. These are simply screwed to the bottoms of the legs. A stem-type caster — it has a metal projection — is available for insertion in tubular legs.

As mentioned, the weight of the item will determine the size caster you buy. However, a general rule is that the larger the caster, the easier it will roll.

Ball-bearing Style. If you want to build an item but head room is at a premium, then consider a ball-bearing caster. This ball bearing rides inside a metal housing. The ball bearing only projects a half inch, instead of the standard 2 inches or more which the average caster wheel projects.

Caster Installation. Installing a plate

Metal ball casters not only offer decorative advantages because they come in so many finishes, but are heavy duty as well. (Shown at left is the plate style; at right is the stem model.)

caster is not a complicated operation. The steps are:

(1) hold the plate on the end of the leg;
(2) mark for the holes;
 3) drill pilot holes;
(4) run the screws through the holes in the plate to secure the caster.

Glide Installation. These come in a wide variety of styles; some screw to the legs while others are nailed to the legs. They are easy to attach, although the installations vary somewhat depending upon the kind chosen. Instructions come packaged with the glide.

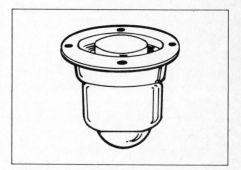

Ballbearing casters are particularly useful where headroom is limited.

SHELF SUPPORTS

For hanging shelves inside cabinets and bookcases you can choose from a number of styles and types.

Standards and Brackets

Several uses for these were discussed in Chapter 2, where it was suggested they be used to vary shelf heights to create maximum storage area.

The standard is the three-sided metal strip with vertical slots that accept the bracket hooks which slip in. The shelves rest on the brackets.

The standards have holes for receiving screws, usually spaced 6 inches to 8 inches apart. After screwing the standard to the wall or back of the cabinet or bookcase, the brackets are just hooked in place in parallel slots and the shelves are laid on them.

Standards and brackets are available in

many different finishes. They can accept shelves up to 18 inches wide, since the brackets the shelf rests on range in size from 4 inches to 18 inches, in 2 inch increments.

Shelves on these hangers may be used to support stereo and other heavy equipment as well as books, as long as the material the screws are being driven into is solid. The standards should be on studs if they will support heavy weights.

Pilasters

Pilasters are similar to standards and brackets. They have metal strips with horizontal slots. These strips screw to the cabinet or bookcase. Short clips fit into the slots. When the shelf has been laid across a pair of pilasters the weight locks the pilasters in place. As with standards and brackets, pilasters may be positioned in different slots to vary shelf height as needed.

Pilasters are made both of steel and aluminum. The steel pilasters are stronger and safer.

Clip Supports

These shelf supports are small clips with ¼ inch diameter projections. The clips are designed to be mounted in ¼ inch holes drilled into the sides of a cabinet. The shelves are then laid across the clips and the weight locks them in place.

The holes for this type of clip must be drilled precisely. For suggestions on how to create such precision-cut holes, see Chapter 9 for jig instructions.

Cleats

Cleats are not really hardware, but they are important when mounting shelves. Cleats are strips or blocks of wood that are screwed to both sides of the cabinet. The shelf is then placed across the cleats. Cleats may be any size you wish, but 1x1 inch gives adequate support.

When using clip supports it is crucial that the holes are perfectly aligned and are all the same size. For instructions on how to build jigs which enable you to drill uniformly sized and spaced holes, see Chapter 9.

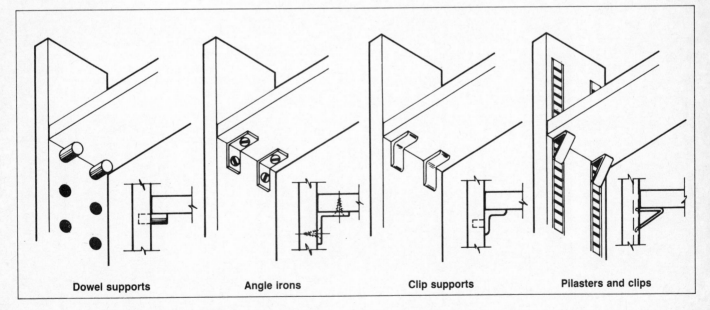

Dowel supports   **Angle irons**   **Clip supports**   **Pilasters and clips**

Any successful attempt to build a cabinet or bookcase, or other carpentry project, requires a solid grasp and some practice of several basic building techniques. One of the more important operations, if indeed there are degrees of importance, is solid joinery — creating the joints used to connect the wood parts that you have cut.

TYPES OF JOINTS

There are many different types of joints that can be used to build a particular project. You can, for example, use rabbet joints to connect the tops and sides of an item, but you could also use the simpler butt joint, or half lap joint. It depends upon the degree of skill you feel you have, the tools at your disposal, and the look you want for the finished piece. A rabbet joint will give a seamless look, while a butt joint will not.

There are a number of alternative tools you can use when making these joints, which can be either hand or power tools. But it is strongly suggested that you use power tools unless you are willing to expend inordinate amounts of time and muscle-power. Here is one gauge of the value of power tools: it is estimated that an inexperienced person with a power saw can cut as much wood as ten experienced carpenters with hand saws over the same period of time.

In this chapter we have concentrated on joinery as used for the projects in Section II and shown in Chapters 1 and 2 of this book. These techniques also can be used on designs of your own creation.

Butt Joint

This is the easiest and simplest of the wood joints. It consists of butting the end of one board or wood section against another. Butt joints can be made using one of a variety of saws; the important point is to cut the stock carefully to ensure that the two pieces will meet flush, with complete contact. To guarantee this, use the measuring hints given in Chapter 5 in order to ensure that the boards will be cut square. Test the joint for fit after cutting, then use a plane or sandpaper — or recut the wood if required — so there will be continuous, total contact between the two adjoining pieces.

Miter Joint

The miter joint can be thought of as a butt joint, except the pieces are cut on a slant, or diagonally.

Frame construction for a cabinet enables you to reduce the weight by using thinner plywood. The frame gives the needed strength. Glue as necessary.

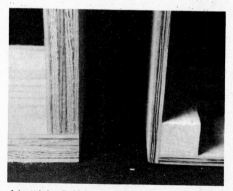

A butt joint (left) is simple to make and suitable for ¾ inch plywood. For thinner panels, use a reinforcing block or nailing strip to make a stronger joint. Glue will make the joint many times stronger than if it were made with nails or screws alone.

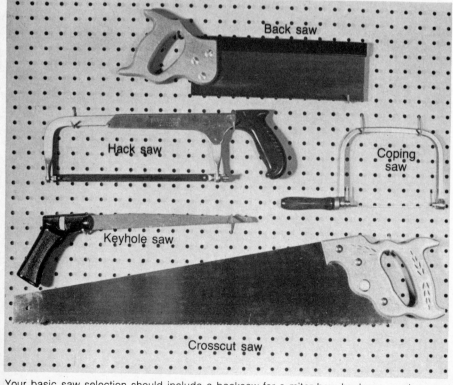

Your basic saw selection should include a backsaw for a miter box, hacksaw, coping saw, keyhole saw, and crosscut saw. You can use metal-working saws to cut wood, but don't use woodworking saws to cut metal.

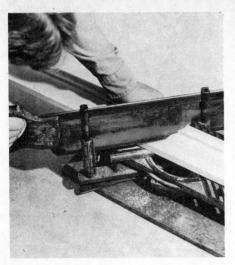

The position of the back saw in a good miter box can be adjusted to cut at any angle.

This joint is very popular in making picture frames. For building purposes it primarily is used for trim, because it results in a clean, finished appearance.

The miter is also used in joining door sections and sometimes on the fronts of cabinets. Its use is usually restricted if joining the main parts of furniture — those pieces that are over 6 inches long — because the miter box that is used to cut the joint does not accept stock longer than 6 inches. Alternate cutting methods for cutting a miter joint, such as using a table saw, prove difficult in most cases.

There are many kinds of miter boxes available. The rule is to get the best you can afford. In addition, use of a good backsaw — one which is long, sharp and solidly constructed — is essential. Once again, buy the best you can afford.

Cutting the Miter. To cut a miter joint, first set the miter box at the angle at which you want to cut the wood. Instructions which come with the tool detail this step, and it is not difficult.

Set the piece of molding that will mate to an adjoining surface firmly in the box and then cut off an inch or two. The purpose here is just to get a clean, finished end. Take the piece of stock (you may have to cut it down into smaller pieces to facilitate working with it) and set it in position on the item on which you are working, at the point where you want the end of the molding to fall. Mark the shape of the adjoining face onto the molding. Position the stock in the box, so that when you make your second and final cut the saw just will follow and obliterate the drawn line as the saw meets the edge of the stock.

If you have cut the miter a little long, you can carefully trim it with a table saw. It is

The first step in cutting a miter is to cut a small piece off the end at the same angle as the final cut in order to have a clean end.

Set the cut piece in its final position and make a square mark at the other, uncut end where you want the other miter to fall. As you cut the miter, the saw should bisect the drawn line just as it meets the edge of the stock.

The completed miter should meet adjacent pieces snugly. If too long, trim the end with the backsaw or run it through a table saw.

better to cut too long than too short; if you cut the stock too short you must start over again.

Proceed to cut the other mating pieces in the same way. When all the pieces are cut, fit them together and nail them in place on your cabinet or bookcase. A good tool for nailing the pieces on is the brad driver. This consists of a wood handle and a hollow metal tube with a spring-activated rod inside and a magnetic head. You pick up the brads with the magnetic head. The rod pushes the head, which pushes the brad into the wood. This is easier than trying to handle the tiny brads and hammer them home.

When the brads are in place, set them with a nailset. Fill the depressions with wood putty and stain or paint to match the stock. (See Chapter 9 for a detailed discussion.)

Dado Joints

A dado joint is useful in a broad range of cases and it gives one of the strongest connections. Basically, a dado is made by cutting a square-edged slot or groove in one piece of wood so the end of another piece will fit snugly into it. You will commonly find dado joints used for shelving; the ends of the shelves fit into dado grooves that have been made in the side pieces.

You can create a dado using a chisel and handsaw. However, this is the hardest method. It is far better to use a table saw or a radial arm saw or a router.

Dadoes are cut easily with these table saw attachments. Fix the two round blades on the outside, the raker blades inside.

If you have a table saw, there are several ways to proceed. First, consider dado blades (a selection is shown in the accompanying photo). There are two round blades, as well as knifelike rakers. Each has a certain thickness — usually ¼ inch for the round blades and ⅛ inch and ⅟₁₆ inch for the rakers. To achieve the desired width of the dado, you use as many round and raker blades as required in order to add up to the width size you require; then set the depth that you wish.

To prevent expensive mistakes when first trying to work this joint — or any joint, for that matter — first experiment with scrap wood until you achieve the correct cut.

Another useful tool accessory when making dadoes is the dado head. This looks like a mini saw blade. It comes with an attachment

The dado head is formed (twisted) to make a cut wider than the blade thickness.

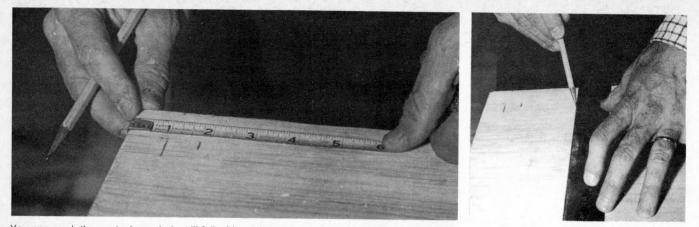

You can mark the spot where dado will fall with a ruler, but always use a square to mark the lines for the dado cut.

Note that a guide board has been clamped to the stock so the base of the router can ride against it, and cut just where it is supposed to.

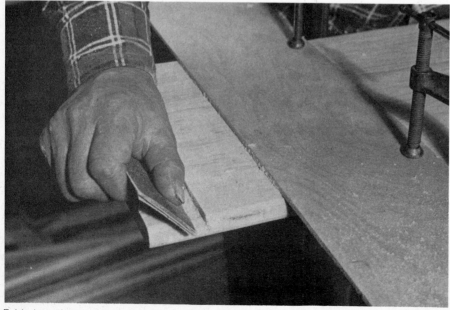

Folded sandpaper can be used to sharpen the edges of a dado.

that allows you to install it on a standard table saw: The dado head is designed (twisted) to provide a cut that is wider than the blade edge. Full instructions for its use come with the device. Again, it is important to practice on scrap until you have the head set to the exact width and depth that you will need.

A dado can also be made with a radial arm saw, but the easiest method is with a router. There are many sorts of router bits available to cut whatever width and depth you wish. Before you begin to cut the dado, use C clamps to secure a straightedge in line with the cut you want to make. The straightedge will act as a guide for the baseplate of the router. Clamp the straightedge so that the cutter will make the dado in the exact spot you wish. You can use a ruler and square to measure and mark dimensions, or you can work it out first on scrap material.

No matter what tool you use to make the groove for the dado, make sure the cut is smooth and the edges sharp so that it can readily accept the mating piece of wood. A piece of tightly folded sandpaper usually works to clean the cut after it has been made. If the cut is very rough, go over it again with the router.

Dowel Joints

Another useful joint is the dowel joint. For this, members are joined using glue and spiral-grooved dowels made for the purpose. Such a joint is commonly used for joining the framing parts of kitchen cabinets, as well as door frames. It looks like a difficult joint to make, but is not hard if you use a dowel jig. This commonly available tool ensures that you drill holes at the correct locations in the pieces of wood that will be joined by the dowels.

Once the parts to be joined have been cut (for the purposes of illustration we will assume that there are four parts — top, bottom and two sides) lay them out in their final relation to one another. Label the joints (for each of the pieces) A, B, C and D, or number them instead. It is necessary to do this because you will be drilling many holes — in this instance 16 — and you want to avoid mixing up the pieces.

Using the Jig. Instructions for use of the jig come with the device, but here is a brief summary of its use and operation. The jig clamps onto the ends of the piece of stock and has holes to guide the drill bit. There is also a guideline on the jig that is lined up with the one or ones you have marked on the ends of the stock. These lines are made to indicate the center (or centers) of the hole(s) to be drilled.

Mark the boards ½ inch in from each side edge; these marks will indicate the positions of the hole centers. Clamp the jig in place, setting it so you can drill a ⅜ inch wide hole which is half as deep as the glue dowel. Use a ⅜ inch bit for the drilling. As a preventive measure, so you don't go deeper than you wish, wrap a piece of tape around the bit at the depth to which you wish to drill. Repeat the clamping-drilling process until all holes have been drilled. Half fill each hole with white glue.

Dowel Placement. Stick glue dowels (each is ⅜ inch in diameter) into these holes, gently rotating them in place until they bottom in the holes. Lay out the cut-out pieces with dowel-sides up; apply glue to the top of each dowel. Let the glue dribble down to coat each dowel well. Place the mating pieces in position but do not attempt to drive them snugly together. If you attempt this, using a hammer or other pressure-exerting tool, it can result in the parts being out of square. Instead, use either bar clamps (which you can rent if necessary) or a jig that you can make out of a length of 2x4 and a couple of short pieces of plywood, as detailed below.

Using Bar Clamps. After loosely assembling the unit, set it on a flat surface. Position one bar clamp over one end of the assembly, and the second clamp at the other end. Gradually tighten the clamps, bringing the pieces of the assembly snugly together, alternating the pressure by tightening first one clamp and then the other — just a little each time.

Making a Wedge-Clamp Jig. If you do not have bar clamps, and are not disposed to buy or rent them, then you can build a jig that will press together the pieces of this particu-

Hardwood dowels cut to length for joining wood have spirals to hold glue for strength.

Parts to be joined by glueing dowels should first be laid out in relation to one another.

Mark the meeting parts a half inch in from the edges — on both pieces for each juncture.

Here is a closeup of the marks for dowels. The line on the jig aligns with the line on the board to center the holes.

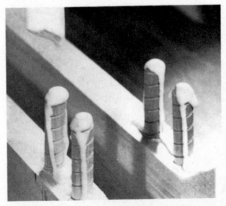
Dribble glue on the projecting dowels.

Loosely join all parts.

The secret to bar clamp use is gradual pressure application, keeping joints square.

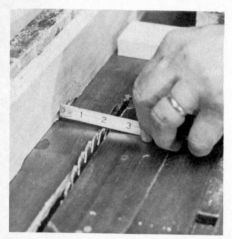

When using a homemade jig, tap on the wedges — first one wedge, then the other — gradually driving parts into square.

For a half lap joint, first set the saw to the width of the cut to be made.

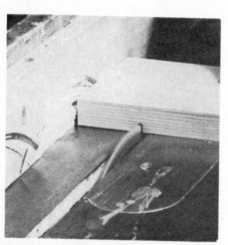

Put the pieces of stock side by side and make the cut to the half-lap depth.

Here is the completed depth cut for both pieces.

lar project, and which can also be used for other projects in the future.

For each end of the assembly to be wedged together, cut a piece of 2x4 (as shown in accompanying photographs) which is about a foot longer than the assembly. Nail a block (approximately ¾ inch x 4 inch x 4 inch or whatever you have handy of comparable size) to the 2x4. The blocks should be square, and located so that when the assembly is laid between them there is about 3 inches of space left open.

Next, cut the wedges. First cut a piece of plywood ¾ inch by 2 inch x 3 inch, then cut diagonally from corner to corner.

Lay the assembly on the 2x4 between the square blocks, on a flat surface. In the open space between the assembly and one of the plywood squares, drive the wedges together gently with a hammer. By driving them in you will take up the slack and push everything together. Alternate hammer taps between the two for steady, even pressure on the assembly being compressed.

As you drive the parts together — either with the wedge jig or with bar clamps — use a framing square or other tool to ensure that the parts are being driven together squarely. When the parts are joined, measure distances between diagonal corners; they should be the same. If the dimensions are not equal, tap the unit so it is square and then hold it with clamps or with jigs until the glue dries.

Half Lap Joint

This is another useful joint, one that is easily made with a table or radial arm saw. It could also be cut with a backsaw. At each end of the board half the width and half the thickness are cut away, and the boards are fitted together in the resulting recesses. The overlap distance (and size of the cut) will be the same as the board width.

To make the joint, first measure in from the end of each board by the width of the board, to find and mark the overlap dimension. Draw lines across the widths of both boards at these markings. Then place the boards next to each other and set the saw so that it will cut across both lines at half the depth (thickness) of both pieces. Make the cuts. Set the fence half the board thickness from the blade. Set the depth (distance) of cut the same as the width of the board. Stand one board on end (turn it 90°, on edge) and push it through the saw, using a push board. The excess piece will fall out. Repeat the procedure on the end of the second board.

It is possible that the fit will not be perfect;

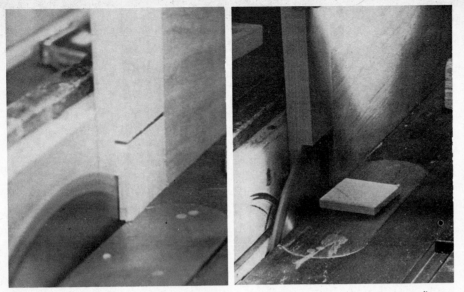

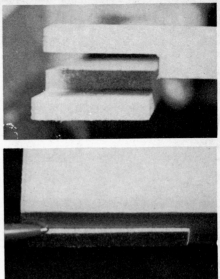

Stand board on end and run through saw blade with a large push board to protect your fingers. Unneeded piece will fall away. Repeat on other board.

Fit the pieces together. If the joint does not fit perfectly, sand or plane off overlap.

one board may overlap the other just a little. If so, use a sharp plane, or sandpaper, to shave off the excess.

Rabbet Joints

The rabbet joint is made by cutting a rectangular recess out of the edge of one piece of stock, to the width of the mating piece. When the pieces are joined, the joint does not show.

The rabbet can be cut in several ways: with stationary power tools, with repeated passes of a circular saw, or with a router with an appropriate bit. Bits are commonly available, but the sizes you can make are limited, up to ½ inch wide. This cut can also be made in one pass with a dado head.

To make the rabbet on a table saw, first draw the outline of the piece to be cut out onto the end of the stock. Set the blade at the depth required (half the thickness of the stock is standard) and run the stock through.

Turn the wood on its side to make the width cut. You can simply set the saw to the intended width, but it is also a good idea to mark the dimension along the top of the board so you can be sure the cut is correct. Run the board through.

That is all there is to the rabbet — make two cuts and a neat rectangular piece of waste will drop out. To ensure that the edges of the cut are square, stick the mating piece of stock in place to see how it fits. If it does not fit well, then adjust the blade or stock position as necessary, and run the joint through again. Sand the cut.

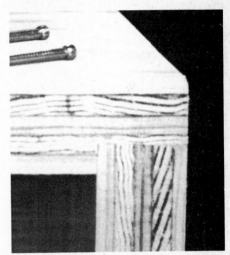

A rabbet joint is easy to make with power tools. This is an ideal joint for drawers, chests, or cabinets.

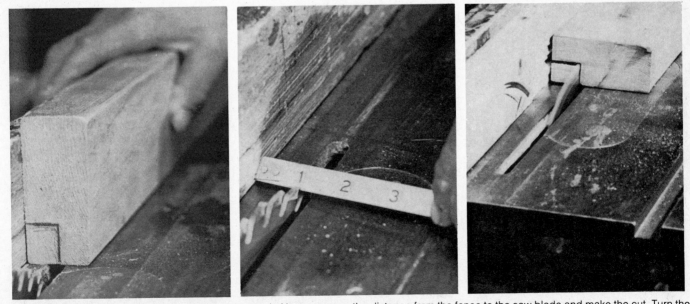

First draw the outline of the joint on the end of the stock. Next, measure the distance from the fence to the saw blade and make the cut. Turn the board on its side and make the second cut.

Dovetail

Dovetail joints are very strong and can handle heavy loads. You can make a dovetail using a router and a dovetail bit, which is certainly the fastest, easiest method. You may, however not want to spend the money for a dovetail bit — which is expensive compared to other bits but is worth buying if you will be building several pieces over a period of time. In this case you may choose to spend the extra time and effort to make the joints by hand, although it requires precise and careful work to ensure a good joint fit.

On one of the ends of the pieces of wood draw the pin outlines. A slope of one in five is most often used, although for exposed, decorative dovetails, a one in six angle is sometimes chosen.

Using a fine-toothed dovetail or backsaw, cut along the outlines, keeping the saw to the waste side of the lines. Make sure the cuts are smooth. To chisel out the wood, use a sharp wood chisel that has a blade which is the same width as the dovetail. File the dovetail smooth, using an emery board.

Use the sawed-out piece of wood to mark the cut-out areas on the second piece of wood. Cut and chisel out the waste; test for fit, filing if necessary. Now apply the glue — not so much that it squeezes out and mars the surface — and clamp until the glue dries.

Finger Lap Joints

No one wants to build a cabinet or bookcase which will become unsteady after a few weeks or months. The sturdiest units are constructed with strong joints, and properly made joints are often difficult and time-consuming to make.

Here we present a joint method which can be used instead of dovetails, and will be appreciated by both the novice and the experienced cabinetmaker. The finger lap joint is relatively simple to produce and is very strong. Rather than the traditional method of cutting notches in board ends which will mesh perfectly, identical, matching notches are cut in all boards and joined with splines — pieces of wood which fit into the notches and give the added strength of a small brace.

Cut all notches the same depth as the thickness of the board, and the same width and the thickness of the splines. This can be done by making several carefully controlled passes with a table saw which has been set to a height equal to the thickness of the board. However, a dado or wobble blade can be purchased for the table saw, and it will assure that all cuts and splines are identical.

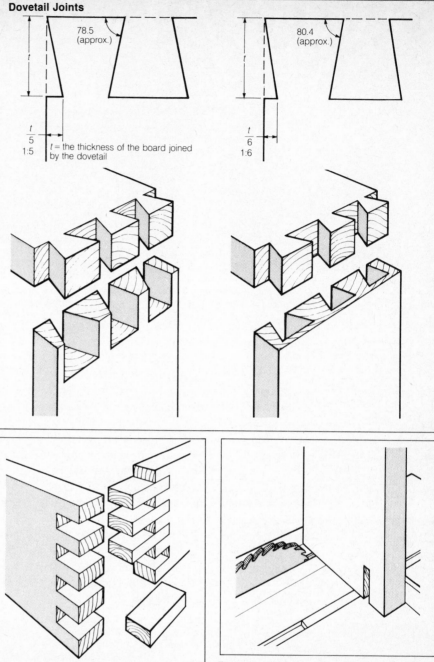

Dovetail Joints

78.5 (approx.)

80.4 (approx.)

t

$\frac{t}{5}$
1:5

$t = $ the thickness of the board joined by the dovetail

$\frac{t}{6}$
1:6

Finger lap joints are strong, inexpensive, and simple to make. Individual pieces of wood called splines are glued into identically cut ends.

The saw blade must be adjusted so that its height is exactly equal to the thickness of the board. The splines determine the width of the cut, which is made by a series of controlled passes with the blade.

Cut all splines so their lengths are exactly the thickness of two boards.

Splines made of plywood or hardwood should be cut to fill the notches exactly. Softwood splines must be cut slightly larger, and forced gently into the notches for reliable strength.

When joining sections of plywood, fewer notches and splines are required because of the naturally greater strength of plywood. Notches need be made only as frequently as every eight inches. The splines for plywood may be either plywood or solid hardwood,

cut or planed to size. Plywood splines will, of course, be stronger than solid. However, splines may be cut out of the same wood as the boards, or of contrasting wood, or of plywood. When using plywood rather than solid wood, you must use more glue because the end grain of any wood will soak up more glue than will the long grain.

To assemble the splines and boards, apply glue to splines and notches for one board, and then insert the splines into the glued notches. Align and let dry before gluing and aligning the second board.

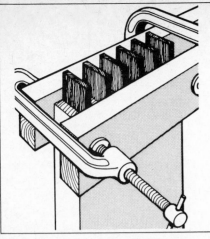

Apply glue and fit splines evenly in the board, clamp a piece of lumber on each side of the board and the splines so that the edges are aligned. To align the splines to the depth of the cuts, place a board over the ends and tap firmly with a rubber mallet.

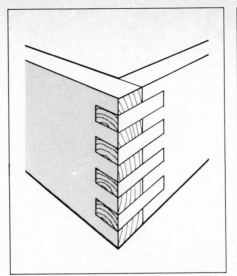

Splines may be made of the same wood as the boards for an unobtrusive joint or contrasting wood for a decorative joint.

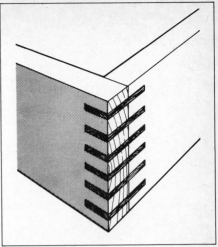

No matter what wood is used for the splines, each must be exactly twice as long as the thickness of the board, and each cut in the boards must be exactly equal to the width of the spline.

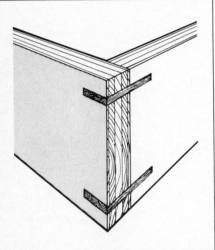

Because of its natural rigidity, lumber-core plywood may be joined with splines as far as 8 in. apart.

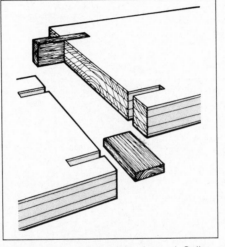

Splines can be used to join plywood. Splines for joining lumber-core plywood need not be thick. You may use either plywood or solid stock, planed down to the proper thickness.

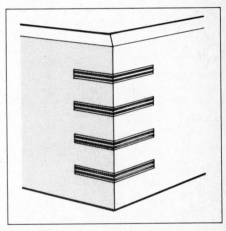

It is possible to use spline joints at other than right angles when constructing something with more than four sides. Multisided objects such as planters may be built using "arrowhead" splines cut to match the mitered corners of the unit being constructed.

"Arrowhead" splines are cut with the aid of a miter box. To ensure a perfect match of angle, it is advisable to cut these a bit longer than the thickness of the board. The splines can be sanded and/or planed down from each direction of the angle until they are at the exact level as the surfaces being joined.

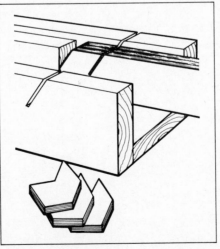

In order for the notches in the boards to be cut to the proper depth and angle, you must hold the miter-angle cut end of the board firmly against the saw table as you guide the board through the saw.

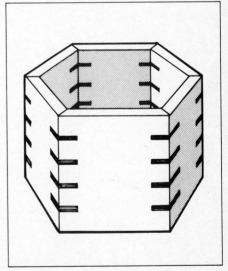

The finished unit will have tight and exact joints which are not only exceptionally strong and rigid, but are very attractive.

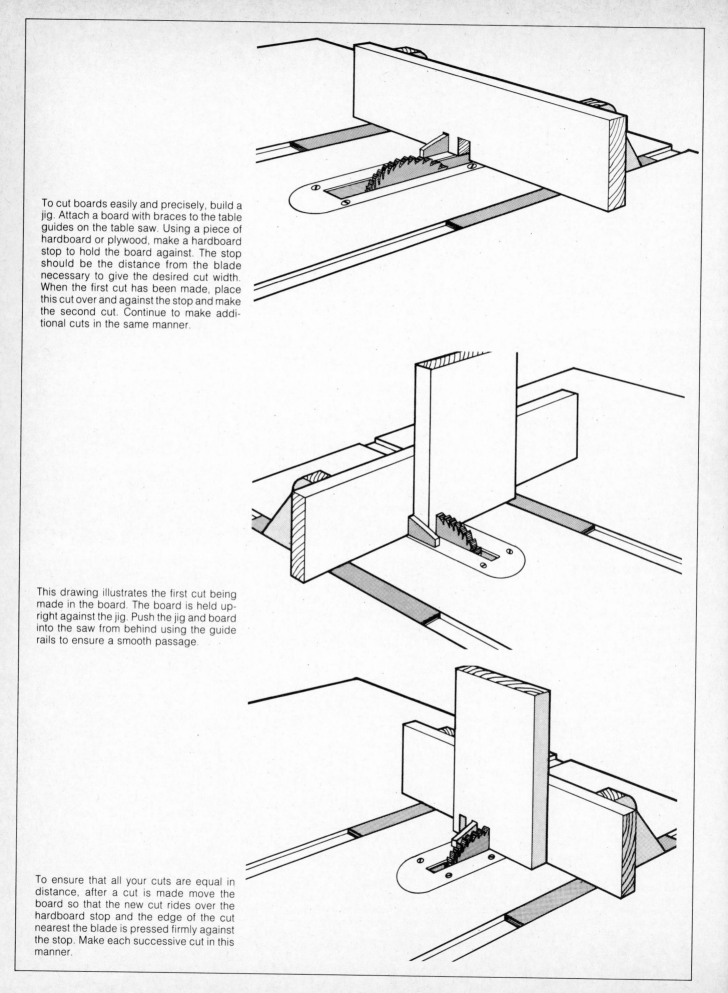

To cut boards easily and precisely, build a jig. Attach a board with braces to the table guides on the table saw. Using a piece of hardboard or plywood, make a hardboard stop to hold the board against. The stop should be the distance from the blade necessary to give the desired cut width. When the first cut has been made, place this cut over and against the stop and make the second cut. Continue to make additional cuts in the same manner.

This drawing illustrates the first cut being made in the board. The board is held upright against the jig. Push the jig and board into the saw from behind using the guide rails to ensure a smooth passage.

To ensure that all your cuts are equal in distance, after a cut is made move the board so that the new cut rides over the hardboard stop and the edge of the cut nearest the blade is pressed firmly against the stop. Make each successive cut in this manner.

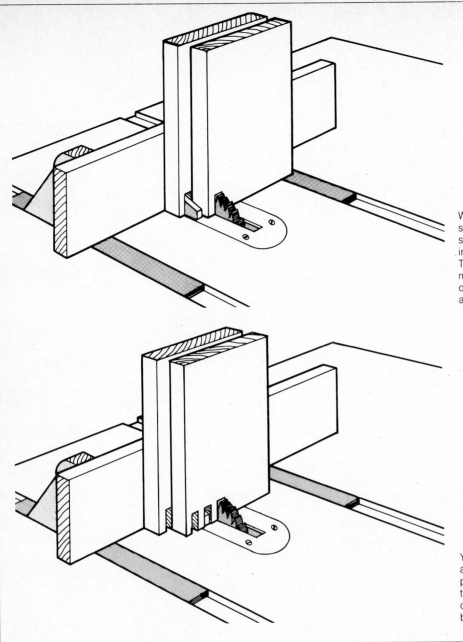

When cutting several boards, time may be saved by cutting two at a time. Place the second board in front of the first after the initial cut has been made on the first board. The first cut on the second board will be made simultaneously with the second cut on the first board. This ensures that all cuts are the same.

Your hardboard stop must be long enough and strong enough to maintain the proper position of both boards when cutting them together. This stop projects from the jig a distance equal to the thickness of two boards.

GLUE

Glue is a backup material for strengthening joints. Even when using nails it is advisable to use glue on the joints. If you use screws, and do not intend to disassemble the item later, then also use glue.

For interior projects, white glue will be adequate. Just apply a wavy bead of it onto one of the mating surfaces. It will spread well when the parts are joined. Take care not to use too much glue; some is bound to squeeze out, but you do not want an excessive amount running down the side of your project. White glue dries clear, but will change the color of any stain applied. If you wipe it off with a wet rag it will raise the grain of the wood, again creating a different surface for the stain.

Before gluing a plywood joint, test its fit. For lasting strength, the pieces should be in contact at all points.

It is best to wipe off glue with a dry rag, then lightly sand the area. If you will be applying a solid material such as laminate or the like, you can use a sander to take off any extra material resulting from inexact cuts. This is detailed in Chapter 11.

Use resorcinol glue for exterior work. This comes as a brown powder which you mix together with water. It is weatherproof.

To control the amount of glue and prevent drips, apply glue to plywood edges using a brush or a stick. End grain absorbs glue so quickly that it is best to apply a preliminary coat. Allow it to soak in for a few minutes, and then apply another coat before joining the parts.

Tightly clamp the joints for units of plywood, using clamps as shown, or with nails, screws, or other fasteners. Use blocks of wood under the jaws of the clamps to prevent damage to the plywood. Since some glues will stain or seal the wood, and make it difficult to achieve a good finish, quickly wipe off any excess. Sand the area once it has dried. Test for squareness, then allow the glue to set.

It is often easiest to assemble and clamp sub-assemblies (rather than the entire unit.) These will be simpler to handle and make joints more accessible, as shown by these partitioned shelves. Apply the clamps with the full jaw length in contact. When jaws are not parallel, as shown at right, pressure is applied to only part of the joint.

Use of special clamps can save work and help you do a better job. Here are various types of edge-clamps, used to glue wood or plastic edging to plywood. Bar clamps or quick C clamps grip the panel which is protected by scrap wood. Then edge clamping fixtures are inserted to bear against the edge-banding material while glue sets.

GLUES FOR WOODWORKING

Type of Glue	Description	Recommended Use	Precautions	How To Use
Urea Resin	Comes as powder to be mixed with water and used within 4 hours. Light colored, Very strong if joint fits well.	Good for general wood gluing. First choice for work that must stand some exposure to dampness, since it is moisture resistant.	Needs well-fitted joints, tight clamping, and room temperature 70° or warmer.	Make sure joint fits tightly. Mix glue and apply thin coat. Allow 16 hours drying time.
Liquid Resin (White glue)	Comes ready to use at any temperature. Clean-working, quick-setting. Strong enough for most work, though not quite so tough as urea resin glue.	Good for indoor furniture and cabinetwork. First choice for small jobs where tight clamping or good fit may be difficult.	Not sufficiently resistant to moisture for outdoor furniture or outdoor storage units. (Thoroughly clean up squeeze-out in areas to receive stain finish.)	Use at any temperature but preferably above 60°. Spread on both surfaces, clamp at once. Sets in 1½ hours.
Resorcinol (Waterproof)	Comes as powder plus liquid, must be mixed each time used. Dark colored, very strong, completely waterproof.	This is the glue to use with Exterior type plywood for work to be exposed to extreme dampness.	Expense, trouble to mix and dark color make it unsuited to jobs where waterproof glue is not required. Needs good fit, tight clamping.	Use within 8 hours after mixing. Work at temperature above 70°. Apply thin coat to both surfaces; allow 16 hours drying time.

The glues described above are those used most often. Other glues sometimes substituted include:

Hot melt glues — for use with relatively small parts, these cool and set quickly.

Epoxy glues — only limited use with wood (expensive; most are not ideally formulated for use with wood), some epoxies may prove successful.

Contact cement — useful when applying laminates and edge stripping to plywood, but not recommended for structural joints.

Wall-panel adhesives — handy for applying decorative paneling for facing, but you may need to use a few nails per panel to resist any slight tendency for panels to pull away due to warping.

Casein glues — these are slow setting, resulting in difficult assembly.

8 Building Doors and Drawers

The very simplest type of drawer can be made using only hand tools. The secret is its bottom, made of ⅜ inch or ½ inch plywood. The bottom extends ⅜ inch beyond the sides of the drawer to form a lip. Ease the edges and apply paraffin for smooth operation.

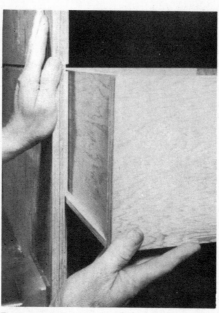

The extended bottom of the drawer fits into slots formed by gluing pieces of ⅜ inch plywood to the inner surface of each side of the cabinet. A gap just wide enough to take the lip is left between these pieces.

BUILDING DRAWERS

Building a drawer is not as simple a process as it seems at first glance. While basically just a well-made box, the parts of a drawer must fit together well enough so the drawer slides smoothly in and out of the cabinet opening despite fairly close tolerances.

The drawers you make should complement the cabinet style and be made of the same material as used for the doors. Basically, there are three major styles. They are, in order of ease of construction, the overlay, the lip and the flush drawer. Each is characterized by the style of the front. Butt, rabbet, and dado joints are used in making these drawers. A preferred practice of the best professionals is use of dovetail joints, but these are more difficult to make and the other joints serve nearly as well.

Following are directions for building all three types. Except for overlay, use 1 inch Number 2 Common pine for the fronts and sides. (One inch is nominal size, not actual size.) If you buy enough of it, you should be able to cut enough clear material from it for all of the parts required and still save money

Here is a drawer (shown upside down) that can easily be built using a saw and hammer. Butt joints are glued and nailed. The bottom should be ⅜ inch or ½ inch plywood for rigidity. The drawer front extends down to cover the front edge of the bottom.

An additional strip of wood, glued and nailed to the front panel, reinforces the bottom of this second type of drawer made with hand tools. The reinforcing permits use of economical ¼ inch plywood for drawer bottom.

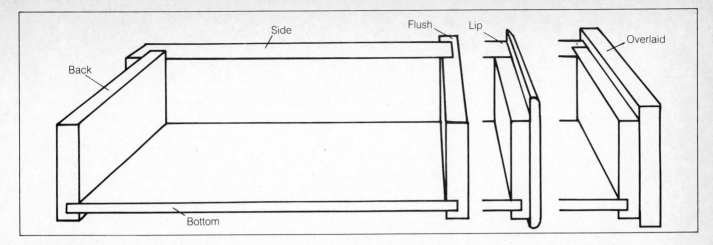

as opposed to buying Clear grade. Bring the measurements for your cut-out pieces with you when you buy the wood so you can check for the necessary lengths of clear material between the knots. Drawer bottoms are normally of ¼ inch plywood, but may be ⅜ inch thick if you expect to store heavy items. Although the standard drawer is 12 inches to 18 inches wide and 18 inches to 20 inches deep regardless of the depth of the cabinet opening, you may wish to adjust the depth if you will have to store longer items.

Remember, as mentioned earlier, to measure any stock before you use it. A piece of wood nominally ½ inch thick can vary slightly in actual thickness and throw off your cutting and calculations.

Construction of Overlay Drawer

Start by measuring the cabinet opening. Cut the front (from ½ inch stock) large enough so that it overlaps the frame around the opening by the same amount as — and can be shaped in the same way as — the doors. (See later, this chapter.) Shape as desired.

Cut the sides to the depth you need, and at least ¼ inch to ½ inch less in height than the opening. Cut back and inside front member of the drawer from ½ inch plywood the same height as the sides, but 1½ inches narrower than the opening. When the parts are assembled this will create a box with ½ inch space on each side — 1 inch in all — to accommodate drawer hardware.

Next, as indicated in the drawings, cut the rabbets and dadoes in the sides and back. You may use a router, radial arm saw or table saw, but in all cases use a fence (adjustable metal guide) and protect it with a wood block. You do not want a metal fence to contact a metal cutter. The cuts should be made in the best faces of the stock, keeping the cleanest edge of the stock away from the fence.

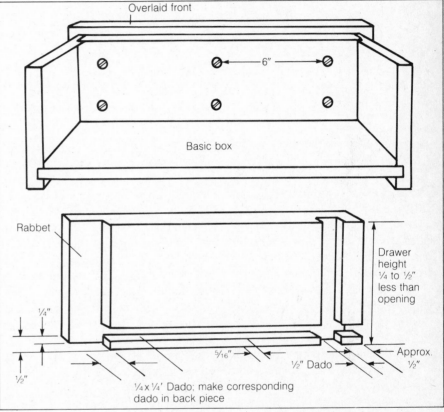

Fit the parts together dry. If dadoes or rabbets are not exact the parts will not fit squarely. Trim the cuts as required, or shim them out with thin strips of wood. When square, measure the distance between the dadoes for the bottom and cut this to size. Fit all the parts together. If the fit is a good one, assemble the parts with 3d finishing nails and white glue, forming the basic box; however, do not glue the bottom in place. If the drawer is not square, the loose bottom will enable you to later pull the box into square. If this becomes necessary, place a square in one corner of the drawer and pull the drawer until its sides are flush against the square. Clamp in position.

Now attach the overlaid front using No. 8 flathead wood screws. The number of screws used will depend on the size of the drawer, but for standard drawer sizes six screws will do, spaced every 6 inches along the perimeter. Whether using nails or screws, always drive flush with the surface except when — as is the case with an overlaid front — they would be visible. To hide the fasteners in an overlaid front, countersink and fill the depressions with wood putty.

It should be noted that if you will be making more than one drawer, you should do all your cutting, rabbeting and dadoing at the same time in assembly-line fashion. Otherwise you will have to reset your machine after each drawer is completed, which will be time-consuming and may introduce error.

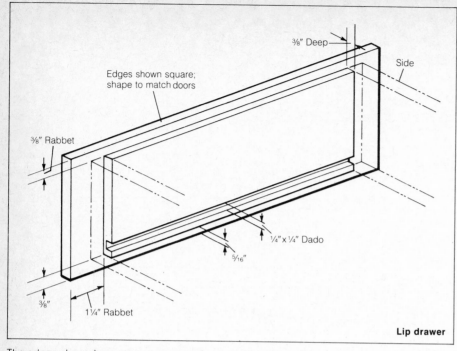

3/8" Deep

Side

Edges shown square;
shape to match doors

3/8" Rabbet

1/4" x 1/4" Dado

5/16"

3/8"

1 1/4" Rabbet

Lip drawer

The edges shown here are square; round or ease the edges of the drawer fronts as needed to match door style.

Making a Lip Drawer

The front of a lip drawer (as shown) is one piece of ¾ inch stock whose back face has been rabbeted and beveled on the edges. Cut the front to an overall size that will be ½ inch wider and ½ inch higher than the cabinet opening. Measure ⅜ inch from the top and bottom; rabbet the backside of the top and bottom of the front edges ⅜ inch x ⅜ inch. Then rabbet the ends ⅜ inch deep x 1¼ inches wide. Cut the dado ¼ inch deep along the bottom of the backside of the drawer front. You can shape the edges with a ⅜ inch quarter round cutter in a router, or use a plane and sandpaper. The rabbets can be done with a plywood cutting blade in a table saw or a dado head in a radial arm saw. If you wish, you can also obtain a special cutter that can do the whole job — both rabbets and edge-shaping — with one pass.

Cut the sides. These should be done in the same manner as the overlay drawer, except that the front ends should be left square instead of being rabbeted. Before cutting the back of the drawer, determine its size by measuring across the inside face of the front — the raised panel — and adding ½ inch to this dimension. This gives ½ inch for the width of each dado required. Cut the pieces out and cut the ¼ inch deep dadoes in the back.

Dry-assemble the drawer, adjusting the cuts (recutting or shimming out — adding thin strips of wood) so that the pieces all fit together squarely. When they fit together

well, measure for, and then cut, the bottom. Assemble the parts with 3d nails and glue.

Flush Drawer

Cut the front of a flush drawer to the exact size of the cabinet opening. When you install the drawer you will have to plane and sand slightly to fit the drawer in, but for now the square edges will make it easier to measure and mark the dado locations on the front.

After cutting out the front, mark and cut the dadoes for it. The dado for the bottom should be ¼ inch deep x ¼ inch wide and ⁵⁄₁₆ inch from the bottom edge; those for the sides should be ½ inch from the ends, ½ inch wide and ¼ inch deep.

Now cut the sides to the length and height, as you did for the other types of drawers. Cut

dadoes for the back piece in the same way, matching the dado in the front piece.

To determine the size needed for the back, fit the sides in the front dadoes, and measure across including the back dadoes. Cut the back to this length.

Dry assemble the parts, shimming or enlarging dadoes as mentioned earlier, then measuring and cutting the bottom. Assemble the drawer with glue and 3d nails. As with the other types of drawers, the bottom should not be glued.

Hardware

When it comes to hardware, a drawer is not the place to cut corners. Even a handsomely constructed unit will become an ugly nuisance if the drawers do not function properly.

If is suggested that you get side-mounted track hardware. This consists of two sections for each side, with wheels. One section is mounted inside the cabinet, and the mating section goes on the drawer.

A number of companies make this type of hardware, including Knape and Vogt, Keil and Grant. Installation instructions come on the package, but they don't tell you how to prepare the inside of the cabinet for mount-

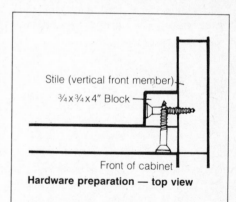

Stile (vertical front member)

¾ x ¾ x 4" Block

Front of cabinet

Hardware preparation — top view

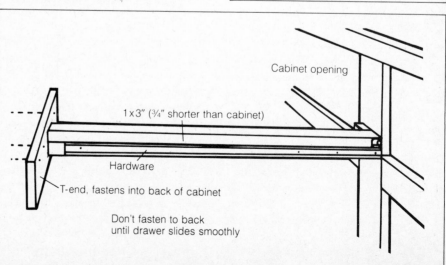

Cabinet opening

1 x 3" (¾" shorter than cabinet)

Hardware

T-end, fastens into back of cabinet

Don't fasten to back
until drawer slides smoothly

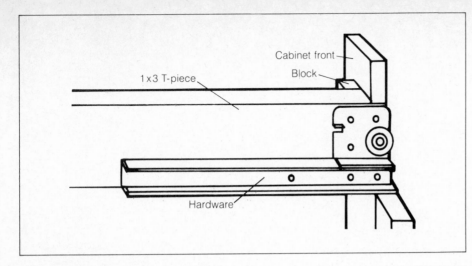

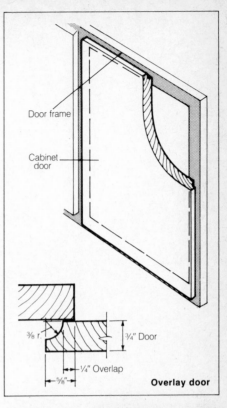

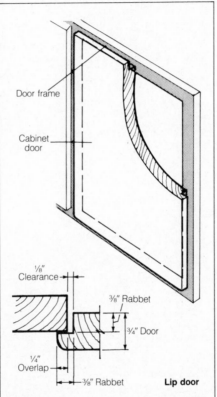

ing the hardware. To do this, cut a piece of 1x3 so that it is ¾ inch shorter than the depth of the cabinet. Cut another piece of stock 1x3x4 inches long and screw this to the end of the first, forming a T shape. Set aside. Cut a block of wood ¾ inch x ¾ inch x 4 inches. Screw this to the front end of the cabinet as shown, then fasten the 1x3 T piece to it, but leave the T-end free. Mount the hardware to the 1x3 T piece and the drawer. Repeat the procedure on the other side of the drawer.

Slide the drawer into place. Adjust the T pieces until the drawer slides smoothly, then screw them to the back of the cabinet. This procedure will enable you to adjust for any errors that have crept in while making the drawers, and which might prevent their sliding smoothly.

DOORS

The three basic styles of doors used on cabinets and bookcases correspond to drawer types: the lip door, the overlay doors and the flush door.

Lip Doors

The lip door is usually made from ¾ inch thick material. It has a lip all around, into which the frame of the cabinet or bookcase fits. The lip door should be cut so that it overlaps the frame ¼ inch in both height and width. For example, if the width of the opening is 10 inches, the door should be cut 10½ inches; if the height is 16 inches, the material should be cut 16½ inches. The door is also rounded on the front edge all around, and it takes a ⅜ inch x ⅜ inch rabbet cut along the edge (running out to the edge).

You can round off the edges with a router and suitable bit, or you can use a sharp plane and fine sandpaper. If the material is covered with plastic laminate, then a router with a plastic laminate bit must be used. Once

mounted, the resulting door will fit snugly into the opening, leaving ⅛ inch space on either side.

Overlay Door

The overlay door (also assuming 1 inch material) should be 1¼ inches bigger in both directions (height and width) than the door opening.

Constructing this door involves using a router to cut a ⅜ inch cove or recess all around the back edges to give a finger pull for the door. This will trim off some of the excess material. When the door is mounted, it will extend beyond the opening ¼ inch. This is the easiest door to make, and if you have some anxiety about mounting hinges,

To install a ⅜ inch concealed hinge use a router to create a cove or recess around the back of the door.

then it is suggested that you make this type of door and use concealed hinges.

Concealed Hinges On Overlay Doors. To install a concealed hinge on an overlay door, first measure 2 inches from the top and bottom of each door to represent the hinge locations. If a third hinge is planned it should be equidistant between the other two.

Slip each hinge onto the back of the door so that it fits neatly into the cove you have made. Position the door on the cabinet to test fit, and to mark where the screw holes fall for the hinges. Then drill pilot holes for flathead screws, and screw the hinge in place.

When all the hinges have been installed, lift the door up and place it in position in the cabinet opening. Using the loose leaf on the

Set the hinge loosely in place. This door was made with a separate back, but the recess is still ⅜ inch so the hinge will fit. The pin on the hinge fits against the outside edge of the door. Now screw the hinge to the door; next, screw the second piece to the cabinet framing.

hinge(s) as a template, mark and drill pilot holes and then simply screw the hinge in place.

Flush Door

This is the most difficult door to install correctly because the tolerances are so close. The door must fit into the cabinet opening leaving just a small amount of space — ¹⁄₃₂ inch — to work properly and to look good. There is little allowance for error.

To make the door carefully measure the opening and cut the door to the exact size required. Use a router or saw to bevel the hinge side ¹⁄₃₂ inch slanting toward the back of the door; the bevel enables the door to clear the frame more easily.

You may find that after installation the door binds on the hinge side. If so, sand it with fine sandpaper as needed until it swings easily.

If you install doors in a free-standing cabinet or in bookcases in any place other than their final location, it is a good idea to check that the unit is level while you install the doors. Level the unit carefully by inserting wood shims under it in the spot where it will be permanently positioned. By following this procedure you will ensure that the doors open and close easily and are properly aligned.

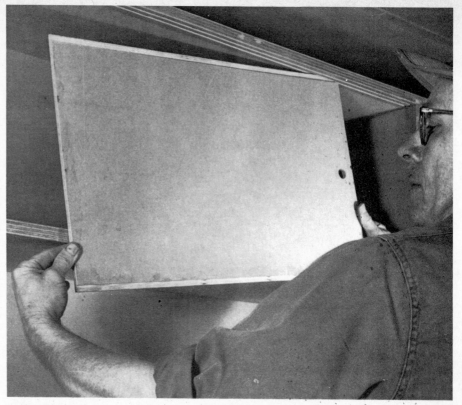

A close-fitting sliding door of plywood can be made by rabbeting top and bottom edges of each door. Also rabbet the back of the front door, and the front of the back door. This means the door will almost touch, permitting only a small gap for dust. It also increases the depth of the cabinet. For ⅜ inch plywood doors rabbeted half their thickness, plow two grooves in top and bottom of cabinet ½ inch apart.

To create removable sliding doors, plow bottom groves ³⁄₁₆ inch deep, top ⅜ inch deep. After finishing insert the door by pushing up into the excess space in the top groove, and then dropping it into bottom. Plowing can be eliminated by use of a fiber track made for sliding doors of this type.

This sliding door can be made with hand tools. Apply front and back strips of stock ¼ inch quarter-round molding. The strip between is ¼ inch square. Use glue and brads or finish nails to fasten strips securely. A sliding door cabinet track also may be used.

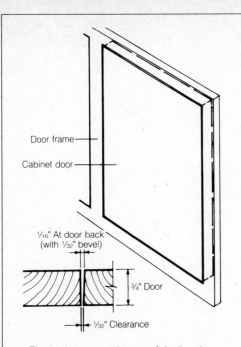

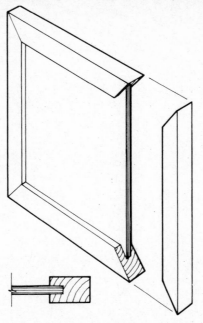

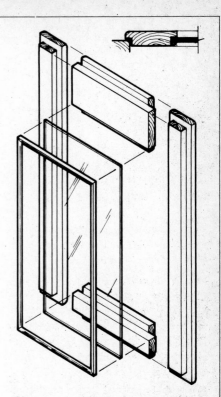

Door frame

Cabinet door

1/16" At door back
(with 1/32" bevel)

3/4" Door

1/32" Clearance

Flush doors require careful planning and measurement, but provide clean lines and styling which may be worth your extra time and effort.

The frame of the recessed panel door is 3/4 inch stock, grooved 1/4 x 3/8 inch to hold a 1/4 inch panel. Test the panel in the groove to be sure it fits. Glue in the panel; use brads at the corners.

Glass or panel insets are secured by quarter-round molding nailed in with brads. The door frame is rabbeted 3/4 inch at the outside edge. A 1/4 inch x 3/8 inch rabbet on the inside receives the inset and molding.

Rout the pieces for the drawer or cabinet sides for the drawer guides, if this is the method you have chosen. If your project is a bookcase, and your shelves are to be permanently installed, you should rout the sides for the shelves. If you are planning adjustable shelves, you will need to drill holes for support tabs or rout the sides for pairs of metal strips which hold similar tabs. The strips allow for smaller adjustments than drilled holes, which cannot be closer than approximately one inch without the chance of damage to the wood. If you find that a tight, side-to-side fit is not necessary for your needs, you may apply the strips without routing. However, your shelves will need to be cut short enough to allow for the thickness of the strips. You could cut notches in the shelves to fit around the strips. While this may seem easier, final installation and adjustments of the shelves may prove more difficult.

Before assembly, sand any rough places on the surfaces and any rough edges on the wood. Careful cutting should have minimized any splintering of the edges, but if your saw has left any jagged places, you must smooth these now. You will avoid two problems: splinters in your fingers and torn surfaces on your wood. Even a small, jagged piece may pull and tear away, taking a length of grain fiber and leaving a mar in the wood which will have to be repaired before you can stain and finish the project.

After checking the fit of the pieces, assemble the top, bottom and sides of the project with glue and nails, countersinking each nail, then clamping until dry and sound. If your project uses a frame, construct that first, using the same technique, then attach the top, sides and bottom, also using the glue and nail procedure. Attach the back with a flush or set-back butt joint or with a flush or set-in rabbet joint. Glue and nail, using clamps for secure drying. If you have used butt joints, bevel the edges of the back so they will not show.

If your project has a door, this should be fitted now. Make any adjustments necessary

A drawer guide may be created by routing the sides of your cabinet and nailing a strip on wood to the sides of the drawers.

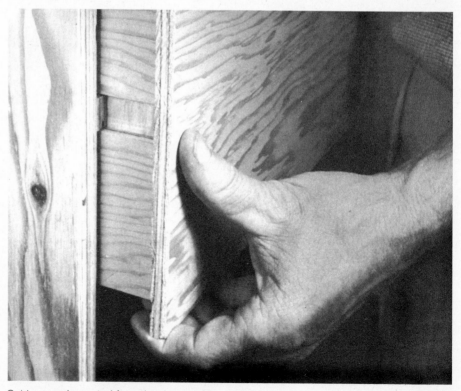

Guides may be routed from the drawer sides and guide strips installed on the cabinet sides.

for a good fit, and allow for changes which will occur when the project surface is finished.

When you are satisfied that assembly is complete and solid, fill any nail holes and sand before finishing.

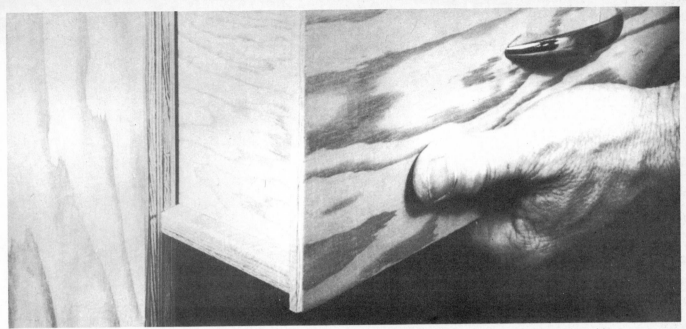

The bottom of the drawer may also serve as the drawer guide. It is cut large enough to fit into routed slots in the cabinet sides.

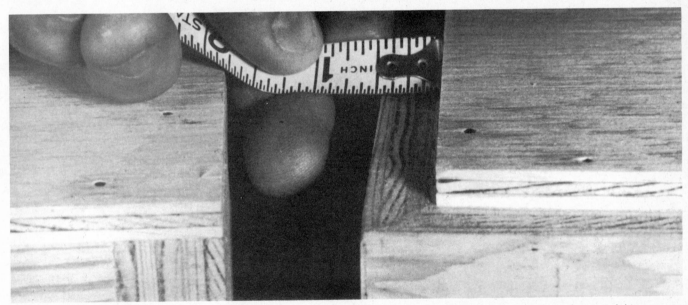

Attaching the back of the cabinet with a butt joint is simple. The back fits flush, as shown at left, or is recessed, as shown at right.

If the back is installed with flush butt joints, the edges should be beveled with a plane for an unobtrusive and finished look.

Cabinet backs may also be finished with either flush or set-in rabbet joints. Both will provide secure finished cabinets.

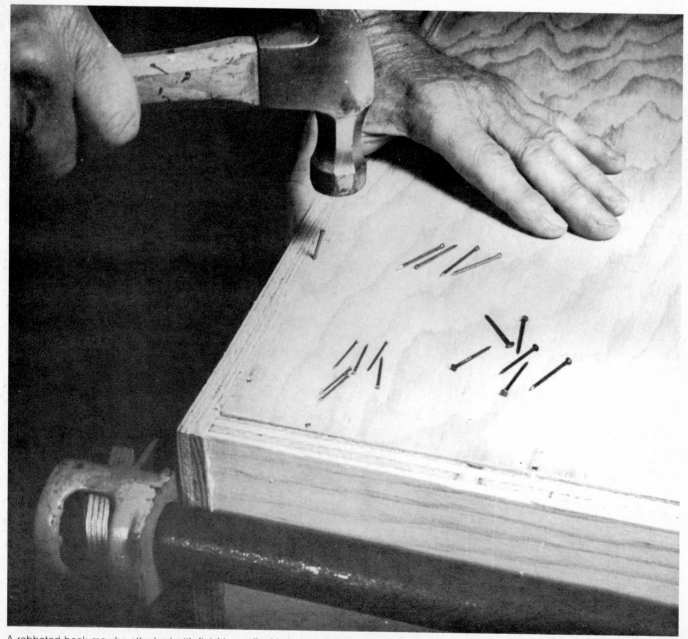

A rabbeted back may be attached with finishing nails driven in at a slight angle to bite into the thickest section of the sides.

A "two-handed" stapler is a useful tool for fastening rabbeted back to cabinets and drawers. A sharp blow with a rubber mallet drives the staple through the back. Staplers can be rented.

A recessed, rabbeted back may be given a more finished look with the addition of quarter-round to conceal the joining of the back.

For security, non-adjustable cabinet shelves should be installed in routed slots, glued, and nailed. If the shelves will bear a heavy load, choose heavier wood and consider bracing it.

The finish for a bookcase or cabinet is like the icing on a cake. It can be an immensely satisfying experience, and will reinforce your feeling that it was well worth all the effort to build your own unit.

There are many different finishes you can apply to wood. Here is a roundup and some finishing tips; manufacturers also provide instructions with their products.

TYPES OF FINISHES

Finishes may be categorized as "clear" or "stain". The clear types are designed to let the beauty of the wood grain show through. Standard stains are used to color the wood; they are coated with a clear finish for protection, since the stains themselves do not offer protection. There are also penetrating finishes which combine both stain and clear finish: they color and protect in the same operation.

Clear Finish

Varnish. This has long been a favorite of some woodworkers, but it is not enough to say "varnish." Under this heading you have a number of different choices.

Standard Varnish. Regular varnish is designed to be used on interior surfaces. It has an oil base. You can apply it with a brush or by spray. It dries to a hard glossy finish, but it takes a long time to dry — 24 hours. Therefore it must be used only in rooms which are dust-free, or in areas where dust cannot get in, such as in a polyethelene tent or booth you put up. This, of course, can be problematic for a do-it-yourselfer to achieve, and it exists with all varnishes to a greater or lesser degree.

Quick-Drying Varnish. Here, quick means around four hours, depending on temperature and humidity in the room. Quick-drying varnish comes in various formulations, each designed for a specific use, such as on boats or cabinets. Hence, when you shop for it, make sure you pick the formulation that is right for your purpose.

Rubbing Varnish. Both regular and quick-drying varnish produce a glossy finish, but if you want an extremely high-gloss finish, buy rubbing varnish. This coating will dry very hard — harder than other varnishes — and can be rubbed with pumice stone and oil to produce a very high gloss.

Cabinet Varnish. This is similar to rubbing varnish in that it can be rubbed to produce an extra high gloss.

Spar Varnish. This type of varnish is designed for extra durability; for example, it is commonly used on bartops. It stands up to liquid well (as do other varnishes) and it is less subject to scratches or other damage.

Spar varnish can be rubbed, but only to a low sheen; it does not take on the high gloss that other varnishes will.

There are interior and exterior types of spar varnish. The exterior material dries in a few hours and will stand up to severe weather conditions.

Polyurethane Varnish. This is another varnish used for exterior cabinetry. It dries in one or two hours and can be rubbed to a low luster.

Flat Varnish. Some people prefer that cabinetry have a low sheen, or flat look, and for this there is flat varnish. Most woodworkers apply it over coats of other varnish which have a gloss.

Shellac. This comes in two types, or "colors": white and orange. In reality, the white shellac is a creamy color while the orange shellac is amber. White shellac dries very clear and will preserve the natural beauty of wood. Hence, it is often used on fine woods where it is desirable to leave the wood grain exposed. Orange shellac darkens wood, although many finishers use it on wood that is already dark. It can also be used to give wood an aged look.

Shellac comes in various cuts, which means the amount of alcohol added to the base that is made from the powdered lac beetle. The lower the number of the cut, the more alcohol it has, and the thinner its consistency. For beginning woodworkers, the two-pound cut is considered best.

Shellac has two distinct advantages over varnish. It is much easier to apply (it has a watery consistency) and it dries in much less

Both the spar varnish, above left, and the polyurethane, right, are clear finishes. By trying finishes first on a sample of the wood, you can see the differences in effect. Here, the difference is minimal, although the polyurethane gives a slightly glossier result.

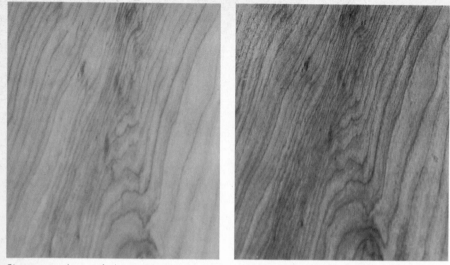

Shown are pieces of plywood before shellac application (left) and after.

time. However, it should not be used as a finish coat if there is an expected use of liquids. Shellac will quickly discolor when exposed to liquid. Because of its easy application, many finishers will apply two coats of shellac as a base coat and then add a layer of varnish. However, it can be used successfully by itself where it will not be exposed to liquid.

When buying shellac, pay attention to the date of its manufacture, which will be stamped on the can. The fresher the shellac, the easier it will be to work with.

Lacquer

Many cabinetmakers use only lacquer on pieces they build, because it combines everything they need in a finish. It dries instantly, and is hard and durable. It comes in flat or gloss colors, or clear. A clear lacquer will change the color of the wood less than a varnish. Since it dries quickly, several coats can be applied, rubbed, and finished within several days.

Lacquer must be applied with a spray gun or spray can. It dries too quickly for a smooth brush application, although brush-on types are sold. Unless you have a very large project, the spray can will be fine. You may have to use two or three cans of it, but the benefits should offset the cost.

Use lacquer finishes only where there will be little chance of contact with moisture. The finish will become cloudy or white if it contacts water. Lacquer should not be applied over some finishes or wood fillers — those with a mineral spirit base. For some woods, such as rosewood, a thin seal coat of shellac must be applied to prevent bleeding.

Penetrating Finish. This is also known as a penetrating sealer. It comes clear and will seep into the wood and protect its surface. Its low luster and clarity will allow the beauty of the wood finish to show through. If you wish, you can also buy penetrating finish with an added color. The most common course is to stain the wood first with one of the other stains and then to apply the penetrating type.

Unlike some other stains and finishes, a penetrating finish can be touched up without the touchups being evident.

Antique Finish

This finish consists first of a base coat, which is applied like paint. Once this is dry, a colored glaze coat is applied and partially wiped off (with more left near the edges) to achieve a grain effect. If may also be striated using steel wool. A clear, protective coat is applied after the glaze has dried. Antique finishes are available in a great many different colors, with special tools for additional effects.

Antiquing is for do-it-yourselfers who have some trepidation (although there should not be any) about applying other finishes. Antique finishes are easy to apply and offer a high probability for a result that will satisfy you. Antiqued furniture can also be subjected to "distressing" techniques to make it look older.

Here are the components used in antiquing: a base color, a glaze and a varnish.

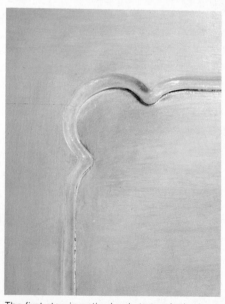

The first step in antiquing is to apply the base coat. The glaze is then applied, once the base coat has dried. Wipe off the glaze, to whatever degree you wish, immediately after application. After the glaze has dried, apply varnish using a bristle brush or a nylon brush.

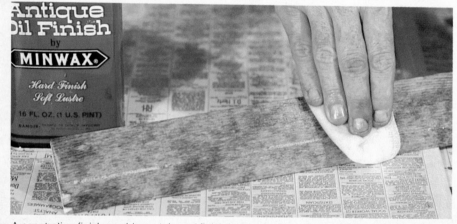

A penetrating finish combines stain and finish (protection) in the same product. Shown is one of the available wood colors.

The French Polish

In woodworking, the ultimate finish for a cabinet or other high-quality piece of furniture is a French polish. This process involves rubbing linseed oil and shellac onto the unit in many layers over a period of time. The mellowness of the finish produced really cannot be equalled.

When To Stain

Many people have the impression that all furniture pieces need to be stained. This is not the case, because there is no protection offered by a stain, just color. Staining will give a traditional color, one that usually is darker than the natural color of the wood, with some additional depth and emphasis of a good-looking grain. The traditional color of a wood is not necessarily close to the wood's actual color; walnut stain, for example, has a browner tone than does the raw wood.

One good reason for staining is to match a newly built bookcase or cabinet to existing furniture pieces. This means that, for example, fruitwood or gumwood — which are less costly than the fine hardwoods — can be used instead of cherry, walnut, or mahogany. The fruitwood or gumwood can then be stained to look like the more expensive woods. Even if you are not trying to match pieces of existing furniture, you may wish to match two pieces of furniture you are building yourself — if, for example, you choose to build both a cabinet and a bookcase. It is difficult to ensure that both pieces will end up the same color without addition of a stain.

There are three common types of stain: water mixed stain, non-grain-raising, and wiping.

Water stain. This comes in colored powder form which you mix with water. Of all the stains it will leave the most natural-looking finish, and it is generally available in many more colors than other types of stain. It does not heighten the wood grain, but gives a uniform color. Water stains must dry between applications, waiting approximately 24 hours between coats.

Non-grain-raising. This stain is used by the professional. It comes as a liquid and is diluted with alcohol or other thinners. Its most useful property is that it does not raise the grain on raw wood, as water stain will. This avoids the possibility of rough areas. These stains also dry faster than water stains — in about 4-5 hours. On the negative side, you should not really consider choosing this stain unless you are prepared to use a spray

Wiping stain is easiest for a do-it-yourselfer to use. Apply it using a lintfree cloth, then wipe it off. Above all, do not leave a wet surface which airborne particles can cling to.

Before using any finish, test it on a scrap piece of the same wood to be finished. Wipe off the stain or complete the steps involved for your chosen finish, so you will know what your final product will be.

rig with it. Otherwise you can end up with a darker finish than you had planned. These stains are not recommended for softwoods with strong grains, but work well on fine cabinet woods. They will stain these more quickly, and darker, than will water stains.

Wiping Stain. This is the most popular stain. It comes in a variety of wood colors, such as maple and walnut. You just apply it from the can, let it sit, and then wipe away excess with a clean, lintfree cloth (a tack rag or cheesecloth works well).

How much stain you wipe off will, of course, determine the final color the piece will be.

Test Finish on Scrap

There is no uniformity when it comes to stain colors or other finishes among companies. The walnut stain of Minwax, for example, is not the same shade as McClosky makes. For this reason, and also because different woods absorb finishes to varying degrees, results will be different each time. Always apply the stain or other finish first to a piece of scrap wood from your project so you will know exactly what you will end up with. One way to find out the right stain is to create a "sample board". Test the different stains so you can compare their colors and effects.

Enamel

Enamel, although considered a paint by many, is really a colored varnish. It can be brushed on, but best results are obtained by spraying it on for a hard, smooth surface. It is particularly suitable for blemished or inexpensive wood. Flat enamel should not be used; semi-gloss or glossy enamels are best for furniture. The level of gloss can be controlled with rubbing to a final finish.

There are hundreds, perhaps even thousands, of colors available. They dry quickly, and are easy to use. The best advice we can give is to buy a high-quality product and a compatible undercoater.

Tung Oil

Tung oil offers a longlasting finish that resists both time and marring. Since the oil deepens the color of any wood to which it is applied, test it first over raw wood, and then over the stain which you had intended to use. In some cases, you can eliminate the use of the stain; in other cases, you may decide to use a lighter stain than you had originally planned. Application of a tung oil finish is time-consuming — requiring two to five coats with a drying time of 36 hours or more for each coat. Each additional coat makes the finish glossier. It is, however, nearly im-

Ipswich Pine — Pine	Natural — Birch	Jacobean — Oak
Special Walnut — Pine	Fruitwood — Birch	Natural — Oak
Colonial Maple — Pine	Red Mahogany — Birch	Golden Oak — Oak
Conestoga White — Pine	Early American — Birch	Provincial — Oak

While the names for stain colors may vary among manufacturers, this sample from one shows how the intensity and character change when applied to different woods. When planning to stain your unit, make sure you have several pieces of scrap on which to try the stain. Keep track of the color and number of coats you use so that when you arrive at the finish color you want, you remember how you got it.

possible to strip and refinish. Be sure you choose a color and tone that will suit you for many years — probably the life of the furniture piece.

FINISHING TECHNIQUES

As mentioned, manufacturers do provide basic instructions with their finishes, but not all of them provide the kind of detail necessary to do a really good job. In light of this, we offer some tips on the basic how-tos involved in finishing: sanding, brushwork, spraying and wiping.

Wood Filler

To produce a fine finish on the bookcase or cabinet you have made, you should try to get it as smooth as possible. The tool for this is sandpaper. Before sanding, however, you should fill any knotholes or other depressions with wood filler. A number of manufacturers make this. It comes as a liquid or

paste. The paste is best; it is applied with a scraper or putty knife, allowed to dry, and is then lightly sanded. This is also a good material for filling holes when setting nails or counterboring screws. You should buy the paste wood filler in cans. It will be available in a cream color that you can color with stain or in a choice of colors.

Wood filler comes thick, and it must be thinned using turpentine or paint thinner before application. Thin it until it is still thick but has a light texture. If you decide to color your own filler you will add color after the filler has been thinned.

Filler seeps into depressions in the wood, where it hardens.

Application. After you have thinned and, if desired, have also colored the filler with the stain you have chosen, you can work it into the wood rather than brushing it on. For best results choose a heavy, slightly stiff, short-bristled paint brush. You can create

this sort of brush by cutting off half the bristles from one of your old but not stiff paint brushes.

For the first coat, brush on the filler with the grain. Sweep it into the surface of the wood and check that you have filled all the pores.

Use a scraper with a flexible blade to smooth material after putty or filler application

Early American   Pine

Cherry   Birch

Fruitwood   Oak

Puritan Pine   Pine

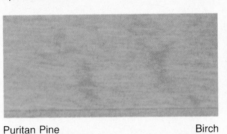

Special Walnut   Birch

Ebony   Oak

Fruitwood   Pine

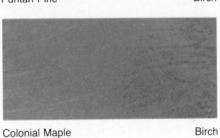

Puritan Pine   Birch

Dark Walnut   Oak

Provincial   Pine

Colonial Maple   Birch

Driftwood   Fir

Now, without wiping off the first coat, recoat the surface. This time work across the grain. The brush should be heavily loaded with filler, so that the wood surface is well coated.

Back off a little and examine the surface. It will look wet, then quickly will become dull. At this point, start scraping off excess filler from the wood surface. The exact moment you should start scraping is critical. If you have waited too long, scraping will be hard and may cause you to gouge some of the filler out. If you begin too soon, you will pull some of the filler out.

To scrape, find a scraping tool that has a straight, sharp edge. A playing card is effective. Stiff cardboard or a wide-bladed knife (often used to apply tape to drywall), or a sharp-edge plastic ruler, are alternatives.

Scrape the wood surface at an angle, and across the grain. Once you have scraped off the excess filler, use a rough cloth (such as burlap) to rub briskly across the grain. With the surface as clean of excess filler as possible, let it dry overnight.

For woods that have quite open grains, you may need two or three coats before the surface is completely filled.

After the surface has dried, closely examine it for any areas that show up dull or rough. Use a fine, wet sandpaper around a felt pad, sanding very lightly. You must be careful not to cut too deeply.

Smooth Sanding

Sandpaper Grades. There are different types of sandpaper available, in different grades of coarseness. Sandpaper is classified under a number system, but it also comes with word classifications. Usually, the three papers used are: Medium — Numbers 60, 80 and 100; Fine — Numbers 150 and 180; and, Very Fine — Numbers 220, 240 and 280. The higher the number, the finer the paper. Medium paper is used for the first sanding; Fine will give very smooth results. Very Fine is often used for smoothing finishes between coats; sometimes it is used wet.

Sandpaper also comes "closed" or "open coat". The closed coat refers to paper where the grit material covers 100 percent of the surface; the open coat refers to grit covering between 60 percent and 70 percent. The open coat will be most suitable for your needs.

There are a number of types of sandpaper, including garnet, flint and aluminum oxide. For cabinets and bookcases the best choice is aluminum oxide. This has a grit material which lasts longer and it should be more than adequate.

Sanding Tips. For sanding flat surfaces, it is best to cut the sandpaper into pieces you can manage easily. Around 5-inch-square pieces are good. You can wrap the paper around a 3 inch x 5 inch block of wood, lining the bottom with felt, cork or other soft material to use as a base, or you can just use your hand. A sanding block is available from 3M for which some sandpaper pieces have an adhesive backing; they are pressed onto the back and peeled off when the paper is worn.

One rule is to always sand with the grain of the wood — never across. Use straight, steady, even strokes; try to apply the same pressure over all the areas. As you sand, dust will clog the paper. This impedes the sandpaper's cutting action. Rap the sandpaper to clear the grit, and use a vacuum or rag frequently to remove the dust. After sanding, make sure you remove every speck of grit before applying the finish.

Manufacturers of finishes recommend the various grits of sandpaper which should be used with their particular finishes. The main idea is to achieve as smooth a surface as possible with the particular paper. Do not rely on just your eyes; feel the wood. It should be smooth to your touch.

Most woods and plywoods will require sanding to remove minor imperfections before applying the finish. Sand slowly on plywood. The veneers are thin and you could inadvertently sand through them.

Curved Surfaces. You may also be required to sand molding or grooves (such as dadoes). If sanding the edge of a groove, fold the sandpaper in half and sand with the sharp edge. For a curved surface, first "shoeshine" the back of the paper over the edge of something to make it as flexible as possible, and then use it. There are also abrasive cords and ribbons for sanding these areas. The only caution when sanding a molding is to make sure that you do not sand too deeply, or you may change its shape.

For the Smoothest Surface — Raising the Grain. If you do a conscientious job with the sandpaper, the wood will reach a point where it seems you cannot make it any smoother. But you can. One method is to raise the grain by swabbing the surface. This also avoids later grain-raising problems. Using a rag or sponge, apply clear, warm water. Do not soak too heavily; add enough to moisten the top $1/16$ inch of the wood surface. Let the wood dry overnight. Then sand the fibers off, carefully, using a very fine paper.

At the point when, after using the finest of sandpaper grades, the paper produces only a light fuzz, some refinishers choose to apply a sanding sealer. This stiffens the fuzz so that it can be sanded off. The result is a remarkably smooth finish, but it is not always appropriate. If you will be applying stain, you should be aware that such sealers will partially seal the wood, which can affect the stain's penetration. The extent of the problem varies depending on the coat, thickness, the type of sealer, and the kind of wood. You should test the sealer, choosing a spot that cannot be seen; for example, underneath a shelf. Apply a thin coat of diluted sealer.

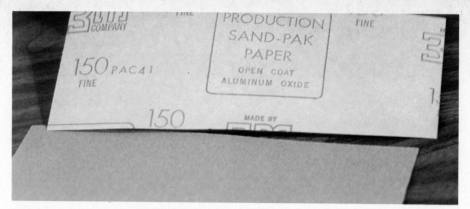
Sand paper comes in many grades for various jobs. Each is clearly identified on the back.

Allow it to dry; sand the area; apply stain. See if the stain penetrates evenly or has blotches.

How to Cut Sandpaper. The easiest way to cut sandpaper is to score it with an awl or screwdriver. Use a straightedge as a guide, and then tear the sandpaper off. Sandpaper also comes precut to fit electric sanders.

Power Sanding. If you will use a power sander, do the last sanding by hand, with very fine paper on a felt-padded sanding block.

The Nylon Test. To check the final surface, slip a stocking onto your hand and sweep your hand across the surface. You will be able to feel any rough spots or snags.

Spraying A Final Finish

For applying finishes, you can usually use either a brush or spray can. Of the two, the author favors the spray, simply because it is easier to get a smooth job. Most of the popular final finishes come in spray cans — varnish, shellac, lacquer, and paint. One drawback is cost. Applying material from a spray can is more expensive than applying it with a brush, but you may want to spend the extra money, particularly if you have invested a sizable amount in the wood or plywood for your project.

It is worth noting that spray units can be bought; spray finishes are relatively inexpensive when applied in this manner. But the original cost of the unit could not be justified for just one or two projects. Spray rigs may also be rented, which is worth consideration.

When spraying an item, one of the most important rules is to (whenever possible) position the item so that you can spray all its surfaces horizontally. For example, you should spray the top of a cabinet first. When this has dried, turn the cabinet with one side up and spray that side. When the side has dried, turn the unit onto its unsprayed side and spray the remaining side. Then the front,

and finally the back, would be sprayed — unless the unit were to be built-in or the back otherwise permanently hidden. By spraying only horizontally, after the previously sprayed surface has dried, you reduce the chance that the liquid will sag or run.

Here are the basic steps, which will vary somewhat depending upon the type of finish and the manufacturer's instructions. It is best to spray several very light coats — in two or three (or more) passes — than one heavier coat. This also guards against runs and sags.

(1) Read the instructions for nozzle adjustment. Usually the nozzle should produce a slightly elongated oval, but this may vary.

(2) Shake the spray can thoroughly until you hear the metal mixing ball jiggling in it, then shake for a minute more.

(3) Hold the spray head about 8 inches from the surface. Press the button, spraying a few inches to the left or right (depending if you are right or left handed) of the item, and then move it towards the item. This means that the spray will pump out at full pressure when the first particles of liquid hit the surface.

(4) Keep the can moving quickly and horizontally (don't arc) to the surface. Spray past the edge to avoid edge buildup.

(5) After the first pass, make another pass, overlapping the first by several inches.

(6) Make additional passes until surface of the piece has been completely covered.

(7) Let dry, then repeat the procedure for the second coat, and additional coats if desired.

Brushwork

Some projects will be too big for use of spray finishes, and a brush will be required. There are a number of techniques that contribute toward the best possible job. Here are general tips; specifics for different types of finishes will follow.

These bookcases are faced with bamboo-like trim created by the designer. The round molding is actually 1⅛" wood curtain rods milled flat on one side. The rings were made by soaking willow (used for rattan furniture), until very soft and wrapping it around a broom handle to dry. The rings were then cut, nailed and glued in place. The rods were nailed to the bookcases, painted to give the desired impression and given a clear sealer finish.

First, use the right brush. Nylon brushes can be used with any type of finish. Bristle brushes — those made with animal hair — may not be used with water-thinned finishes; water will soften these bristles to the point where they are unusable. You should buy a good brush; a poor quality brush will give more problems than any possible savings.

(1) Position the piece, as much as possible, in horizontal sections. As with spraying, this helps prevent a sagging or dripping finish coat. If paint does sag, feather it out immediately.

(2) Start applying the paint, varnish, or stain, across the grain. Flow it on well, concentrating on getting even coverage. Each new stroke should overlap slightly (about 2 inches) the old one.

(3) Brush out the paint with the grain.

(4) Use the brush as a wiping tool. Wipe the brush on the edge of the can; brush again, with the grain. As the brush collects liquid, wipe the brush off. This smooths the liquid and removes excess.

(5) Wipe the brush dry again and tip off the applied liquid. That is, pull the brush across the unit's surface with the bristles held almost vertically. Overlap the strokes and go the full length of the piece — with the grain.

(6) Repeat the procedure for the other sides, letting each side dry between coats.

(7) Depending upon the finish used, read the manufacturer's instructions as to whether or not you should sand lightly between the coats.

Wiping Stain On

Stain should be brushed or wiped on with a lint-free cloth (cheesecloth is good), allowed to set a minute (or as specified on the container), then the excess wiped off.

The real secret in doing a good job when wiping a stain is not to leave a wet surface, and to wipe evenly. Wipe it as dry as you can. If you leave a wet surface, airborne grit can contaminate it. If you have applied wood filler, be sure it has dried completely before applying stain.

Varnish

Once again, we emphasize the need to avoid dust when applying varnish. To help avoid dust problems, use the fastest-drying varnish available. Try to work in a warm room — 70 degrees Fahrenheit or above. The air should be dry; humidity will make the varnish set-up time longer. Vacuum the room thoroughly, and then wait about 24 hours to let any dust settle. After applying the varnish, keep movement and people in the area to a minimum. Wear lint-free work clothes. If you will be rubbing the finish after the varnish has dried, the dust problem will not be as crucial. The final rubbing should get rid of most of the dust specks. It is very frustrating, however, to work hard on a finish and later discover little irregularities due to dust. Use a tack rag to remove dust before applying the coating, and between coats.

Urethane Varnish. When applying urethane varnish, do not apply over a coat of shellac or lacquer. Check the varnish can to find out if any specially-formulated stain must be used in combination with the brand of varnish. Read the label for drying times between coats. Many specify a deadline during which the next coat must be applied. If that deadline is missed, there may be a wait of 24 to 48 hours before application of the next coat, with the added requirement of scuffing-and-sanding between coats. Again, check the label to make sure you are using a thinner specified by the manufacturer.

Use a natural-bristle brush to apply the urethane varnish, after tapping the brush to dislodge any loose bristles. Buy a good quality brush, even if comparatively high-priced, for this work. You will need to apply at least two coats; three is recommended. The first coat will be a light, seal coat. (See ''Brushwork,'' earlier in this chapter.)

Between coats, wet-sand the finish. Sprinkle a little water onto the wet-or-dry sandpaper, and rub the surface until it feels smooth. Wipe off any residue. Once the surface has dried, apply the next coat. To get an even better finish, rub with fine pumice

This is a representative sample of softwoods and hard-woods. The end grain of each is shown at the top. The tight, parallel grain of the quarter sawn wood is shown in the center and each bottom section shows the plain sawn wood. (See Chapter 4 "Basic Materials" for details.)

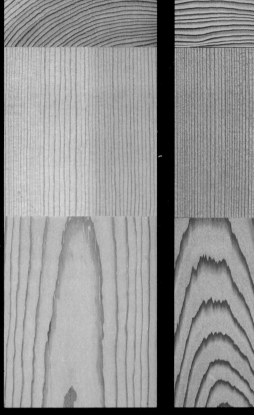

Ponderosa Pine

Western Red Cedar

Sugar Pine

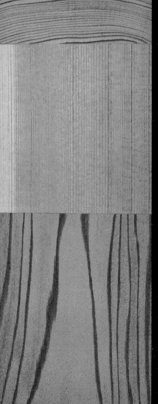

Redwood

Douglas Fir

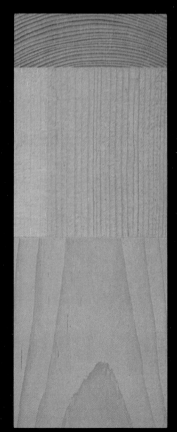

Western White Pine

Sugar Maple

Yellow Poplar

American Elm

Yellow Birch

Black Cherry

White Ash

Black Walnut

White Oak

and mineral oil rather than sandpaper. Mix a creamy, thin mixture made up of the pumice and oil. Pour some of it onto the surface and, using a firm cloth pad, rub parallel to the grain with long strokes. After rubbing the entire surface evenly (being careful not to go over the edge onto any adjoining surface) wipe off the surface with a damp cloth. Check that the surface is uniform and smooth. If not, rub again. Be careful not to rub too long in any one spot, or you might cut through the last coat — which means you would have to begin again.

Do not work too near the edges of the bookcase or cabinet, or you might have a drip and run of varnish down the sides.

For a beautifully soft glow, rub down your final coat using a thin paste made up of rottenstone and mineral oil. Use a rubbing pad of clean felt — either a new pad, or one that has never been used for anything but rubbing with rottenstone.

Let the finish dry completely before adding a protective wax. This means waiting at least several days — perhaps even a week. Choose a hard paste wax, and buff it with a lamb's wool pad.

Shellac

A shellac finish is built up of several layers. The number of layers depends upon the cut used; the heavier the cut, the thicker the coat. We recommend a 2-pound cut, as opposed to the 3-pound cut (which is usually how it comes in the can) because it gives a better assurance of a good finish to someone who has not worked with shellac before. To create a 2-pound cut from the 3-pound cut in the can, mix 5 parts shellac to two parts denatured alcohol. If mixing from 4-pound cut, combine 4 parts shellac with 3 parts alcohol; if working with 5-pound cut, add equal parts shellac and alcohol. When using a 2-pound cut, three coats is recommended, although some people prefer to add a fourth coat.

Work in a warm, low-humidity area. Use a full brush, moving slowly across the surface to avoid creation of bubbles. (See "Brushwork" earlier in this chapter.) Plan on a half hour to an hour for each coat to dry; this will depend on the humidity.

Once the first coat has dried hard to the touch, sand thoroughly. This first coat gives a rough surface. Use a sanding block and very fine sandpaper. Use an open-coated paper, and lots of it, because shellac clogs the paper.

After sanding, wipe off the surface using a clean, dry cloth. Carefully clean off all dust;

add the second coat. Sand again, but this time not as hard because you will have a smoother surface to begin with. Repeat for however many coats you choose.

Once the final coat is completely dry, it will be glossy, smooth, and even. Rub down with the finest sandpaper available to take away the high gloss and to remove tiny irregularities. Wait at least one day and add a coat of paste wax. Buff using a lamb's wool pad.

Lacquer

Lacquer usually is sprayed. It is applied in many thin coats, building up the coats to the necessary thickness. One of its advantages is that you do not have to sand between coats; the solvents in each new coat will soften the undercoat enough for good adhesion. For a smoother finish, rub between coats to work out imperfections in the surface.

Safety Precautions. Equipment for spraying lacquer has become inexpensive enough to buy or rent, depending upon how much work you will be doing. However, spraying lacquer can be dangerous — it will coat the lungs without adequate protection and ventilation. Wear a breathing filter or mask and work in a room with a large fan that can exchange the air in a short time. Another warning: do not allow any heating appliances or smoking in the room; lacquer is combustible and can be a serious fire hazard. Follow these same precautions if using lacquer from a spray can.

Working Conditions. Spray the lacquer in a room that has a temperature between 70 degrees and 85 degrees Fahrenheit. Choose a day and place with low humidity; moisture in the air will not only extend the drying time, it can result in a clouded finish (called "blooming").

Timing. This basic technique for spraying lacquer is the same as that given earlier in the chapter under "Spraying A Final Finish", with the added warning that timing is very important. You must keep the gun in motion, but you cannot move it too fast or too slow. If too fast, you will end up with an incomplete coat. If the gun is moving too slow, there will be sags and runs. Even the distance you are from the cabinet or bookcase makes a difference. If you are too far away, the lacquer drops will start to harden before reaching the surface, causing a rough finish (called "orange peel"). If you are too close, the lacquers builds up quickly, and can sag or be uneven.

The key to proper distance and timing is practice. Practice until you have the feel of

it, and also can gauge the corresponding finger pressure and the resulting coat thickness. Two passes (complete coverings) of the surface will be considered one coat. Wait about 2 to 3 hours (again, check brand instructions) before applying the next coat.

If you decide to use lacquer, be sure to follow *all* the safety recommendations, and practice on scrap wood before trying it on your newly built cabinet or bookcase.

If you buy a clear acrylic lacquer in an aerosol spray can (for example, Krylon or DuPont Spray Enamel) be warned that aerosol spray cans do not offer as even a spray pattern as do the spray guns. We do not recommend that you spray large surfaces this way. These cans are best for smaller projects.

Rubbing between coats. When rubbing between coats use rubbing compound (such as an automobile rubbing compound), rather than water with the wet-and-dry sandpaper as was recommended for varnish. Experiment with the compound before trying it on your finish. You must first learn just how fast the abrasive will cut the finish. Be careful and do not rub too long in any one place.

Brush-on Lacquers. Lacquers do come in forms that can be brushed on. These lacquers have retarders added to their formulas; they will not dry as quickly as do the sprays. You cannot apply spray lacquers with a brush, but you may thin out some brushing lacquers so they can be used in spray guns.

When brushing on a lacquer, choose a wide brush that has short bristles. Apply a somewhat heavy coat and do not brush it out any more than is necessary. Try to work using wide, extended strokes. Be sure the lacquer is thin enough so it will brush easily. Add thinner if you find you have brushing problems. Always choose the thinner indicated by the manufacturer of the lacquer that you are using; check again before mixing. The chemical combinations of unsuited lacquers and lacquer thinners can result in a poor finish. If you decide to rub down the surface between coats to eliminate small flaws, use rubbing compound and work carefully.

Enamel

First apply the undercoater. It is often a good idea to color the undercoater to match the color of the enamel. As mentioned previously, spraying the enamel offers the smoothest finish (see tips in "Spraying a Final Finish," above). However, enamel can be brushed on.

When applying the enamel, always use a brush that is either brand new or absolutely clean. Pour the enamel and the undercoater out of their original cans into small pans or paint buckets. Then tightly close the cans to avoid formation of a "skin" along the top of the paint.

Do not stain furniture that you will be enameling. Do apply a wood filler to ensure a smooth surface, and to keep the grain from showing through.

To enamel wood that has knots or streaks, or a new soft wood, first apply a seal coat of thin shellac, then apply the undercoat. This will prevent bleeding. Once the shellac has dried, sand lightly. For the seal coat, mix up a small batch using one part denatured alcohol and one part 3-pound cut shellac.

Brush on the undercoat, working it until you have a smooth, even coat. Let it dry overnight.

Now apply two coats of enamel, making the first coat a mixture of undercoater and enamel, half of each. Follow this with one coat of just the enamel, full strength.

For an even better finish, follow the undercoat-enamel mixture with two more applications of enamel. Sand between the coats and finish by rubbing down using a paste of water and fine pumice.

When brushing on the enamel, use the same steps given for brushing on varnish. Wait 12 hours between application of coats. Before rubbing on the pumice paste, make sure the enamel has cured completely. This time will vary from a few days to as much as two weeks. Check the label; it may give guidelines for drying and curing requirements.

Use the same procedures for lacquer enamels. The undercoater you will use in this case is a lacquer formulation. The drying time required between each coat is usually less — only four to five hours — but (as always) check the label.

Distressing

"Distressing" techniques are designed to give the impression that the furniture piece is an antique. There are a number of different ways for distressing a piece (including one case where the author saw a finisher shoot a piece full of buckshot to simulate worm holes). We give a roundup of these, which you can use in whatever combination you wish.

Denting. This is just what it implies — creating a series of dents that might have occurred naturally over time.

This table top shows a variety of deliberately made tiny dents, long scratches and small spatters. All gouges were filled with a dark wood filler so the surface could be given a smooth, fine polish while still showing the distressing.

One way to accomplish this is with a ballpeen hammer. Just lightly tap the piece in random locations. You can also use a large link chain. Ball it up in your hand and hit the piece with it. Be careful of any backlash. If you wish, you can add dots of color at the same time. Coat the chain with enamel and then pound the piece. Every now and then reposition the chain in your hand so the color will be applied evenly. Denting should be done after a base color has been applied. Practice first on scrap pieces to get the feel of how hard you must swing to get the desired effect.

Spattering. This also leaves dots of color, but not dents. Dip a long-haired brush in the paint. Hold one end of a stick on the surface and rap the ferrule of the brush against the stick. The paint will spatter in an even pattern. Again, prior practice is recommended.

Worn Edges. Every piece of furniture is subject to wear, but before using this technique you should determine exactly where the wearing would naturally occur (usually on the corners) by examining other pieces of furniture. Once you have determined the most common areas of wear, use a rasp or file to very slightly round off the edges. Then sand them smooth. Proceed very carefully and slowly with this technique.

Burning. Another sign of age in furniture is darkening at various points, such as in crevices and corners. To achieve these touches you can use a propane torch. Keep-

ing the flame back and always moving, apply the flame on the wood just until it chars a bit, then remove the loose material with a wire brush. Follow by rubbing well with 00 steel wool. Use all safety precautions indicated for a propane torch, and be sure to work where there is no combustible material nearby. Working out of doors is best, if possible.

Simulated French Polish

Once you have completed any final staining and sanding, rub the wood with boiled linseed oil. Now make a "French Polish Applicator."

This applicator will be made from a lint-free material such as a soft T-shirt or stockings wrapped in an outer cloth of lint-free material, usually cotton. Cut the outer cloth so it is 6 inches by 6 inches, or a little larger. Place whatever filler you have chosen in the middle and then fold the corners up to cover the filler.

Wait until the linseed oil application has dried completely. Now saturate your pad with 1-pound cut shellac. To make 1-pound cut shellac from 3-pound cut, mix 3 parts shellac and 4 parts denatured alcohol. To mix from 4-pound cut, combine one part shellac with 3 parts alcohol. When working with 5-pound cut originally, add one part shellac to two parts alcohol (also see "Shellac," this chapter).

The pad should be uniformly wet but should not drip. Rub the surface, working in a continuous, circular movement. This movement is the key to the French polish. Try to start the movement in the air over the surface, and just continue the motion as you contact the surface. Your arm should not be stopped while touching the finish, or you will leave a tacky, rough spot. Keep going until the pad begins to leave shellac deposits. Then lift off the surface with a sweeping movement.

Reload the pad with shellac, but add a few drops of linseed oil. Apply as many coats as you want — the actual number is a matter of choice. Each coat will be very thin. If you use heavier shellac, the coats will be thicker, but this makes it harder to control even distribution. If using a heavier cut of shellac, such as 5-pound cut, sprinkle several drops of alcohol on the pad each time you lift the pad from the surface.

The last step is to take off excess oil and to remove any marks caused by the pad. To do this, wet a clean pad with denatured alcohol and then wring it out. This will give a damp pad. Quickly skim this across the surface, moving with the grain. This should be done carefully, because alcohol softens shellac.

A Fast French Polish. To produce a French polish that is almost as good as the more time-consuming method above, first apply two or three thin coats of shellac. Use a brush, applying the coats and sanding between them, as described above. Then use the French polish procedure just given, but only for the last coat.

Veneering

Ordinary furniture can be dressed up by addition of a veneer, especially if you choose an unusual wood. Veneers are available for over 100 exotic and beautiful woods. You can order them from catalogs or from woodworking supply houses; prices will vary, but they are relatively inexpensive compared to what you would pay for a prefinished piece.

Veneer should be applied only to flat surfaces such as cabinet sides or drawer fronts. It is hard to veneer oddly shaped or curved pieces. These more difficult surfaces should be stained or otherwise matched to the veneer.

If stains do not work, try artist's oils. Rub them on with your finger after testing the match. To soften a too stiff compound, mix in a little turpentine. You can often get the exact shade you need by mixing several colors. Let dry at least 72 hours. Staining or coloring of adjoining areas should be done before the veneering.

Veneering uses extremely thin sheets of wood that are cemented to a core material.

Preparation. Veneers may come wrinkled and stiff. If so, spray them with water and, when they are quite damp, set a heavy even weight on them and let them sit overnight. The next day they should be flat and ready for installation.

Cut veneer pieces a little larger than the area that will be covered. Sand, very gently, the underside of the veneer and the surface on which the veneer will go. Use a tack rag to clean off sanded surfaces. Work off any ridges or grain that might swell and raise. Since veneer is so very thin, it will show any irregularities on the surface to which it is bonded. This can cause difficulties at the later stages, during finishing.

Before applying veneer, lay out the pieces in order to match up grain pattern and color. Number the undersides of the pieces from right to left so that you will know exactly where each piece should go.

Veneering Smaller Surfaces. If you are applying only one piece of veneer, which means that you will not have to match seams, here are the steps involved.

(1) Brush contact cement onto the bottom of the sheet of veneer.

(2) Brush a coat of the contact cement onto the area where the veneer will be bonded.

(3) Let both surfaces dry. The required drying time will vary; you can determine if the cement is dry by placing brown wrapping paper against the dried cement. If the paper will not stick to the cemented surface when pressure is applied, then the cement has dried sufficiently.

(4) Take 2 sheets of kraft paper and cover the surface to be veneered. The paper should overlap in the middle by about 1 inch and cover the area to be veneered.

(5) With the cement side down, place the veneer on the kraft paper. You will be able to adjust as much as necessary, because the paper will prevent contact.

(6) Once you have the veneer exactly as it should be when bonded, press it firmly in place with your hand, pressing near the center just beyond the overlap so that you can (with your free hand) pull out one sheet of paper beneath the veneer. As the two cemented surfaces meet, they will bond. Remove second sheet.

(7) Use a veneer roller across the newly veneered surface for an even, firm bond. Work from the middle out to the edges.

As soon as the two surfaces come in con-

tact they will form a permanent bond. There will be no adjustment or changes possible.

After you have achieved a good bond, trim off excess veneer from the edges. This is best accomplished by turning the veneered surface over so that it rests against a hardwood or other similar surface with perfectly straight edges. Then trim along the edge using an extremely sharp knife or a veneer saw; if the latter, it should have a small sawtoothed blade with an offset handle. Use gentle strokes, carefully keeping the saw flush against the edge of the hardwood in order to trim the veneer off evenly. If using the veneer saw against the grain, you should reverse the stroke when you reach the last few inches to be cut. This will keep the veneer from splintering along the edge.

Veneering Large Surfaces. The biggest problem you will probably encounter is in making smooth joints between pieces of veneer when covering a large surface. In these cases the following steps should prove helpful.

Again, first match up the various pieces of veneer for even continuation of color and grain. Take two of the pieces and position them on the surface to be veneered. Arrange them until you have the pieces as they will be once they have been cemented. Then turn over the piece on the left, just as though it were a page in a book. By turning it over it will rest on the other piece of veneer. The left edges of the pieces will meet to form a seam once the veneer pieces are in their final positions.

Carefully adjust the two "pages" until they are true and square. To cut the edges that will form the seam, clamp the veneer pieces between two lengths of hardwood. About ¼ to ½ inch of the veneer will hang out beyond the hardwood. Using an extremely sharp knife, trim off the veneer which is hanging out, following along the hardwood edge and using it as a guide. At this point you will have two matching straight edges of the veneer that will meet in an exact seam once the veneer has been applied to the surface.

Disconnect the hardwood clamp. Pin the two pieces of veneer to a board, underside facing you, keeping the edges that will form the seam snug and tight. Tape the edges together. Lift the veneer slightly to expose the surfaces inside of the seam's taped edges, and run a very thin bead of white glue down the seam. Lay the veneer flat. Now tape the face of the veneer at the seam while the glue dries. Match and join all the pieces

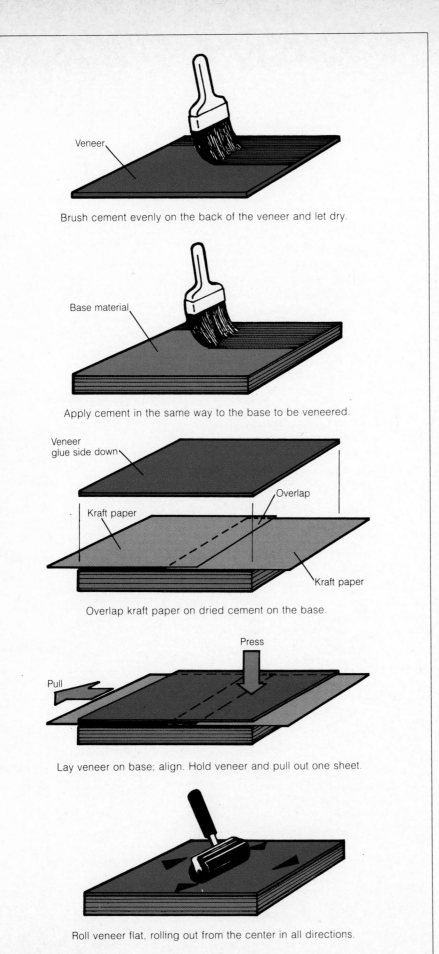

Brush cement evenly on the back of the veneer and let dry.

Apply cement in the same way to the base to be veneered.

Overlap kraft paper on dried cement on the base.

Lay veneer on base; align. Hold veneer and pull out one sheet.

Roll veneer flat, rolling out from the center in all directions.

of veneer until you have connected enough veneer to cover each surface.

Now draw up patterns (templates) for each surface which will be veneered, using brown paper. Label each template indicating left side, right side, and which side will face upward. Use these templates to cut the veneer for each surface. Use a veneer saw if possible.

To apply veneer to the surfaces, use the overlapping kraft paper system as described above, but make one of the pieces of kraft paper about twice as long as the other. Overlap the two sheets so that one piece covers about two-thirds of the area to be veneered and the other piece covers the other third. Have a helper firmly hold down the veneer near but not on the overlap, over the longer piece of paper. Otherwise, clamp one end of the veneer (over a protective piece of plywood) to hold it down. By clamping the longer of the two pieces of kraft paper near (but not on) the overlap, you can pull the shorter piece of kraft paper out. Smooth it down and then unclamp. The area that has now bonded acts as your clamp and anchor, letting you carefully pull out the longer sheet of paper. Smooth down, and then remove the tape.

How to Finish the Veneer. Veneer can be sanded and finished just the same as other wood surfaces. It is not often stained, however. Remember that the veneer is extremely thin and you must take care not to sand through it. Only use the finest of sandpapers; always sand lightly. If possible, use the sandpaper with a sanding block.

Finishing Particleboard
Particleboard presents difficulties when painting because it is porous. A wood filler applied before undercoating will avoid uneven coverage. Because particleboard has no grain, you can scrape off excess filler once the surface has been filled and is smooth.

In addition to the standard finishes, you can use other materials to cover surfaces of cabinets and bookcases, as described in Chapter 1.

PLASTIC LAMINATE

One of the most popular materials for covering a cabinet top is plastic laminate. This thin, hard plastic is commonly used to cover countertops and vanities — wherever a durable, liquidproof, easy-to-clean surface is required — and is frequently used as a covering on kitchen cabinets. It also is desirable for its intrinsic good looks. Laminate comes in a tremendous array of colors and textures, including some which simulate wood. Hence, you might use an inexpensive wood on top of the cabinet — plywood or particleboard — and then cover it with laminate for an elegant result.

Handling Plastic Laminate

Plastic laminate comes in several sizes, but the 1/16 inch size is best suited for cabinets or counters. You must observe several cautions in order to get the best from it — and to avoid cracking it. Although strong and durable on the job, laminate in sheet form can crack easily and must be handled with great care.

For use under laminate, particularly in a kitchen or bathroom, ¾ inch plywood is the minimum thickness.

The best tool for working laminate is the router. Before using the router, check that all edges of the piece being worked on are square. Any flaw — such as a dip in the edge — will show up on the laminate. Use a ball-bearing bit on the router; the ball-bearing guide rides against this.

If you are going to be cutting a curve, the laminate should have a radius of at least 6 inches or more. If it is smaller than this you will risk a crack.

When buying laminate, buy enough so that you have sufficient to allow for at least a half-inch overlap on the piece that you are covering, plus a half-inch waste for each cut; the router bit will cut a half-inch swath.

Techniques

In cutting laminate for the various projects here, or for projects of your own design, you will be dealing with large pieces and possibly edge strips. We will give details on the best procedure to follow; the overall idea is to have closed edges visible, facing in the direction where they will look best.

Several router bits will be helpful, no mat-

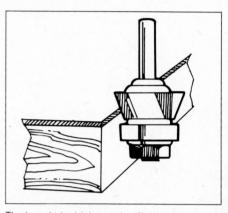

The bevel trim bit is used to finish plastic laminate edges at an angle.

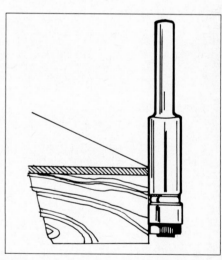

The flush trim bit cuts a perfectly vertical face on the laminate and base.

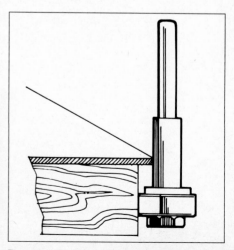

The overhang bit is used to trim base beneath laminate to leave laminate overhang.

A router is extemely useful in cabinet building. It will make the application of any plastic laminate much easier, faster and more professional looking.

Clamp plastic laminate to a piece of plywood which you then use as a straightedge to guide your cut. The plywood will also give support as you cut.

ter what you are cutting. One is the flush trim bit which cuts the laminate exactly flush with the edge of a piece. Another is the overhang trim bit, which cuts the material so it will overlap ⅜ inch. Also helpful is a homemade straightedge: a piece of plywood cut about 9 inches wide and 8 foot long. Secure the laminate to this using C clamps, then cut the laminate down to manageable size before you begin the project. To ensure a clean, true edge, attach the laminate to the plywood's factory-cut edge.

Cut Edge Strips. If there will be edge strips, cut them on the straightedge and clamp the laminate in place so that ⅛ inch overhangs. Trim the laminate with the flush trim bit, adjusting the guide on the tool if necessary so it rides on the middle of the laminate edge. The objective is to cut a clean edge.

Reclamp the laminate on the straightedge so that the laminate overhangs by the width of the bit plus the width of the edge. For example, assume the edge is to be 1½ inches wide. The bit is ½ inch and will make a ½ inch wide cut. Since the edge is 1½ inches then clamp the laminate leaving a 2 inch overhang. When you cut, a clean 1½ inch edge will fall off. Repeat for as many edges as you have.

Cutting Top Section. Follow the same general procedure as given above for cutting the laminate piece that will cover the top of the item. Cut it ⅜ inch to ½ inch larger in both length and width than the dimensions of the top.

If you need to cut curved pieces, clamp the piece onto the top of the item to be covered. Then cut with an overhang trim bit. This will leave a ⅜ inch overlap, which you can trim later with the flush trim bit. A flush trim bit could also be used to trim the curved laminate, but you would have to be cautious and careful not to cut the material too small; the overhang bit is safest.

Applying Adhesive. Contact cement is the adhesive used to secure plastic laminate. Always try to work outdoors with it, or make sure interior ventilation is adequate and that any possible source of fire or sparks has been removed or extinguished.

A good tool for applying the adhesive is a mohair roller. You can also use a bristle brush (not Nylon) or a notched spreader, which dealers will furnish.

Apply the cement to all the laminate surfaces, then to the bases. If the base is plywood or particleboard, coat it twice (particleboard is very porous). The best procedure

Apply contact cement for laminate with a roller. Spread an even coat of cement on your base and let dry. Spread evenly to the edge of the base. Apply two coats to particleboard.

Cover the back of the laminate evenly and as near the edge as possible. Good coverage means that there will be very little chance of separation from the base after installation.

After one hour, check to see that the cement is dry to the touch. Do not let dry too long.

Use a file to finish inside corners of laminated cabinet. The router cannot make an absolutely square corner.

Lay lath strips or other lengths of wood on base material and align laminate on top. Pull wood separators out and press laminate flat, then tap with wood block and hammer.

Hold file at angle shown to smooth edges of laminate after it has been applied to the base material.

for adequate coverage is to pour the adhesive onto the laminate then spread it. Keep all foreign matter out of the adhesive.

Let the adhesive dry to the touch. This will take up to a half hour, depending on humidity.

Apply the top piece of laminate first, then the edging strips. Since contact cement will adhere the parts instantly, be very sure to align the laminate exactly with the base. To help you do this, lay thin strips of wood (molding or sticks) on the base, a foot apart. Then lay the laminate on top, lined up so that its edges overlap the base evenly all around. Remove the sticks one by one, and gently but firmly press the laminate in place as you go. When all the strips have been removed, bond the laminate securely by tapping it all over with a softwood block and hammer.

To install the edging, put the first piece in place so it butts tightly against the overlapping edge of the top piece, and one end is flush with the corner of the unit and overhangs it at the other end. Repeat the procedure on each side of the unit. Then trim the laminate, cutting excess off the main piece first, using a flush trim bit. Then trim off the pieces of the edge strips that extend beyond the corners.

Smooth off the cut edges with a file. There is a special file for plastic laminate, or you can use a regular file with a mill or bastard cut. You can also use a bevel trim bit to give the laminate a beveled edge, if you can afford another bit.

Cabinet Fronts

If you will be applying plastic laminate to the front of a cabinet, you can cut and fit individual pieces of laminate on the edges, although it is a difficult and precise operation. It is far easier to apply laminate to the entire front — with a piece that overlaps a little — and to punch holes where the cabinet openings are and trim them out with a router, using the edges of the openings as a guide for the bit.

Doors

Doors need to be covered front, back and edges; you can follow these steps.

(1) Cover the back of the door with laminate; trim flush with a flush trim bit.

(2) Cut a piece of laminate that overlaps the front all around by about $\frac{1}{16}$ inch.

(3) Cut four pieces for the edges, also overlapping the back by $\frac{1}{16}$ inch.

(4) Secure laminate to the front with adhesive, then butt edge pieces against it.

(5) Use flush trim butt to trim the front of the cabinet, then the edges.

WALLCOVERINGS AND PANELING

One type of surfacing material mentioned in Chapter I was wallcoverings. This can be applied to the cabinet or the bookcase using the same methods that you would use in installing them on a wall. That is, use a level or plumb bob to establish trueness or a vertical, then install the wallcovering as suggested by the manufacturers in their instructions. If you will be using the wallcovering in a bathroom, use a vinyl or vinyl-clad type. These will stand up to moisture and are also a good idea for the kitchen, where one is required to clean the coverings frequently.

Paneling

One alternative cabinet material is paneling, especially if you are planning to remodel or update a room with matching paneling. This can be done quite easily by building a framework for the basic unit out of 2 x 4 stock (as for the Built-in Bathroom Vanity in Section II), designing it to your specific needs and space. You can plan to have drawers or doors, as desired. The most interesting and pleasing part of the project is that the top, sides and front of the unit are faced with the paneling. Whether you have planned drawers, doors, or a combination, they will have a perfect fit. In designing the unit, however, keep in mind the overall size of paneling, which is usually 4 x 6 feet.

First build the framework. To cut the front, lay the panel over the face of the built-in unit and carefully mark the location of the doors or drawers. Using a drill for a starter hole and then a keyhole or sabre saw, cut out the pieces which will cover the doors or drawers. Cut carefully and evenly because these will become the door and drawer fronts. You will find that there is a perfect match because the front is "all of a piece" and the saw has removed enough material for perfect clearance. Another possibility is to use a router, as for plastic laminate. Attach the paneling to the frame, drill a pilot hole in the panel, and use the router to trim out the excess.

Attach these cutouts to the drawer or door frames, add hardware, and install. Your room will have a unified look and the final finishing of your piece will be minimal. Cover the top and ends of the unit with the same panel material. Edges may be covered with matching panel moldings which are available from the paneling dealer.

TILE

Both ceramic and resilient tile are alternatives for covering surfaces of cabinets and bookcases, but it is suggested that you restrict use of resilient tile to horizontal surfaces. The adhesive, whether the tile is self-stick or applied with a cement and a trowel, secures the material to a horizontal surface such as a floor. Its ability to hold the material in place vertically is questionable. While this is not the type of material you would choose to cover the top of an elegant piece of furniture, it works well for work benches, children's units, and similar situations where easy cleanability is an advantage.

Ceramic Tile

For this popular material, installation instructions do not come packaged with the product. Dealers are often knowledgeable, and some offer do-it-yourself films for the buyer.

The following installation steps will give you an idea of the basic procedures. As starting points, draw horizontal and vertical

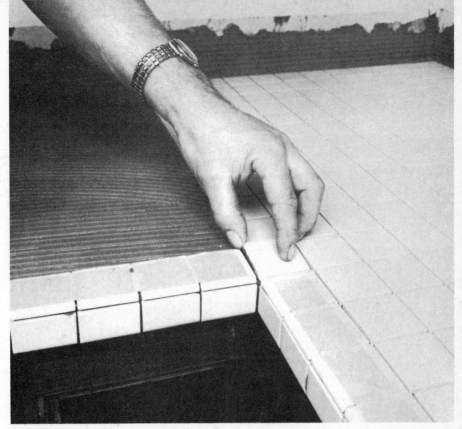

Set ceramic tile into adhesive with a slight twisting motion. You will be able to adjust the alignment of each tile for a perfect match in both directions.

A tile cutter may be rented from a tile dealer and will make trimming tiles very easy.

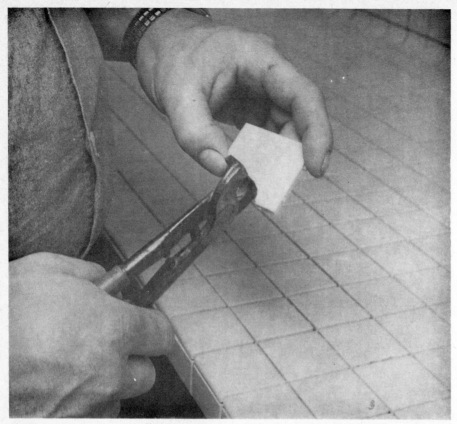

A tile nipper is used to cut odd shapes and curves in tile to fit around obstructions.

Apply grout with a non-abrasive trowel. Sweep the grout into the spaces between the tiles using a broad motion. Excess is wiped away after spaces are filled.

lines in the center of each area to be tiled, using a plumb line and level. If the area to be tiled is 3-sided, plan so that the horizontal starting point will be one continuous line extending to all areas that will be tiled.

Lay out a course of loose tile. Then adjust the vertical lines to the left or right so that the least amount of cuts are necessary. If possible, arrange it so there will never be less than half a tile.

Apply the adhesive with the notched trowel, holding it at a 45° angle for 100 percent coverage. Spread only a small area at a time, so adhesive does not dry out before tile is positioned.

Set each tile with a slight twisting or scrubbing motion. Press and tap firmly into place. Align and adjust tile until all joints are uniform and straight.

Many tiles come with built-in spacers to ensure that joints will be uniform. However, keep checking the alignment. If a line is not straight, wiggle the tiles back into place until the joint line is even. If you have applied the adhesive in a small enough area, it will remain soft for quite some time, and you can afford leeway in retracing your steps. Be sure to clean off excess adhesive on the face of the tile right away.

When cutting tiles to fit, rent the cutter offered at most dealers. Practice cutting with the device before you start. Since few corners are perfectly plumb, so do not cut a whole row of tiles at one time. Cut each one as you get to the end of each row. A tile nipper is used to cut to fit around pipes or at angles. Nip off only little bits at a time, or the tile might break. Use carborundum stone to smooth rough edges. However, don't bother to file down tile that will be hidden.

Wait approximately 24 hours after tiling before grouting. Then mix and use the grout according to the manufacturer's instructions. Apply the grout with a rubber float or squeegee, spreading it diagonally across the joints. Using a wet sponge, wash the excess grout from the face of the tiles. To shape the grout lines strike the joints with the handle of an old toothbrush. Clean the tiles and dress the joints with a damp sponge. Wet the joints regularly to help them harden. When joints are dry, use a silicone spray and polish with a clean cloth.

If you are tiling both a counter and back-splash or wall area, then make sure that you keep the tiles in line. It is best to tile the flat surface first, then the vertical one.

12 Time Saving Jigs

Cutting and drilling stock can be made easier with a few tricks. In this chapter we offer four time-saving aids or jigs which you can easily build to make these operations faster, simpler and, perhaps, more precise.

JIGS FOR DRILLING HOLES
Holes to the Same Depth

One operation that frequently is required is drilling a series of holes to the same depth. Achieving accuracy can be difficult, but you can put together a little jig which will ensure uniform depth.

First, cut an 8 inch length of ¾ inch by ¾ inch softwood. Clamp the piece in a vise, then use the same drill you will be drilling with when making the holes, drill into one end of the piece the full depth of the bit, as shown. Then mark onto the stock the depth which you have drilled; next to this mark indicate the depth you want the bit to go. For example, if your bit has penetrated 3 inches, and you wanted ½ inch depth, you would make a mark 2½ inches from the end. Then, cut the piece off at your second mark. Slip this piece over the bit; the bit will project the exact depth (½ inch) you want.

Equally Spaced Holes

Drilling holes equal distances apart can be problematic. For this jig, cut a length of furring (1 inch x 2 inches) which is long enough to accommodate all the holes required. Use your measuring tools to mark equally spaced holes down the center of the strip, and then drill the holes.

That is all there is to it. To use the jig, just stand it against the surface to be drilled and use its holes to guide you in drilling holes in the piece you are working on. If holes must be a particular depth, use the spacer discussed in the preceding section.

JIGS FOR CUTTING STOCK

On some projects you may have a fair amount of stock to cut to the same size. For accomplishing this quickly, there are two other jigs you can make — one is for short boards, the other is for long boards.

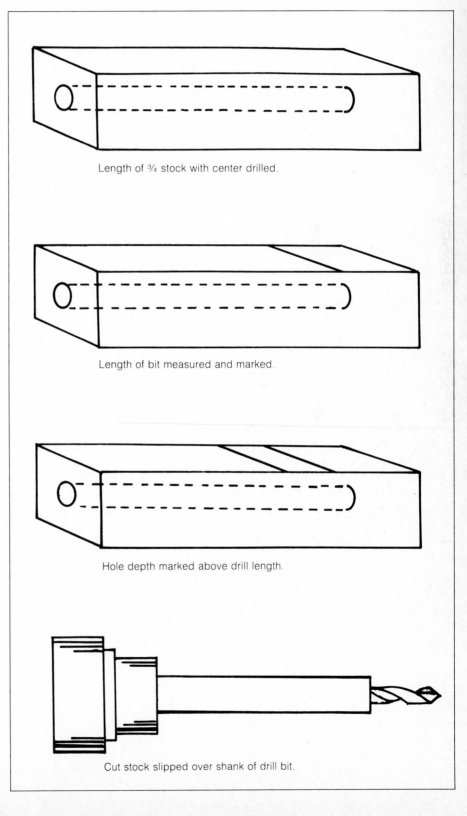

Length of ¾ stock with center drilled.

Length of bit measured and marked.

Hole depth marked above drill length.

Cut stock slipped over shank of drill bit.

Long Stock

To make the jig for the long stock, cut a piece of ¾ inch plywood so it is about 8 feet long and 24 inches to 36 inches wide. Flush with the edge, on one long side of the plywood, nail a length of ⁵⁄₄ x 2 inch stock. Nail a much shorter piece (a foot or so) to the opposite side, at the corner, aligning it with the outside edge of the plywood. Then nail a piece of 1 x 3 (or wider) stock across the two other pieces, forming a pocket. Fasten a strip of lath on top of this piece to guide the saw. The circular saw will ride against it as it cuts the stock. Then nail a 2 x 4 stop at a distance equal to the length of stock you need to cut.

To use the jig, slip a board through the pocket and up against the 2 x 4 stop. The saw baseplate rides on the ⁵⁄₄ piece, with the lattice (as mentioned above), serving as a guide. To vary the length, reposition the stop. Nail it in a different spot each time to match different lengths.

Short Stock

The jig for cutting short pieces to length has the same basic idea. As detailed in the accompanying drawing, cut a rectangle from ¾ plywood; it should be the same length as the piece you will be cutting. Then, cut a stop whose width is the same as the distance from the edge of the baseplate to the edge of the saw blade. As shown, screw the stop underneath the piece of plywood, at one end.

Use a large C clamp to secure the stock to be cut to the jig, slipping it underneath the plywood square to butt against the stop. Set the assembly on a bench and cut, keeping the saw flush against the outside edge of the plywood square. The excess stock will fall away.

It is important, when making either of the two jigs discussed above, to make sure that all the parts are square to one another. Only then can you be assured that the pieces you cut will be accurate.

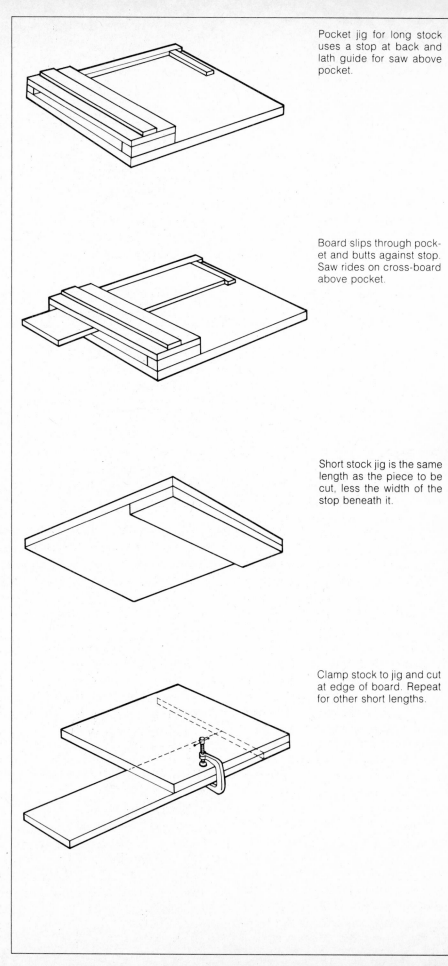

Pocket jig for long stock uses a stop at back and lath guide for saw above pocket.

Board slips through pocket and butts against stop. Saw rides on cross-board above pocket.

Short stock jig is the same length as the piece to be cut, less the width of the stop beneath it.

Clamp stock to jig and cut at edge of board. Repeat for other short lengths.

A number of the projects in this book call for hanging items directly on a wall or, if built in, installing items between the wall studs.

IN, ON, TO THE WALL

It is always desirable to hang a unit on the studs using screws because this is the strongest way to attach it.

Your first job is to locate the studs, and there are a number of ways you can do this.

First, you can lightly tap the wall with a hammer. The studs in most rooms of modern homes are commonly located on 16 inch centers, from the center of one to the center of the next. In older homes — 50 years or more — the studs are likely to be 24 inches apart or, if the carpenter was not careful, at random distances. When your tapping results in a solid sound or feeling, as opposed to a hollow one, a stud is located there. Make a mark, then measure and mark at 16 inch intervals along the wall.

Usually, feel is more accurate in determining where studs are than sound, but if this does not work there are alternate methods, as follows.

In checking Sheetrock (or wallboard) walls you sometimes can see the edges of the panels, which will be nailed to studs. To do this, hold a lamp, with the light on and shade removed, close to the wall. If you can find the flanking edges of the joint compound used to cover the edges, then the stud will be at approximately the center of these edges. The compound edges will usually be 16 inches to 18 inches apart.

If you are checking plaster for studs, close examination will sometimes reveal vertical hairline cracks which are directly over the studs.

If there is a high baseboard, then the baseboard molding will be, or should be, secured to the studs with nails driven through the top of the baseboard. Just draw a square, vertical line above a nail; drive a nail through the line, and the stud should be there.

Sometimes, despite use of the tests above, you will not be able to locate the studs. In this case, the only alternative is to drive a 10d finishing nail into the wall at one-inch intervals along a horizontal line (do it in an area that will be covered by the installed unit). Eventually you will find the solid feeling and resistance, indicating you have hit a stud. Then measure at 16 inch (or 24 inch for older homes) intervals.

Kitchen Cabinets

The techniques involved in hanging kitchen cabinets can be used to hang any kind of cabinets. A few other situations will be dealt with later.

Kitchen cabinets consist of base cabinets and wall-hanging units. It is suggested that you familiarize yourself with their basic structure, in Chapter 2, to help you better understand the steps that follow.

Removing Existing Cabinets. Before you can install your new cabinets you may have to remove old cabinets. This is messy, but within the capability of the homeowner. You will need a hammer, pry bar, crosscut saw, hacksaw, screwdriver, pipe wrenches, electrical tape, butt chisel, adjustable wrench, containers for junk.

Look for the molding at the back bottom edge of wall cabinets and along the wall at end cabinets. Pry off this molding first, since it helps hold the cabinets in position.

Wall cabinets may be held by screws or nails to the studs. Sometimes cabinets are fastened to the wall with toggle bolts or Molly anchors. If the walls are masonry, the cabinets probably are held with lead anchors and screws.

Look for these fasteners along the top and bottom inside edges of the cabinets and remove them with a screwdriver. If held by nails, place a pry bar in back of the cabinet and against the wall and lift out.

The cabinets probably will be fastened together at the fronts, along the inside framing or at the top (and even along the bottom) with nails or screws. Remove these fasteners.

If the cabinet tops butt up against a soffit, the tops may be fastened to the soffit, which

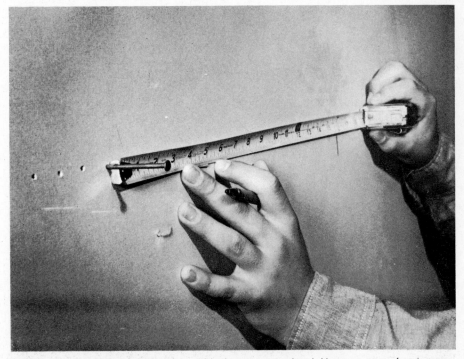

Studs (and most framing members) are 16 inches on center (o.c.). However, some framing may be 24 inches o.c. especially in garage, carport, and patio structures. Find the first stud, mark it on the wall and measure from this point.

is a framework of 2x3s or 2x4s covered with gypsum wallboard.

Once you remove one cabinet, the rest will be easier since you will know where to find most of the fasteners. Enlist the aid of a helper to steady the cabinets while you remove the final few fasteners.

First check for any electrical and plumbing connections that might be in the way. You will probably find these only at the sink unit and on the wall over the range. Plan to remove these cabinets last, since you want to have water and electric power as long as possible, but be sure to disconnect this wiring before removing the cabinets. When you are making disconnections, turn off the water and electricity at the main service entry. The range hood is fastened to a valance or soffit, usually with screws.

First disconnect the electricity that powers the exhaust fan and hood light. To identify this circuit, turn on the fan and/or light. Turn off the power at the main circuit breaker or fuse box until you find this circuit. When the power is off, the light will go out and the fan stop working. Leave this circuit *off*. You may turn the others on, if a voltage test shows no current leaking to this circuit. It is now safe to make the disconnections. You will probably have to unscrew the metal pan covering that hides the junction box housing the electrical connections.

Use a screwdriver to open the terminal screws far enough to remove the wires. Separate the wires, taping the ends heavily with electrical tape before going on.

Now remove the hood unit by backing out the screws that hold it in place. Then remove the valance, which probably is fastened to the wall cabinets with screws or to the soffit with metal brackets, screws, or nails. The hood will have a vent duct. This duct will have to be unscrewed from the main vent hub above the exhaust fan. The duct may go directly through the outside wall, or through a soffit to the outside wall.

Now for the base cabinets. Remove countertops first. If they are laminate, they will be screwed to metal or plastic brackets located at the inside top of the base cabinets. If the counter is of tile, remove as described in the previous chapter, using a cold chisel and a sledge hammer.

Remove any molding or trim around the ends, kickspace, and back of the base cabinets. The base cabinets probably are fastened to each other with nails or screws along the front inside edge. Pull these fasteners out.

Begin with the end cabinets and work toward the sink cabinet. When you remove an end cabinet, the cabinet next to it will be easier to work with, and the job will start to quickly "unravel." Use a hammer and a pry block of wood for the nails, and a screwdriver and pry bar for the screws, toggles, Molly bolts, anchors, and large nails — 10d and up.

You may have several preliminary jobs at the sink cabinet. If the sink has a disposal unit, disconnect the power from it. The wires may be in a junction box on or near the unit. Or the wires may come from a wall outlet or both. Tape the ends of the main supply wires.

The disposal is connected to the sink with a mounting ring and two (usually) set screws. You can get at the screws from inside the cabinet at the top of the disposal unit. Also disconnect the disposal drain. You will need a pipe wrench or large adjustable wrench for this. The drain pipe fits a connection at the side (usually) of the disposal unit.

If you don't have a disposal, disconnect the kitchen sink drain using pipe wrenches at the first joint down from the sink drain opening. This will be a U or P trap fitting, and the fitting will slip down and off the drain tailpipe that is connected to the drain in the sink. Also disconnect the water supply pipes to the

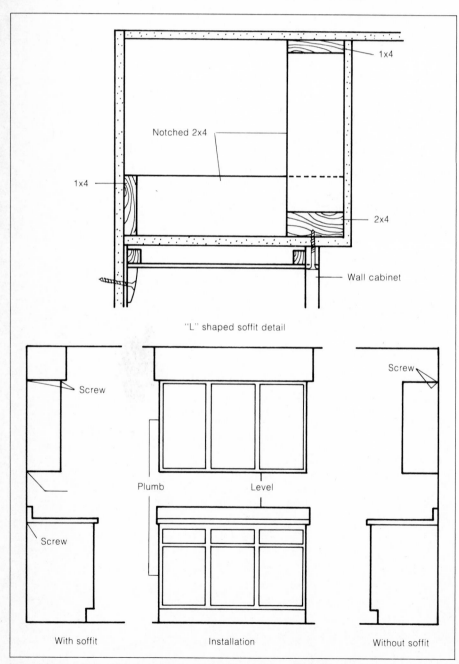

In most homes today kitchen cabinets are installed with a soffit to fill unusable space between cabinets and ceiling. However, it is possible to install cabinets without soffit.

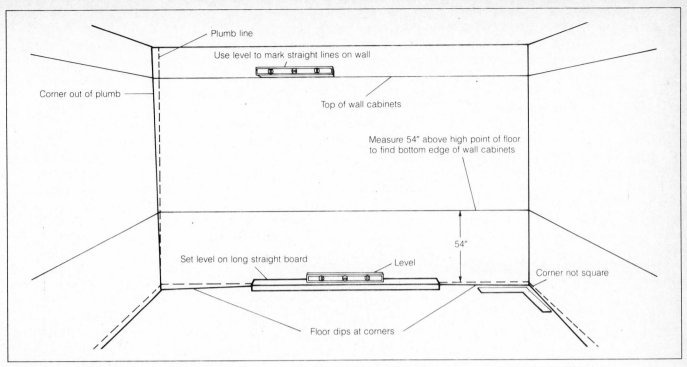

Plumb line

Use level to mark straight lines on wall

Corner out of plumb

Top of wall cabinets

Measure 54″ above high point of floor
to find bottom edge of wall cabinets

54″

Set level on long straight board

Level

Corner not square

Floor dips at corners

Cabinets must be installed level. Locate plumb and square and mark your kitchen walls. Shims will be needed here to level cabinets.

sink faucets. But first, turn off the water at the shut-off valves where the water supply comes through the wall. Or turn off the water at the main water entry. Do not disconnect the water supply pipes until the water is off.

If the supply pipes are copper, you will need an adjustable wrench to remove the pipes at the faucet connections. If the pipes are galvanized steel, you will need pipe wrenches to remove them — also at the faucet.

Disconnect water supply and drain pipes to your dishwasher at this time. Water supply for the dishwasher may be connected through the floor. You will have to go into the basement to shut off this valve and (perhaps) disconnect the pipe. Or the water supply may come from a tee fitting off the faucet supply pipe. A compression fitting, which may be turned with an adjustable wrench, is usually all you need to disconnect from the main supply line.

The dishwasher probably has separate electrical power, which comes up through the floor or through the wall in back of the unit. The dishwasher may be on a separate circuit. Make sure the power is off before you start working.

The dishwasher drains into the kitchen drain pipe or the air gap, which has an inlet/outlet tube. Simply trace the hose and you will find the connection.

Installation, Base Cabinets. The base cabinets go in first if the countertop has a high backsplash. The backsplash area will be

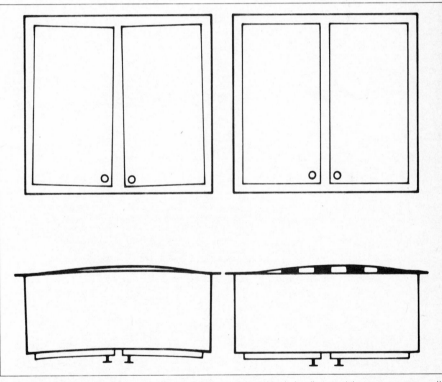

Cabinet doors may become misaligned if the cabinet back is distorted by an uneven wall. Shimming out the back to level will restore doors to plumb.

handy for setting the wall cabinets (before the final surface material has been applied to the backsplash). To adjust and level, obtain a bundle of Number 2 undercourse shingles to use as shims.

Put in two base cabinets, leveling their top surfaces, with one another by driving shims under them as needed. However, first measure the distance they are out of level. If less

than three quarters of an inch, use the shims to prepare them for final fastening. If more than ¾ inch, it is better to trim the cabinets down. To do this, use a scribing tool to make lines on both the fronts and sides of the cabinet. The lines will be parallel to the floor, with the line half the shim thickness from the floor — a one inch shim would call for a line ½ inch from the bottom edge. Trim the cabinets at the bottom according to these lines, then replace and reshim them.

With all cabinets level and in place, mark a line along the wall where their top surfaces reach. Remove cabinets and secure a nailer to the wall. The top edge of the nailer should be just below the line you have drawn. This nailer normally will be of 1¼ inch x 2 inch stock, but it can vary to fit the cabinets you install. Reinstall the cabinets, making them level again if the shims have slipped out of position. Secure the cabinets to the nailer with No. 10 flathead screws 16 inches to 18 inches apart. First, though check to see that the cabinets fit together side by side at the front. If not, adjust them until they do.

Connect the cabinets together at the stiles using No. 10 screws of sufficient length (see Chapter 6). Counterbore the screws if the cabinets are hardwood.

No Backsplash. If there is no backsplash, install the wall cabinets first; you will be able to get closer to them for working. You can rest them against a nailer which has been leveled and secure to the wall, but if you don't have a strong helper, use a T-Brace to support cabinets as you screw them in.

If there is a space above the cabinets, you can cover this with wallboard and molding. Before installing the cabinets you should tack a 1x2 nailer to the top edge, recessed ⅜ inch. Tack another nailer to the ceiling above the cabinets, also recessed ⅜ inch. Secure lengths of wallboard to these two nailers and tape and paste joints. Then cover the edges with the molding.

Installation of Wall-Hanging Cabinets. It is important that you hang kitchen wall cabinets on studs. In a kitchen studs are likely to be at random points; they are installed this way to allow for pipes used with fixtures and appliances. Locate them and mark their positions. Place the marks so they will be visible when the cabinets are up.

As mentioned earlier, you can use a high backsplash as a place to rest the cabinets as you install them.

Start installation with a corner cabinet, if you have one. Hike it into position and drive a 10d nail through the top rail into the stud to temporarily hold the cabinet up.

Use your level to check the cabinet and level and plumb both the front or sides; a cabinet secured to a warped wall can make it difficult or impossible to open and close doors smoothly. Hammer shims behind the cabinet as required to make it plumb.

Next, screw it to the studs with No. 10 screws; make sure they get a good bite in the studs; at least 1 inch (drill pilot holes). If a corner cabinet, also screw it to a stud on the adjacent wall.

Lift the other cabinet in place next to the first. Determine how the front edges fit together. If necessary, scribe the edge of the cabinet, take it down, and trim as needed so the edges go snugly together. Planing the edges at a slight angle towards the rear will enable them to fit together more easily.

Mount all the cabinets like the first two, then connect them by driving screws through holes counterbored in the stiles.

Other Cabinets and Bookcases

You can hang other cabinets and bookcases using most of the same principles involved in hanging kitchen cabinets. Wherever they are hung, cabinets and bookcase must be plumb and level, using shims as required or trimming them as needed with a plane. In all cases, screws are driven into the studs.

In cases where studs do not fall in the spot needed for cabinet attachment, you may use hollow wall anchors or toggle bolts. However, unless the cabinet will support very little weight, you should connect it to at least one stud.

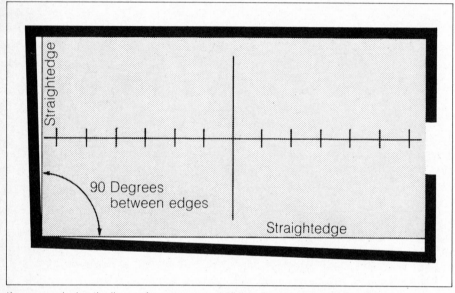

If your room is drastically out of square, snap chalklines from one corner with a 90° angle between the edges of the lines. Use these as baselines for your cabinet installation.

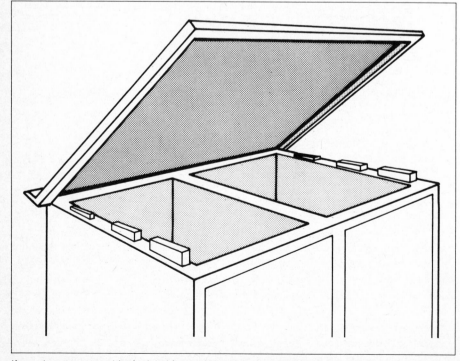

If you do not want to shim for level from underneath the cabinet, you may level a countertop with shims. Place shims on the cabinet base below the countertop and secure.

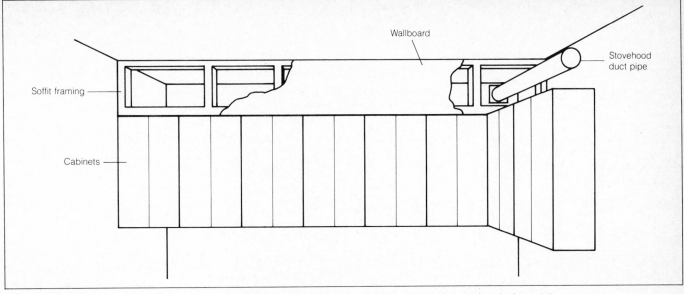

While the primary purpose of a soffit is decorative, the space can be used to hide ductwork and electrical conduit.

Working with Gypsumboard

Nail panels to the framing members with gypsumboard nails. Space the nails about three inches apart. When the nailheads are flush with the surface, hit them one more time with the hammer. This creates a "dimple" in the surface of the panel and countersinks the nailheads below the surface of the panel. These dimples will be filled later with spackling compound.

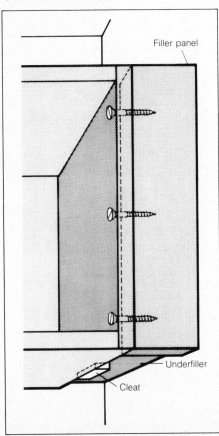

If cabinets do not meet the wall, the space left can be disguised with a filler panel.

When the panels are in place, check the edges to make sure that they do not project above the surface of any surrounding wall. If the edges do project, you may be able to trim them down slightly with the razor knife. It is likely, however, that the panel will fit perfectly.

Mix a stiff batch of spackling compound. With a putty knife or wall scraper, trowel on a thin layer of the spackling at the joints and along the ceiling line. Then embed the joint tape into the spackling compound. Run the wall scraper down over the tape, pressing it into the spackling.

With the tape embedded, fill all dimples with spackling coumpound, leveling the compound in these depressions using the wall scraper or putty knife.

Let the spackling dry one day. Apply a layer of spackling over the tape; let dry another 24 hours. Add a third coat. Once dry, sand the spackling lightly and prime the panel with paint. Once the paint has dried, give the panel a light sanding and dust off the residue. Add a second coat of paint or apply wallpaper.

OPENING UP WALLS

For certain projects you will be required to open up the walls; i.e., remove the wallboard, sheetrock or plaster to let recess cabinets and install cabinet units between studs. The number one rule is not to cut the studs.

The first step, of course, is to find the studs. Once you have found them, draw horizontal outlines of the units to guide your cuts. The stud edges will serve as guides for the vertical cuts.

Next, drill a hole between the studs with a drill or chisel as close to a stud as you can, then cut out the material with a keyhole saw. When you reach the edges of the studs they will, as mentioned, serve as your guides for vertical cuts. There are various ways to cut the wall, depending on the material.

Plaster Walls

Opening up a plaster wall is bound to be messy. If the walls are very old (forty or fifty years) you might want to decide against it. It is difficult to cut into old plaster without creating a mess and ending up with ragged outlines. For plaster that is relatively new, and in good condition, the procedures depend upon the type of lath, or base, to which the plaster is adhered.

Whatever the lath, the first step is to score the plaster. Do this with a broad bladed chisel, tapping through the plaster to the lath, but do not attempt to cut through the lath itself. Once you are through the lath and have cut the outlines, use screws to hang the cabinets on the studs.

Wood Lath. If wood lath, cut through it using a keyhole saw. Cut slowly and carefully, using a very sharp saw, and taking great care not to damage the wall around the outline.

Rock Lath. You can follow the same procedure for rock lath, which is a Sheetrock-like base.

Metal Lath. If the wall has metal lath, use the chisel to break through both the plaster and the lath. Metal lath is sometimes used on the body of the wall, but is more often found near and in wall corners, where it is used for reinforcement.

BENCH/CABINET

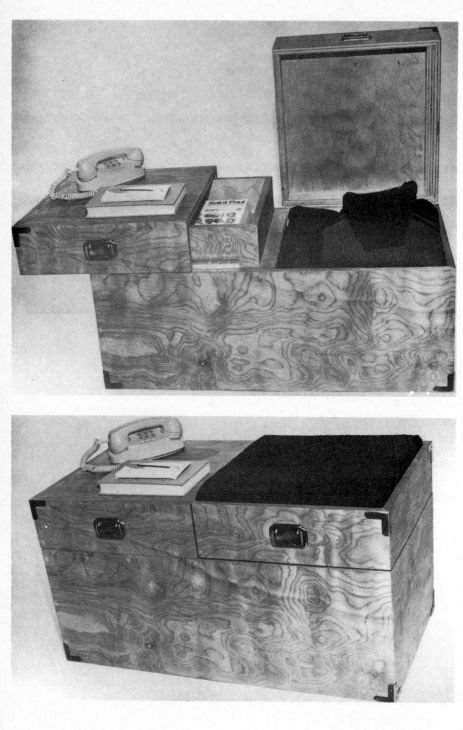

This piece serves two purposes: (1) a storage unit with a lift-up lid for access; (2) a bench. The side, slide-out hide-away compartment is a convenient place for telephone books, and the telephone itself could be placed conveniently on the top.

Construction

The unit is made entirely of ¾ inch birch plywood except for the ¼ inch Masonite bottom.

Typical of "Campaign" style chests, the lid of this unit is not a simple, flat top, but includes five inches of sheathed vertical framing which meets and matches the sides. In fact, you will build the basic box and then cut off the top five inches to serve as the framework of the top before completing the lid. Cut the parts as detailed in the sketch and on the materials list. The front, back, and side pieces on the list include the five inches needed for the top. Cut the hardboard bottom and then cut dadoes for this bottom piece in the front, back and side pieces. The chest is shown in the photos with mitered corners; however, if this seems too difficult, the chest may be constructed with rabbet joints.

Assemble the four sides and hardboard bottom with No. 4 1½ inch long finishing nails and glue. Let dry. Set your tablesaw at 5 inches and cut the top off the chest by rotating it through the saw. (This is a common trick when making any box to assure exact fit on the top.)

Use the tablesaw again, cutting the top in half in the other direction to obtain the two pieces shown in the drawing.

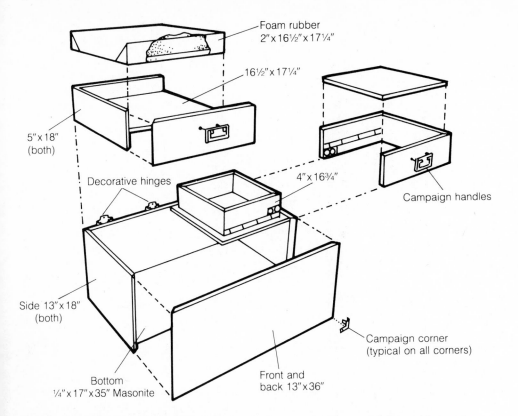

Foam rubber
2″ x 16½″ x 17¼″

16½″ x 17¼″

5″ x 18″
(both)

Decorative hinges

4″ x 16¾″

Campaign handles

Side 13″ x 18″
(both)

Bottom
¼″ x 17″ x 35″ Masonite

Front and
back 13″ x 36″

Campaign corner
(typical on all corners)

Next cut four pieces of plywood, each 16½ inches x 17¼ inches. Attach them to the two top pieces and the lower chest using finishing nails and glue. These fit inside box frame. Save the fourth piece to support the cushion.

The four pieces that form the box for the phone books on top of the chest can be made next. Cut them out and assemble them. Attach the box to the chest, again using finishing nails and glue.

Cover all exposed plywood edges with veneer tape; set all nails and fill with wood putty. Sand the unit with fine sandpaper. Finish with a clear finish.

Attach the hardware and slide in a cushion of a suitable size. If you wish, you can get a piece of foam rubber cut to size and cover it with material of your choice.

Materials List

¾″ Birch plywood
2 pcs.   18″ x 36″ for front and top
2 pcs.   18″ x 18″ for tops and sides
4 pcs.   16¼″ x 17¼″ for top, bottoms and cushion support
2 pcs.   4″ x 16″
2 pcs.   4″ x 16¾″
22′ veneer tape
1 pc.   ¼″ hardboard, 17″ x 35″
16 campaign corners
2 campaign handles
2 campaign hinges
No. 4   1½″ finishing nails
1 pair 15″ to 16″ drawer slides
White glue
Contact cement

BASIC KITCHEN CABINETS

Most professional kitchen remodelers do not build the cabinets they install. They find this unfeasible because of the time required to build them.

The do-it-yourselfer, however, usually has time on his or her side, and making kitchen cabinets can both reduce kitchen remodeling costs and provide a satisfying accomplishment.

Following are instructions on how to build two basic kinds of kitchen cabinets: (1) hangers, those mounted on the wall; and (2) base cabinets, those mounted on the floor (for information on installing cabinets, see Chapter 13).

The dimensions given are standard; base cabinets are designed 34½ inches high so that their tops will be level with a dishwasher or range when the countertop (1½ inches) has been added. Before installing such items, however, it is suggested that the appliance sizes be double-checked to see if they are compatible with the cabinet dimensions. You may have to adjust cabinet heights or widths for comfort, convenience, or fit.

Construction of Wall-Mounted Unit

Following illustration A, cut out the sides for the hanging cabinet from ¾ inch plywood. Make ¾ inch dadoes in the top and bottom as indicated, and ⅛ inch dadoes along the back of each side. Cut a bottom and top to the dimensions indicated, and nail and glue them between the sides. Nail and glue the back in place, then attach the back mounting members at the positions indicated. Cut and assemble the front members with glue dowels (See Chapter 7 for details). Secure this assembly to the unit using glue and nails.

Assemble doors to suit (See Chapter 8) and attach them with hinges of your choice, as indicated in Chapter 6.

Construction of Base Cabinet

Illustrations B and C detail construction of a typical base cabinet. Cut out sides from ¾ inch plywood. The dimensions will be 23⅝ x 34½ inches before cutting out the 3½ x 3 inch notches for the kickplate.

Cut the necessary dadoes into the sides as indicated, to hold the top back support rail and the bottom shelf. Then cut and assemble the front members with glue and dowels, and attach to the sides with countersunk screws. Note that the side stiles (vertical members) are rabbeted to link up with the sides. Cut out the kickplate as indicated in Figure B, from ¾ inch x 5-inch wide stock. This piece is glued and nailed to side panels as shown in C.

Cut the back from ⅛ inch plywood, and glue securely to the ½ inch dadoes made in the sides. After installing the back you can nail through the back and sides to secure the middle and bottom shelves. The final step is to install a ¾ inch reinforcing piece along the top edge of the back.

You will usually use at least ¾ inch exterior plywood or backer board as the support for the countertop, depending upon the counter material to be used. Be sure that drawer glides are installed before adding the countertop.

Materials List

Hanger Cabinets (Standard)
2 pcs. plywood* ¾" x 11¼" x 31" for sides
2 pcs. ¾" x 2" x 31" for side stiles
1 pc. ¾" x 2½" x 27" for center stile
1 pc. ¾" x 2" x 26½" for top face rail
1 pc. ¾" x 2" x 26½" for bottom face rail
2 pcs. ¾" x 1¼" x 29" for mounting rails
2 pcs. ¾" x 10⅜" x 30" for top and bottom
2 pcs. ¾" x 10¼" x 29" plywood for shelves
  (shelf track thickness might differ, measure interior width to insure proper shelf length)
1 pc. ⅛" x 30" x 30" plywood for back
½" x 2" stock for door panels
¾" x 2" stock for side and bottom door frame stiles
¾" x 4" stock for top door frame stiles

Base Cabinets (Standard)
2 pcs. ¾" x 23⅝" x 34½" plywood for sides
2 pcs. ¾" x 2" x 31" stock for face stiles
1 pc. ¾" x 2" x 26¾" stock for center stile
1 pc. ¾" x 2¼" x 26" stock for top rail
1 pc. ¾" x 2" x 26" stock for bottom rail
2 pcs. ¾" x 2" x 12" stock for drawer rails
1 pc. ⅛" x 29½" x 31" plywood for back
1 pc. ¾" x 1¾" x 28½" stock for top back support rail
1 pc. ¾" x 11¼" x 29½" plywood for shelf
1 pc. ¾" x 2¼" x 21¼" stock for top support rails

Bottom Frame
1 pc. ¾" x 5" x 30" stock for kickplate
2 pcs. ¾" x 5" x 20½" stock for bottom end support
1 pc. ¾" x 1½" x 28½" stock for back support
1 pc. ¾" x 1½" x 21¼" stock for center support

Doors
½" x 2" stock for door panels
¾" x 2" stock for door frames

Drawers
6 pcs. ½" x 3½" stock for drawer sides
2 pcs. ¼" x 11" x 20" plywood for drawer bottoms
2 pcs. ¾" x 4" x 14" stock for drawer fronts
1 pc. 2" x 3" x 20¼" stock for center drawer
2 sets 18" drawer guides

*Birch veneer plywood
  (or veneer of your choice).

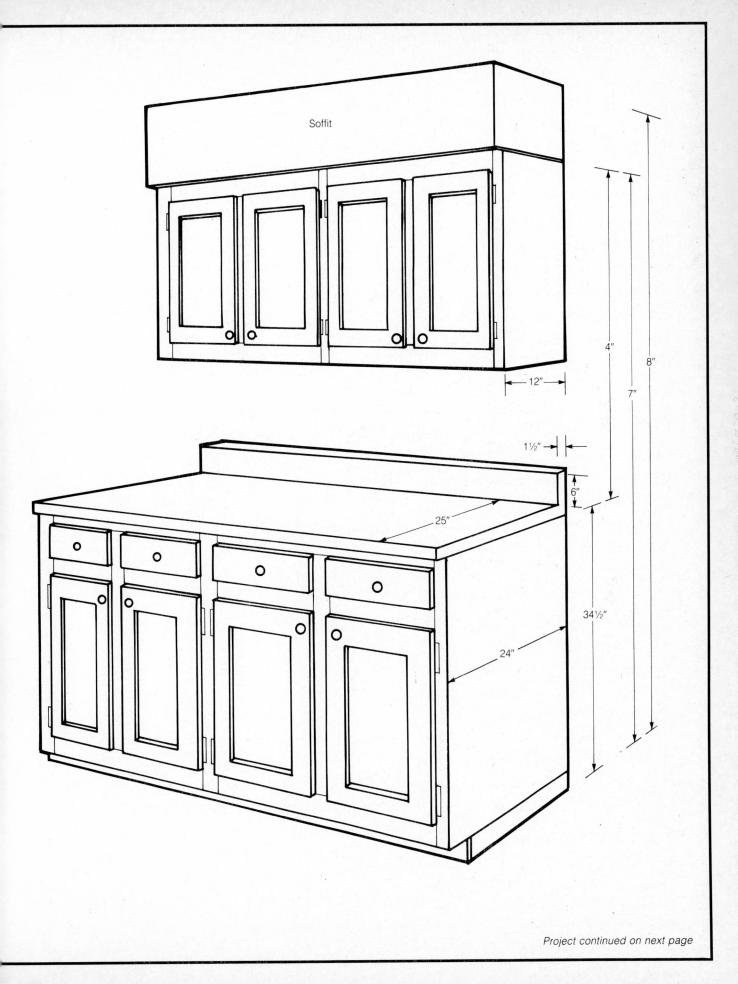

Soffit

12"

4"

7"

8"

1½"

6"

25"

34½"

24"

Project continued on next page

KITCHEN CABINETS continued

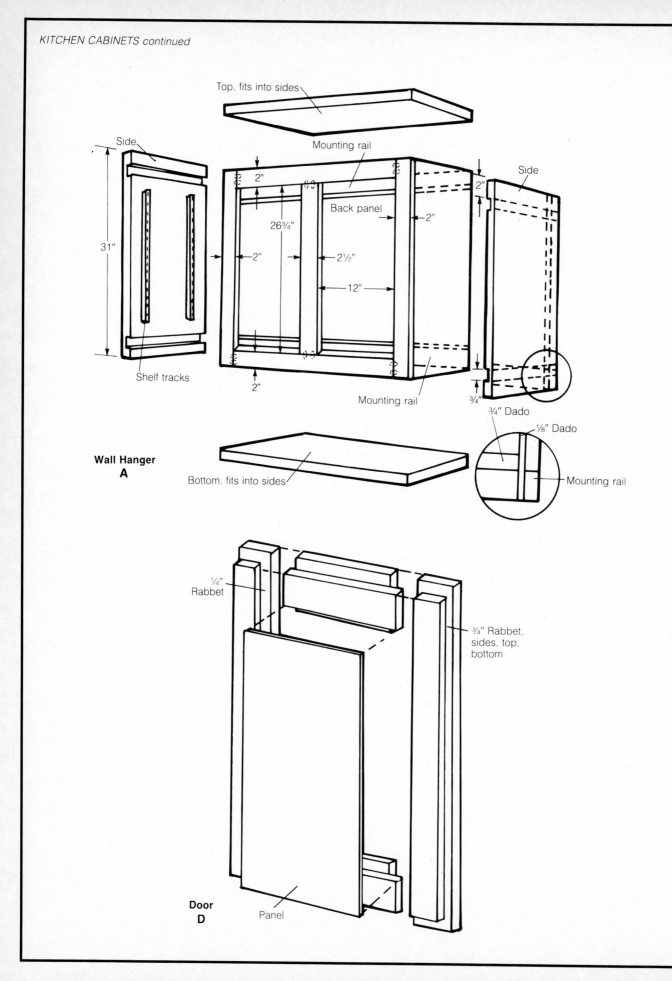

Top, fits into sides

Mounting rail

Side

Side

Back panel

2″

2″

2″

26¾″

31″

2″

2″

2½″

12″

Shelf tracks

2″

Mounting rail

¾″

¾″ Dado

Wall Hanger
A

Bottom, fits into sides

⅛″ Dado

Mounting rail

¼″
Rabbet

¾″ Rabbet,
sides, top,
bottom

Door
D

Panel

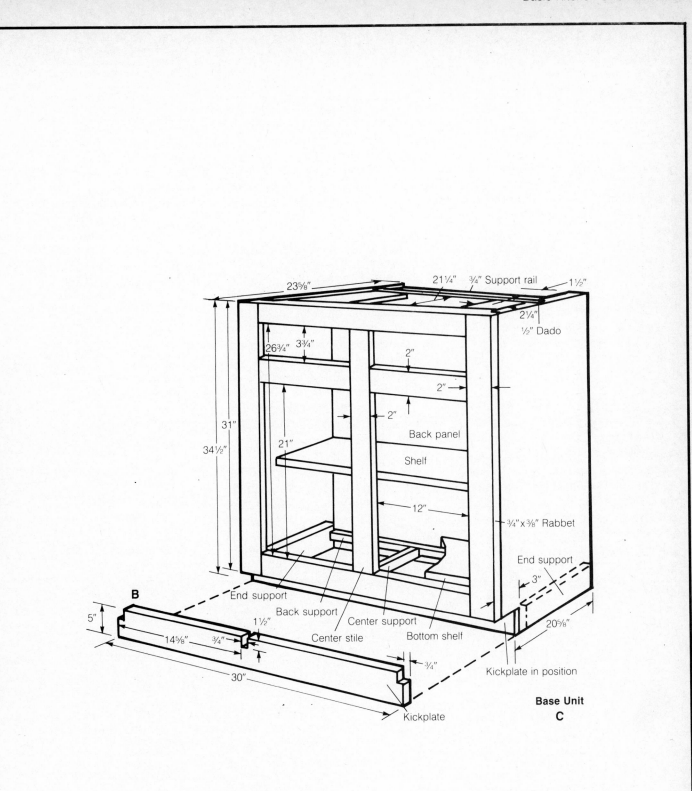

23⅝"   21¼"   ¾" Support rail   1½"

2¼"
½" Dado

26¾"   3¾"

2"

31"

2"

2"

Back panel

Shelf

34½"

21"

¾" x ⅜" Rabbet

12"

End support

3"

B

End support

Back support

5"

Center support

20⅝"

14⅝"   ¾"   1½"

Center stile

Bottom shelf

¾"

Kickplate in position

30"

Base Unit
C

Kickplate

SHELVES INSIDE WALLS

Shelf space inside walls can store a wide variety of items. One of the most desirable uses is for canned goods in the kitchen. There are many can sizes which have a diameter that allows them to be stored on the shelves in walls.

The drawing shows three shelves installed inside each pair of studs, but the distance between shelves can vary depending on your particular needs. The depth of the shelf will be the depth of the inside of the stud to the backside of the opposite wall (usually a 3⅝ inch stud depth). You may wish to let a portion of the shelf or cabinet project from the wall for greater shelf depth.

Constructed as shown, the shelves can accommodate fifty to sixty cans, depending on size. For example, standard soup cans would fit five per shelf, while jars or No. 2 cans would fit four abreast. Quick access to and inventory of your canned goods supply are some of the bonuses of this system.

You can make the shelves any height you wish. However, if you plan to use standard swing-out doors, try to locate the opening above head height of anyone who might be sitting nearby.

Construction

After opening the walls (see Chapter 13 for details), cut and install 1 x 1 cleats on the studs to hold the Marlite® brand panels that line the recesses. Use screws and glue to secure the cleats in place.

Cut out the pieces of paneling used to line the recesses. Use a notched spreader to apply waterproof adhesive to the backs of the panels. (Lumberyard dealers carry adhesive, panels and spreader). Leave 1 to 1½ inches uncoated near the edges so the adhesive will be able to spread.

Following the drawing, secure the panel pieces in the recesses. The back panel is installed first and rests on the cleats. Install the bottom shelf next, then pairs of side panels on which the upper shelves rest. Install each shelf as each pair of side panels are put in place. Check each shelf installation with your level and correct to perfect horizontal.

You can trim the opening with 2 inch molding. The doors can be made of ⅜ inch plywood and can be lipped or overlay doors (see Chapter 8).

Paint the trim to match the paneling and the rest of your decor.

Materials List

Marlite® Brand — Tongue & Groove 16"x96" Plank sheets
4 rear panels   14¼"x 19"
4 bottom shelves   3⅞"x 14⅜"
8 side panels   3⅞"x 5½"
8 side panels   3⅞"x 5½"
8 side panels   3⅞"x 5⅝"
4 top panels   3⅞"x 14⅜"
2 end facings   3¾"x 21⅝"
2 top and bottom of cabinet frame facing   2"x 62"
3 divider facings   2"x 17⅝"
4 door   14½"x 18⅛"
4¾" plywood bottom shelves   3⅜"x 14⅜"
8⅜" plywood shelves   3½"x 14⅜"
4⅜" plywood doors   13¾"x 17⅜"
4 door pulls
4 magnetic latches
8⅜" offset hinges

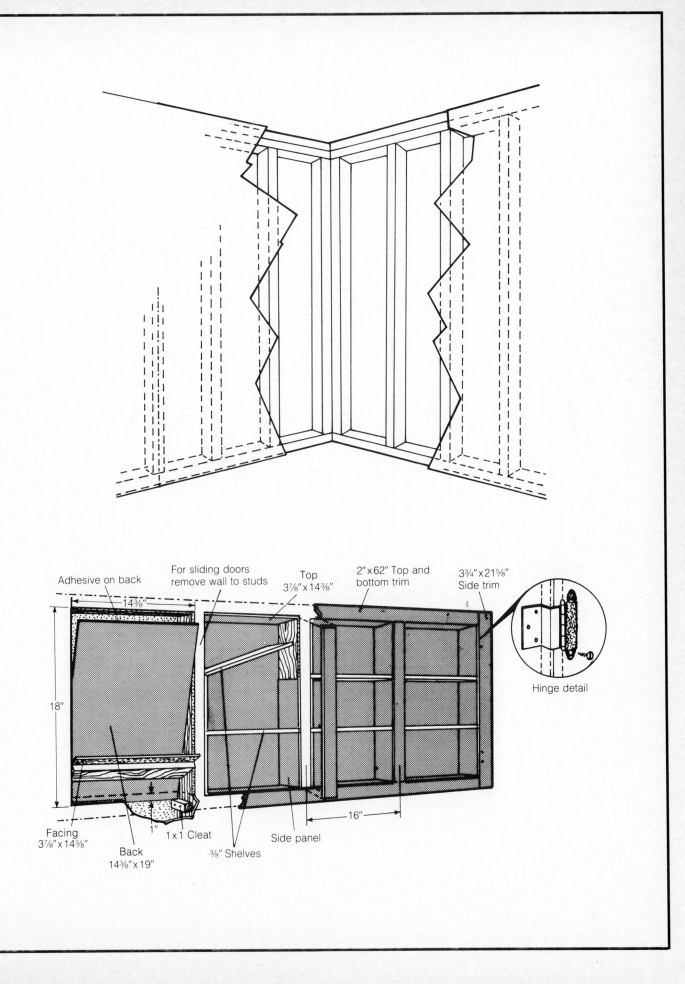

Adhesive on back

For sliding doors
remove wall to studs

Top
3⅞″ x 14⅜″

2″ x 62″ Top and
bottom trim

3¾″ x 21⅝″
Side trim

14⅜″

18″

Hinge detail

Facing
3⅞″ x 14⅜″

1″   1 x 1 Cleat

Back
14⅜″ x 19″

⅜″ Shelves

Side panel

16″

BUILT-IN TWIN CHINA CABINETS

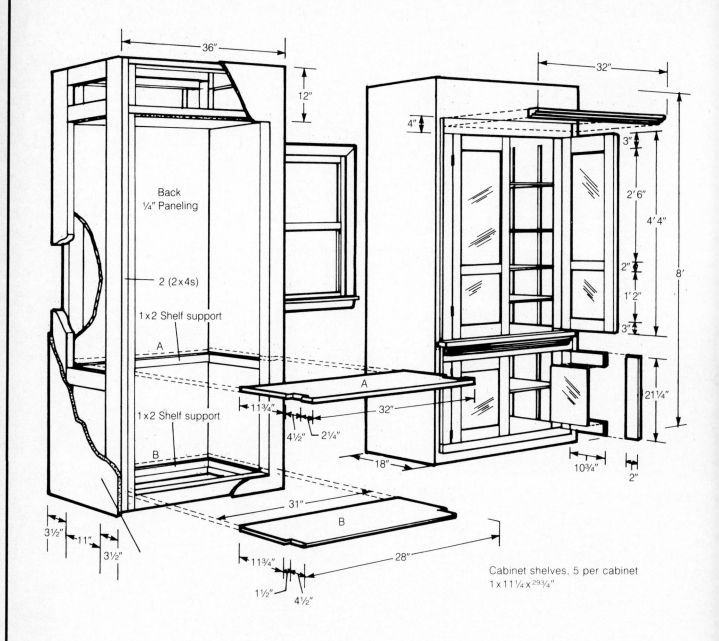

Back
¼" Paneling

2 (2 x 4s)

1 x 2 Shelf support

A

1 x 2 Shelf support

B

36"

12"

3½"

11"

3½"

11¾"

4½"

2¼"

A

32"

18"

31"

B

28"

11¾"

1½"

4½"

32"

4"

3"

2' 6"

4' 4"

8'

2"

1' 2"

3"

21¼"

10¾"

2"

Cabinet shelves, 5 per cabinet
1 x 11¼ x 29¾"

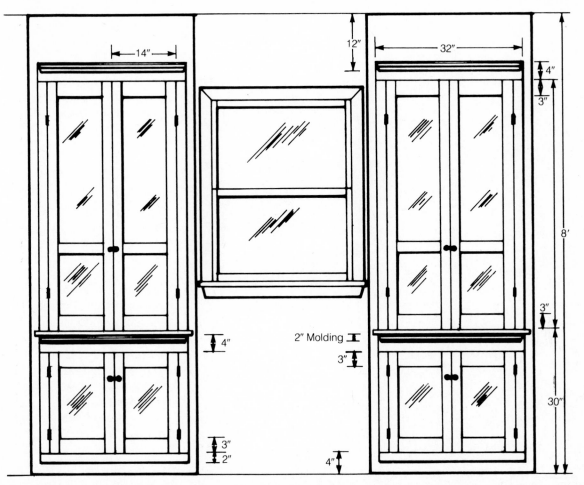

Begin this project by anchoring 2x4s flat to the wall, 32 inches apart, measuring to the outside edges of the 2x4s. Then anchor the 2x4s to the ceiling and floor, and frame in the soffit as shown (the cabinet is 18 inches deep, including a ½ inch drywall sheet). The 2x4 on the front edge of the cabinet should be placed 17½ inches from the wall. Apply ½ inch drywall sheet to framework, leaving cabinet opening as shown. Tape and sand all seams.

Anchor 1x2 inch shelf supports, as shown. The top edge of shelf support A is 29¼ inches from the floor; the top edge of shelf support B is 3½ inches from the floor.

Cut shelves A and B from ¾ inch hardwood plywood, as shown. Shelf A has a lip that extends past the front of cabinet by 2¼ inches. Shelf B is flush. The notch that is cut is 1½ x 4½ inches. Measurements might differ slightly depending on the accuracy of the framework. Measure and make any necessary adjustments.

Nail hardwood framework to cabinet front.

Assemble cabinet doors. Cut a ⅜ x ⅜ inch rabbet on inside edges of vertical and horizontal pieces, as well as ends of horizontal pieces. Glue with a white glue, and clamp.

Measure door frames for glass and secure with ¼ bead molding on the back side. Add cabinet doors and hardware. Attach shelf brackets.

Cut shelves to length. Shelves are cut from 1x12 (¾ x 11¼) and are 29¾ inches long. The length might differ depending on the thickness of shelf bracket available. Check dimensions of your cabinet before cutting. Sand and finish to suit.

Materials List (for one cabinet)

---

12   2"x4"x8' uprights and framework
1   1x2x12' hardwood shelf supports
3 Sheets   ½" drywall
1 Sheet   ¼" paneling   Cabinet back
5   1x12x29¾"   Shelves
Drywall coumpound
Drywall tape
Drywall nails
White glue
2   ¾x4" hardwood   Cabinet trim
51 feet of ¾x2" hardwood   Cabinet trim
Hardware
Nails; hinges 4 sets; knobs 8
2   32x2" decorative hardwood trim

VANITY BUILT-IN

This bathroom vanity may be adjusted to fit various spaces. It is given visual distinction here by the addition of rough sawn redwood paneling to the faces of the doors and drawers.

Construction

The dimensions of the piece may vary according to the space available. A useful height is 30 inches with a depth of 2 feet.

Begin construction by cutting parts to size as indicated in the illustration, or adjusted as required in your situation. First, assemble the base, composed of 2x4s screwed together. You may prefer to use 2x6s. On top of the base build the 2x4 rectangular framework as shown in the drawing, using dowel joints. Nail the frame to the base, forming a toespace.

Build the main framework for the cabinet from 1x2s. Adjust your plan from the drawing provided to conform to your requirements. Assemble the parts with glue and finishing nails. Secure the assembly to the base with screws.

Make the top of ¾ inch plywood. Cut the plywood 24⅝ inches wide and to the length you need. Add a 1x2 reinforcing strip faced with a lip of ¾ inch plywood underneath the front edge of the top, as shown in the detail.

The cabinet is faced with redwood paneling, as mentioned. Drawers are the overlay type, made and installed as specified in Chapter 8. The overlay (face of the drawers) can be finished with redwood molding, mitered at the corners.

If you wish, you might construct the translucent light box. Details are provided in the drawing. The framework for the light box is made from 2x2s, nailed together and covered on the bottom with strips of the redwood paneling. The underside is faced with strips which create a rabbet on which sections of translucent plastic rest.

Materials List

2x4s or 2x6s for base cut to size for your requirements
2x4s for frame assembly on base cut to size
1x4s for cabinet framework   draw plan and calculate needs ¾" plywood for top
1x2 reinforcing strips for tops
Resawn redwood paneling for vanity front and drawer fronts.
Plastic laminate for vanity top
Stock for drawers plan and calculate needs
Drawer hardware

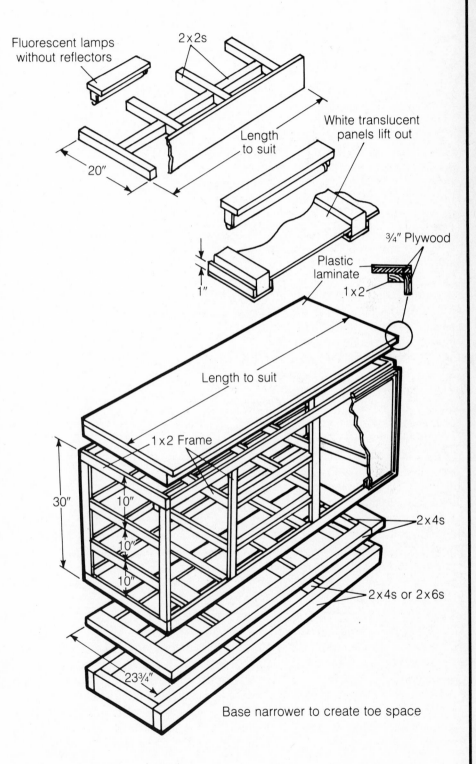

Fluorescent lamps without reflectors

2x2s

20"

Length to suit

White translucent panels lift out

1"

Plastic laminate

1x2

¾" Plywood

Length to suit

1x2 Frame

30"

10"

10"

10"

2x4s

2x4s or 2x6s

23¾"

Base narrower to create toe space

DESK PLUS SHELVES

This handsome unit combines shelf space with a small desk and drawer. It uses the back of the wall as its own back, and can be fitted into a hall, kitchen, office or den.

Construction

The unit gets its sturdy look from the 2 inch redwood stock used for the sides and shelves.

It is best to build the unit separately, then mount it on the wall. The unit shown uses 1 x 4 stock to trim around the top edge, but you can use any material that suits the decor of your home.

Cut the parts as indicated in the Materials List or drawing. As you can see, the sides of the unit are curved. They are 8¾ inch at their narrowest point and 20 inches at their widest. You will have to add, using dowel joints, a section of stock to each side to make the wooden standards wide enough for the full 20-inch depth. You will not have to add to the full length; work out a to-scale plan to determine how large a piece you will have to add. It would be advisable for you to first determine the curve which you would like and then to draw a pattern to full scale. You can tape the pattern onto your wood to guide you when cutting. You can use a saber saw to cut the curves.

Measure the locations of the shelves and the desk top carefully. Mark these points; check your measurements again. Then rout dadoes for the shelves. You may prefer to face the front below the writing surface with a single piece of 2 inch stock. If you want to include the drawer, you can build it to size for the middle third, or for half or the full width. (See Chapter 8 for details of drawer construction.)

A light stain followed by a clear finish was used here, after the edges had first been rounded off with plane and sandpaper.

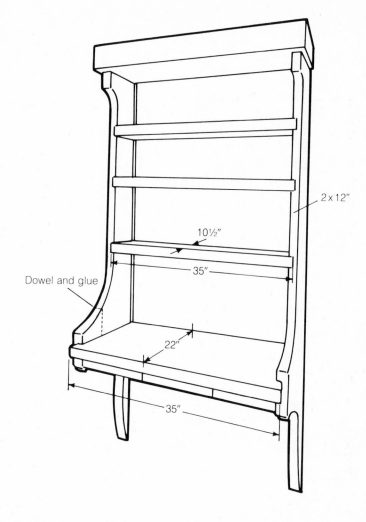

You can hang the unit by driving screws through each of the side pieces near the bottom where the stock is narrow; counterbore the heads. At the top, the sides can be notched in order to have a 1 x 4 nailer screwed to them; the nailer, in turn, can be secured to the wall with screws which go into the studs. You may also attach, with screws, a pair of 1 x 4 strips at the back of each side support. These 1 x 4s can then be used to mount the unit to studs. Angle irons may also be bolted to studs and the sides of the unit; add a bracing strip nailed to the wall below the desk top or any of the shelves. The wood is heavy, so you want to be sure it has been sufficiently secured.

Materials List

2 pcs.   2 x 12 x 8' for standards
2 pcs.   2 x 12 x 18", to be dowel-joined to standards for full width desk shelf support.
3 pcs.   2 x 35 x 10½" for shelves
2 pcs.   2 x 35 x 22" for desk top
          (2 pieces of 12" stock dowel-joined)
2 pcs.   2 x 12 for desk facing
1 pc.   2 x 12 for drawer front
¼" plywood for drawer sides, back and bottom
1½" No. 10 flathead screws.
White glue
Finish

TAKE-APART CABINETS

The construction technique used in these cabinets consists only of tabs which fit into slots. No other fastening is required. As such, the cabinets can be taken down and the pieces stacked up for easy transport. The process may appear to be very simple but this is deceptive; the project should be approached with care.

The cabinets are also modular. In the drawing, three tiers are shown. But you can build just two, as shown in the photographs, or one — adding other tiers as time and budget permit.

Construction

It must be stressed emphatically that this is not a project for a beginner. While cutting tabs to fit into slots seems easy, it is precision work. If your cuts are not just right, the tabs will not fit in; they might fit loosely and the unit will be weak and unsightly.

It is best to cut parts out by tiers. Build the first tier; check for square and level and true. Then build the tier above, and finally build the top one. The slot can be cut with a saber saw or a router. Follow the drawings for construction. Refer to the "Sides" and "Shelves" drawings for the size and cutting details, which are keyed in by letter and/or number to the main drawings. The drawers may be made as indicated in Chapter 8, and installed with suitable hardware.

Finishing the unit is, as with most of these units, optional. The units in the photo are painted with semi-gloss enamel and the edges are painted a contrasting color.

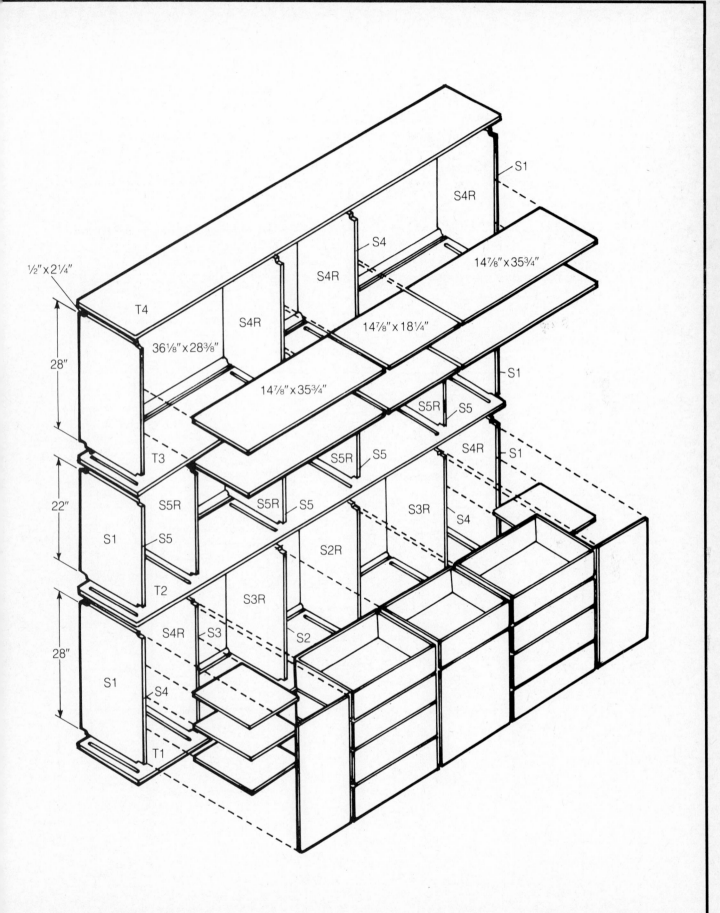

½" x 2¼"

28"

36⅛" x 28⅜"

T4

S4R

S4R

S4

S4R

S1

14⅞" x 35¾"

14⅞" x 18¼"

14⅞" x 35¾"

S1

S5R   S5

T3

S5R   S5

S4R   S1

22"

S5R

S5R   S5

S3R   S4

S1   S5

S2R

T2

S3R

28"

S4R   S3

S2

S1

S4

T1

Project continued on next page

TAKE-APART CABINET continued

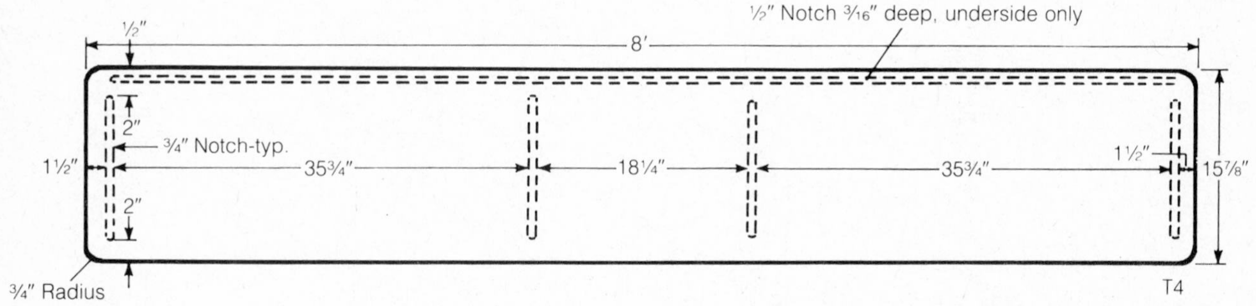
½" Notch 3/16" deep, underside only
½"
8'
2"
¾" Notch-typ.
1½"
35¾"
18¼"
35¾"
1½"
15⅞"
2"
¾" Radius
T4

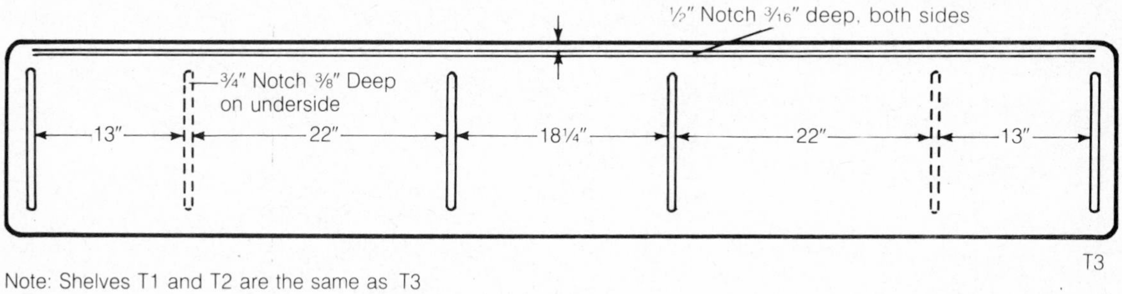
½" Notch 3/16" deep, both sides
¾" Notch ⅜" Deep on underside
13"
22"
18¼"
22"
13"
T3

Note: Shelves T1 and T2 are the same as T3

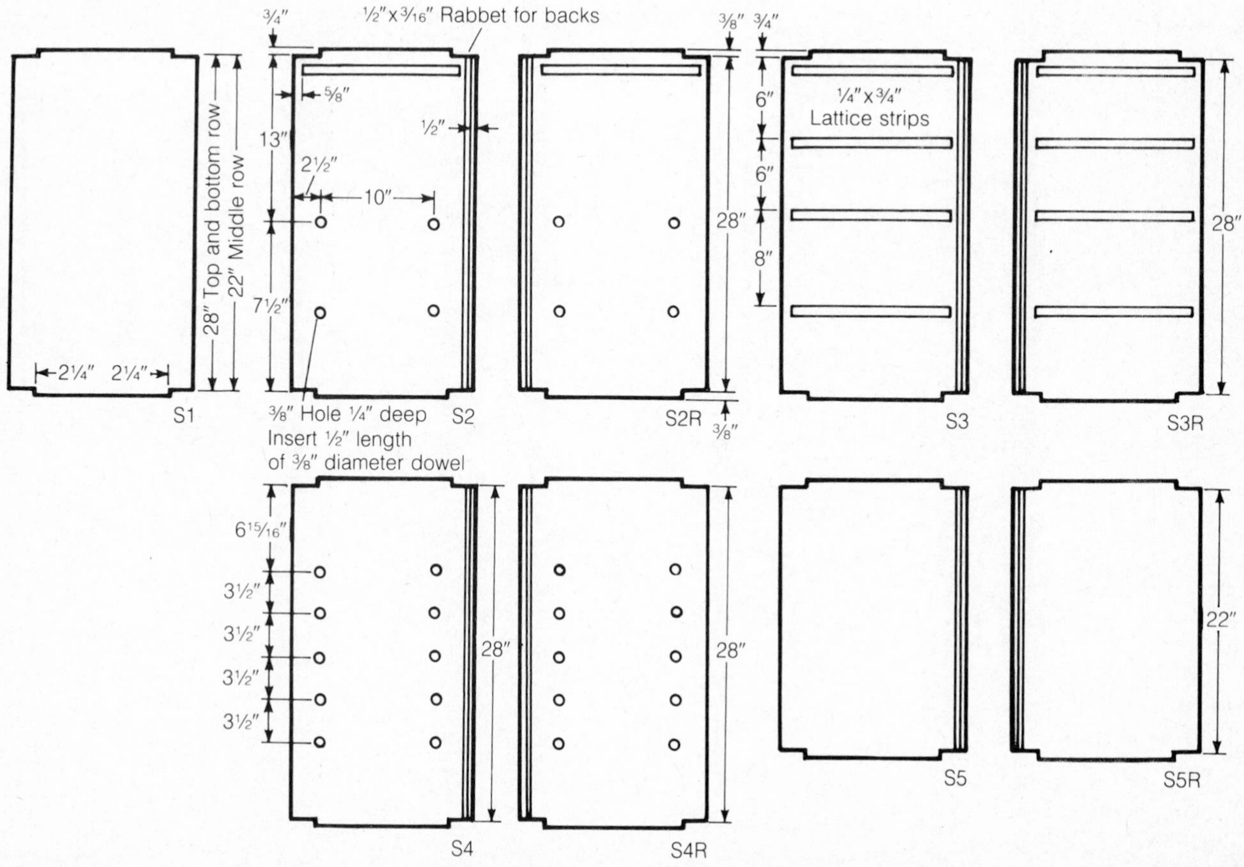
¾"
½"x3/16" Rabbet for backs
⅜" ¾"
⅝"
½"
13"
2½"
10"
7½"
28" Top and bottom row
22" Middle row
2¼" 2¼"
S1
⅜" Hole ¼" deep
Insert ½" length
of ⅜" diameter dowel
S2
28"
S2R
⅜"
6"
6"
8"
¼"x¾"
Lattice strips
S3
28"
S3R
6 15/16"
3½"
3½"
3½"
3½"
28"
S4
28"
S4R
S5
22"
S5R

MAGAZINE RACK

This magazine holder is really a cabinet in its simplest form — a box with one open side. Nevertheless, its simple lines and plastic laminate finish are attractive.

Construction

Following the sizes given in the drawing and Materials List, cut all pieces. Prior to assembly, laminate the inside faces of the sides, ends and bottom; rout the edges flush.

Predrill the laminate for the assembly screws and fasten the sides and ends into a butt-jointed box, with the laminated faces on the inside. Screw the bottom piece to the four sides. Countersink the screws; putty and sand any holes. Laminate the outside of the rack, shorter sides first; trim top flush, bevel sides.

Join two ¾ x 1½ x 6½ inch pieces with white glue and nails to form one of the feet. Repeat for the second foot. Laminate the ends and sides of each foot, beginning with the small ends; rout flush. Laminate the long sides and bevel trim the edges. Do not laminate the top or bottom faces.

Laminate the top with an 8½ x 14½ inch piece, centering it on the top to allow a ¼ inch overlap on all sides. Drill a hole through the laminate, insert a flush router bit and rout the inside edges. Allow a slight radius at the corners to guard against cracking. Bevel trim the outside edges.

Turn the rack over, setting it on its top edges. Use white glue to attach the feet to the bottom. Once the glue has dried (at least an hour), the feet may be made scratch-free by covering the bottoms with cork, felt, or urethane bumpers.

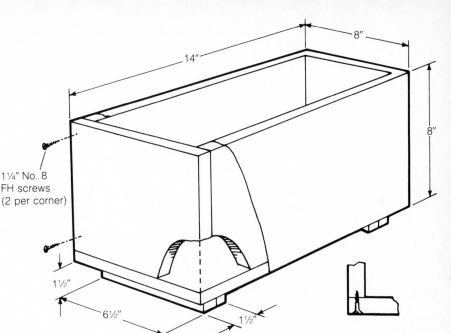

1¼" No. 8 FH screws (2 per corner)

Materials List

¾" plywood

2 pcs.   7¼" x 8" for the ends
2 pcs.   7¼" x 12½" for the sides
1 pc.   8" x 14" for the bottom
4 pcs.   1½" x 6½" for the feet

Plastic laminate

4 pcs.   8½" square
4 pcs.   8½" x 14½"
2 pcs.   8½" x 14½" for bottom and top edges
4 pcs.   2" x 7" (for solid casters)
4 pcs.   2" x 2"

Misc. and Hardware
White glue
20 or more 1¼ No. 8 flathead wood screws
Choice of cork, felt or urethane bumpers for magazine rack solid casters

FOR THE BARBECUE

Equipment needed for a backyard barbecue can include many items of various sizes, but this 6 foot wide, 3 foot deep and over 4½ foot high unit should be able to accommodate everything easily. The cabinet is designed to fit against one wall, or a fence, but it could be made free-standing just as easily.

It should be noted that this is a large, challenging project and you should not attempt it until you have considerable experience with your tools.

Construction

Select a well-drained site on which to place a floor of foot-square concrete patio blocks. Stake the area out, level the ground, then place the blocks: the frame will rest directly on the perimeter of these blocks. The unit can be constructed directly on a wood deck, using the deck as the floor.

Refer to Illustration A, and, following the measurements of the drawing, make two end sections and one middle frame section with dowel joints. The middle and one end section (right side in Illus. A) are identical, so the first can be a pattern for the second. Cut and fasten horizontal back braces to side and middle frames to tie the sections together.

Refer to Illustrations B, C and D for details to cut pieces for the roof. Assemble the roof, sloping it ¼ inch to the foot.

Note that a metal- or plastic-clad quarter-inch plywood is used for the roof and the slide-out shelf. (This provides a shelf that is easily cleaned and

will not be scarred by hot pans or utensils.)

Attach the roof to the frame with neoprene washers and roofing nails, 12 inches apart, over the five rafters. Add 1 x 4 inch fascia around the unit at the top, cutting it out at the back for drainage along an extended center rafter which has been routed and sealed against rot. This rafter leads to an Oriental-style chain drain as shown in Illustration D.

A wide storage shelf above the pull-out shelf fits in easier if it is sawn in half, then set together in place. After other shelves have been installed, nail the

½ x 3½ inch tongue-and-groove western red cedar siding to the 2 x 4 inch cross members. Corners can be mitered, or lapped.

Make the doors next. A jig of cleats on a workbench or plywood sheet facilitates fabrication of built-up doors and blind-nailing the board siding to the 1 x 4-inch Z-braces, which should be assembled with corregated fasteners for stability before nailing door boards in place. Hang doors, add door handles, then stain units, or paint to match or complement house siding. If it is to be stained, saw-textured siding is attractive.

Materials List

INTERIOR

2 x 4s
2 pcs. 6'
3 pcs. 4' 7¾"
3 pcs. 4' 7"
1 pc. 3' 5"
4 pcs. 3' 1"
7 pcs. 2' 9¾"
11 pcs. 2' 5"

2 x 2s
2 pcs. 2' 9¾"
2 pcs. 1' 1"

1 x 4s
2 pcs. 2' 3½"
4 pcs. 2' 2"
2 pcs. 1' 8½"
2 pcs. 1' 6½"
14 pcs. 1' 4¾"

1 x 2s
6 pcs. 2' 9¾" trim for end of
  supports
2 pcs. 2' 7" top shelf supports
1 pc. 1' 4½" for sliding frame

1 x 1s
3 pcs. 2' 9¾"

EXTERIOR

1 x 4s
2 pcs. 6' 2"
1 pc. 3' 2½"
2 pcs. 0' 6"
1 pc. 0' 3½"

¾" Plywood
1 pc. 3' ¾" x 2' x 11¼"
1 pc. 3' ¾" x 2' x 8½"
1 pc. 3' ¾" x 1'
1 pc. 2' 10¾" x 1' 6"
1 pc. 2' 9¾" x 2' 9¾"

1 x 2s
2 pcs. 6' 3"
1 pc. 3' 4"

½" Plywood
1 pc. 4' 6" x 2' 10"

½ x 3½
63 pcs. 5'
3 pcs. 2' 9¾"

Metal or Plastic Clad Plywood
1 pc. 6'1" x 3'5" (cut to fit roof)
1 pc. 1'11" x 2'9¾" (sliding shelf)
2 pcs. 0'10" x 0'2" (runners)

Nails
10d common
8d common
6d finish
roofing, with neoprene washer

Hardware
7 pulls
6 pair hinges
6 friction catches

Miscellaneous
caulking (to seal roof)
18—12 x 12 patio blocks (floor)
5' chain (for drain)
stain for desired finish

NOTE: If unit is covered on both ends, 12
     pcs. of 5' T&G siding will be
     required.

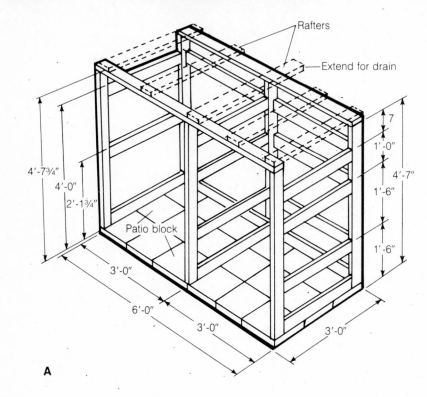

Rafters

Extend for drain

4'-7¾"

4'-0"

2'-1¾"

Patio block

3'-0"

6'-0"

3'-0"

3'-0"

7

1'-0"

4'-7"

1'-6"

1'-6"

A

Project continued on next page

FOR THE BARBECUE continued

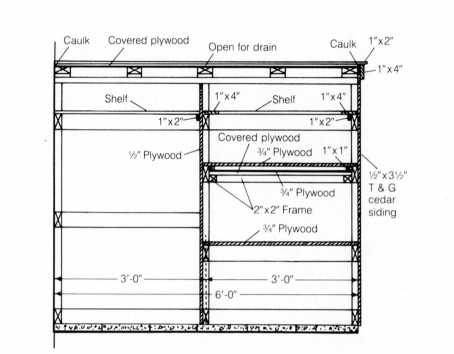

Caulk   Covered plywood   Open for drain   Caulk   1"x2"

1"x4"

Shelf   1"x4"   Shelf   1"x4"

1"x2"   1"x2"

½" Plywood

Covered plywood

¾" Plywood   1"x1"

½"x3½"
T & G
cedar
siding

¾" Plywood

2"x2" Frame

¾" Plywood

3'-0"   3'-0"

6'-0"

B

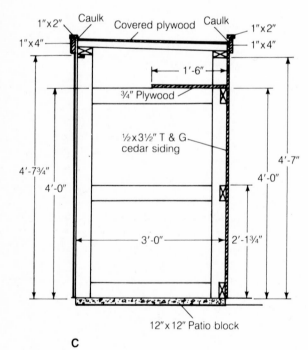

1"x2"   Caulk   Covered plywood   Caulk   1"x2"

1"x4"   1"x4"

1'-6"

¾" Plywood

½ x 3½" T & G
cedar siding

4'-7¾"   4'-7"

4'-0"   4'-0"

3'-0"   2'-1¾"

12"x12" Patio block

C

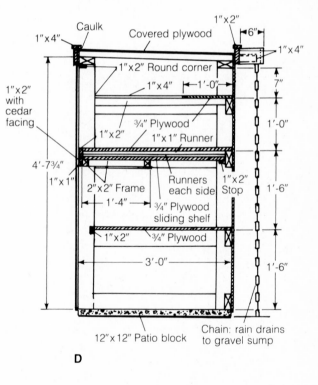

Caulk   Covered plywood   1"x2"   6"

1"x4"   1"x4"

1"x2" Round corner

1"x2"
with
cedar
facing   1"x4"   1'-0"   7"

¾" Plywood

1"x2"   1"x1" Runner   1'-0"

4'-7¾"   Runners
each side   1"x2"
Stop

1"x1"

2"x2" Frame   1'-6"

1'-4"   ¾" Plywood
sliding shelf

1"x2"   ¾" Plywood

3'-0"   1'-6"

12"x12" Patio block   Chain: rain drains
to gravel sump

D

LAUNDRY STORAGE

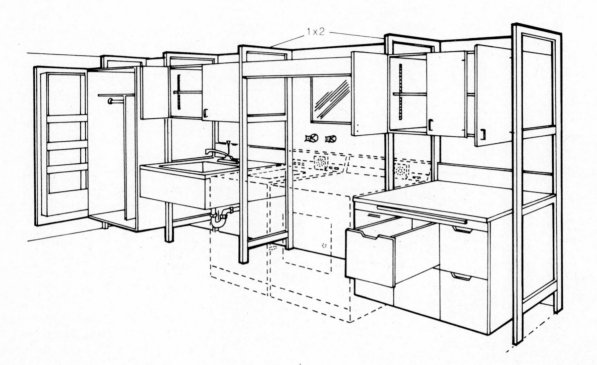

The most significant component in these laundry storage units is the framework between the units. The framework adds a simple stylistic touch. In addition, it enables the storage units (shown here are a tall cabinet on the left, two pairs of hangers, and a base cabinet on the right) to be suspended from the framework, which is either attached to the wall with finishing nails or screwed in place. This latter alternative is particularly useful if you must restore a house to original condition when you move.

This project must be done to fit your available space; therefore, you must draw your own plans and develop your own materials list. Plan each step of the construction before you start, including locating your studs and joints,

since the framework sections will have to be attached to these in order to safely and securely support any cabinets or drawer units you design.

Construction
The Framework
The 1 x 2 framework can be built of pine, or it may be cut from ½ inch plywood. If you use boards, you should use the dowel method given in Chapter 7 for joining the pieces. If you cut the framework from plywood, no joinery will be required because each piece is a half sheet of plywood with sections cut out, but you should plan your cutting layout so your "waste" pieces can also be used in constructing the cabinets. Careful framework layout on the plywood will minimize waste.

The Cabinets
The cabinets themselves can be made with ½ inch plywood using one of the joinery procedures mentioned in Chapter 7. The cabinets may be finished with a wide variety of materials, as detailed in Chapters 10 and 11.

The cabinets can be attached to the framework in several ways. However, it is probably easiest to install the framework, then lift each of the cabinets into position, and mark the location on the framework in level and true position.

One means of attaching the cabinets is with dowels, but screws may also be used. This system gives the cabinets stability in position, but they may be taken down or removed from the framework without great difficulty.

TWO-SIDED STORAGE DIVIDER

This two-faced room divider has enough room to solve many storage problems. The front face has a handy dropleaf desk, space for a television set, stereo equipment, records and storage drawers which may be reached from either side. The rear face has cupboards for china or glassware. Decorative accessories may be seen from both sides of open shelves. Brightly painted sliding doors have curved edges instead of finger pulls.

Construction

Cut all plywood parts to overall size as indicated in Materials List or drawings. Rabbet end, top and bottom panels as indicated in the drawings. Measuring carefully make dado cuts for shelves in partitions and end panels at heights shown in Illus. A and B. Be sure to provide a blind dado in front for shelf of desk compartment (as shown in Illus. C). Make dado cuts for partitions in top and bottom panels. Follow with dado cuts along shelf edges for compartments with sliding doors. Install metal drawer track in these last dado cuts. Provide dadoes in bottom face of shelf for ¼ inch partitions of record storage compartment.

Drive 2-inch finishing nails into both edges at bottom of desk front and drill pivot holes. Now assemble shelves above and below to form the desk compartment.

Install back as shown in lower drawing on page 113 and in detail on page 114. Assemble remaining shelves and partitions with top, bottom and ends using 6d finishing nails and glue. Check the unit for square while assembling.

Place ¼ inch plywood spacers into position in bottom of record compartment. Slip record partitions into place using a little white glue along top and bottom edges. Install panels A and B into positions shown using glue and 6d finishing nails.

Next, make necessary rabbets and dadoes and assemble the filing box for the desk compartment.

Build flush drawers as detailed in Chapter 8 (sizes required are in the Materials List). There are seven, three for the desk compartment plus four larger drawers for the compartment directly below the desk. For style you can cut the curves along the top as shown in photograph.

Variation: Sliding Doors

Large sliding doors of ¼ inch plywood may be added to close off either or both faces of the unit. This can be accomplished by fastening wood strips along the top face and the bottom edge of the divider (shown in the photograph). Install track, door hangers, divider strip and door fascias.

After filling nail holes and edges with wood filler, sand the divider until smooth and finish it to match the room decor. Three coats of paint were used here — an undercoater followed with two coats of semi-gloss enamel.

Finally, fasten caning or other fill material in place with painted ½ inch quarter round molding. Drill holes in large sliding doors to set finger pulls flush with surface. Slip sliding doors into place to complete the unit.

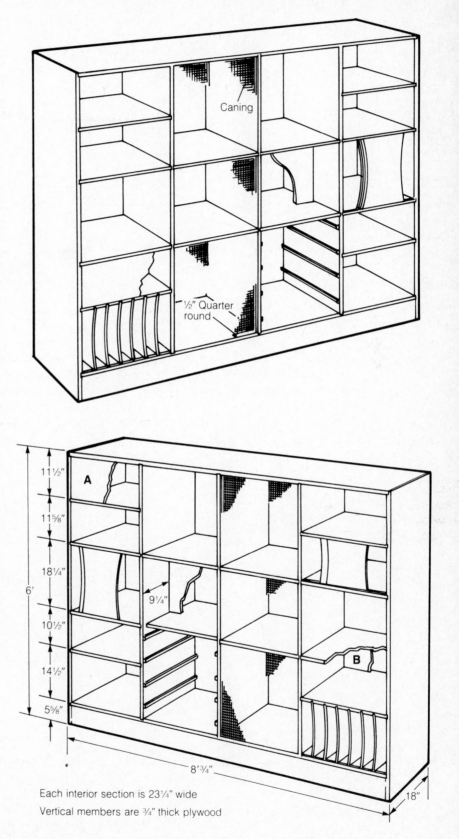

Each interior section is 23¼" wide

Vertical members are ¾" thick plywood

Project continued on next page

TWO-SIDED STORAGE DIVIDER continued

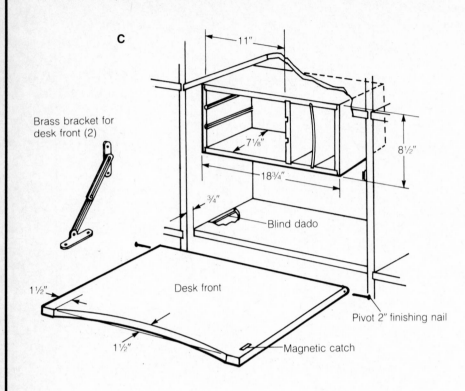

Brass bracket for desk front (2)

C

11″

7⅛″

18¾″

8½″

¾″

Blind dado

1½″

Desk front

1½″

Pivot 2″ finishing nail

Magnetic catch

Materials List

¾″ plywood
2 pcs. 18″x95¾″ for top and bottom
2 pcs. 4⅞″x95¼″ for base
2 pcs. 18″x72″ for end
11 pcs. 18″x23¾″ for shelves
1 pc. 17¼″x23¾″ for shelf
3 pcs. 18″x66⅛″ for partitions
8 pcs. 6″x23⅛″ for drawer front
1 pc. 17½″x23¼″ for partition
1 pc. 10¾″x23¼″ for panel
1 pc. 18¼″x23¼″ for desk front

⅜″ plywood
1 pc. 9¾″x23¼″ for panel
3 pcs. 2½″x10⅞″ for drawer front
1 pc. 7⅛″x7½″ for side — desk
2 pcs. 7⅛″x18½″ for top and bottom — desk
1 pc. 7⅛″x8″ for partition — desk
1 pc. 7⅛″x8½″ for side — desk

1″ plywood
8 pcs. 6″x17″ for drawer sides
6 pcs. 2½″x6⅛″ for drawer sides
3 pcs. 2″x10½″ for drawer backs

¼″ plywood
1 pc. 7⅛″x8″ for partition — desk
7 pcs. 3⅛″x18″ (approx.) for bottom — record storage
6 pcs. 14″x18″ for partitions — record storage
4 pcs. 17″x21⅝″ for drawer bottoms
3 pcs. 6⅞″x10½″ for drawer bottoms
4 pcs. 13″x17⅞″ high for small sliding doors
2 pcs. 13″x11¼″ high for small sliding doors
4 pcs. 1⅞″x96″ for fascia
8 pcs. 24″x66½″ for sliding doors

Other Materials
80 ft. ½″ quarter round to hold caning
8 · ½″x2⅛″x16½″ slides for drawers
8 ¼″x⅝″x18″ guides for drawers
4 ¼″x¼″x7⅛″ slides for drawers
2 ¾″x5½″x8'-¾″ support for sliding doors
2 1¼″x1⅞″x8'-¾″ support for sliding doors
6 ⅞″x23¼″ long metal track for sliding doors (small)
8 prs. hangers and track for sliding doors (large)

Miscellaneous
No. 6 1¼″ flathead wood screws
6d finishing nails
24″x9'-6″ caning
Finishing materials
Drawer hardware as required
2 lid supports for desk front
16 ¾″ round finger pulls for sliding doors

BASIC BOX

The box shown in the drawing can be used as the basic module for the unit shown in the photograph or for any unit you can design using a cube plan. The essential component is an 18 inch x 18 inch cube constructed of ½ inch plywood. The cube has an open back and a door in the sketch, but it could be built with a back. The cube interiors may be fitted with compartments if you wish, or half size boxes 9 inches high may also be constructed easily. This is truly a project where you can elaborate and put your imagination to work, or you can construct the unit in the photograph.

Construction

Building the basic box shown is simple. Cut the parts as indicated in the drawing, then assemble them with finishing nails and white glue. Attach the door with a butt hinge. The boxes can be painted, covered with laminate, veneered, or stained. All exposed edges should be covered with veneer tape or painted, depending on the final finish you wish to give the piece. Here, the edges are painted. You may also finish the edges with molding strips.

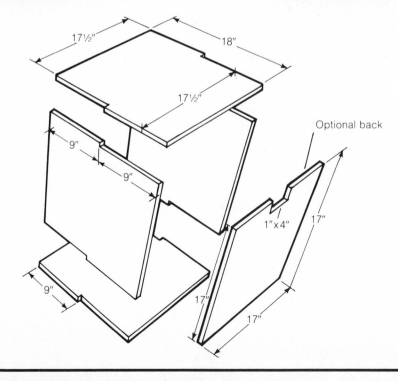

VERTICAL BATHROOM STORAGE

Cinnamon-colored clear all-heart redwood or sap-streaked clear grade redwood would be an excellent material for this bathroom unit. These grades are available in a variety of lengths. The bath cabinet unit is designed to use short lengths.

This unit can be custom fitted from floor-to-ceiling for a built-in look. You also can fit the cabinet over a basin or other bath fixture — wherever you need to solve a storage problem.

Construction

Cut all lumber to size as indicated in the Materials List. Lightly sand saw-cut edges. For all construction, use only noncorrosive finishing nails, such as aluminum, stainless steel, or hot-dipped galvanized.

Construct two cabinet support boxes. For the lower box, join two 28½ inch long 1 x 4s with two 2½ inch 1 x 4s. Then join two 28½ inch 1 x 4s with a 5 inch 1 x 4 for the upper box. Use 6d finishing nails throughout.

Now start building two door panels using four 1 x 4s; cut them 36 inches long for each door. Choose the 1 x 4 lumber with the best grain if you plan a clear finish for the cabinet. Use glue to attach 1 x 2 x 13 bracing pieces 1 inch from the top and the bottom of the back of each door panel, clamping firmly. Fasten braces with #8 x 1¼ inch brass screws. The ends of the bracing pieces should be about ½ inch from the sides of the door panels.

On each side of the long side panel (Detail A shows how to measure length of panels) measure and mark a 1½ inch diameter circle, centered 3 feet, 7¼ inch down from the top edge of each panel (Detail B). Drill only half way through each panel with 1½″ hole saw to accommodate the towel rod or pole.

Place the towel rod between the side panels and attach the cabinet support boxes at the top and bottom with glue and 6d finishing nails (nails in the side panels should be countersunk and the nail holes filled with wood putty for a better appearance). The back of the top box should be flush with the back edge of the side panels, while the bottom box is recessed slightly at the back to allow for notching the side panel to fit molding or tile near the floor (Detail B).

Shelving

All exposed 1x8 shelves measure 28½ inches long. Glue one shelf to the lower support box. Other exposed shelves can be attached at convenient heights, using shelf hangers, glue, 6d finishing nails, or brass screws, depending on the look you prefer. Allow at least 24 inches from the towel rod to the next lower shelf.

Shelves in the enclosed cabinet section are 1x6s each 28½ inches long. Attach a shelf between the side panels so that the bottom of this shelf will be 3 feet, 1½ inches from the top of the side panel. If you want more shelves in the cabinet section, attach them at convenient heights or install with adjustable pilasters.

Cabinet doors can now be fixed to the side pieces with two 1½ inch (minimum) hinges per door panel; for extra convenience use self-closing hinges. A decorative pull or knob can be attached to each door. To hold doors closed, use one magnetic catch per door.

Here, the cabinet was given three coats of polyurethane varnish, sanded

lightly between coats. You can use whatever finish you desire, mindful of the fact that if done in redwood you would probably not wish to hide the grain.

Securely fasten the unit to the wall with screws or wall fasteners, running the fasteners through the back of the support boxes.

Variations

To place a bath cabinet unit over a bathroom fixture put the first shelf piece on cleats that are 1x1s, 7¼ inches long, attached to each side panel. This allows removal of the shelf to service the fixture. The lower support box should be attached to side panels with screws so it will be removable if the cabinet is to be moved. Attach the support box after the unit is in place.

The first (lower) shelf should be a 1x8, but other shelves can be 1x6s, each 28½ inches long.

Materials List

1x2s: 4 pcs.   13″ door bracing pieces
1x4s: 2 pcs.   5″ for cabinet support boxes
       2 pcs.   3½″ for cabinet support boxes
       4 pcs.   28½″ for cabinet support boxes
       8 pcs.   36″ for doors
1x6s: 1 or 2 pcs.   28½″ for enclosed shelves
1x8s: 3 pcs.   28½″ for exposed shelves
       2 pcs.   7½′ for side panels* (or to the length necessary for height of bathroom)
6d finishing nails
#8x1¼″ brass screws
#10x2½″ screws with washers
Hinges
Magnetic catch
Wood towel rod 29⅜″ long
* (Side panel lengths depend on height of bath ceiling; see Detail A.)

Project continued on next page

VERTICAL BATHROOM STORAGE continued

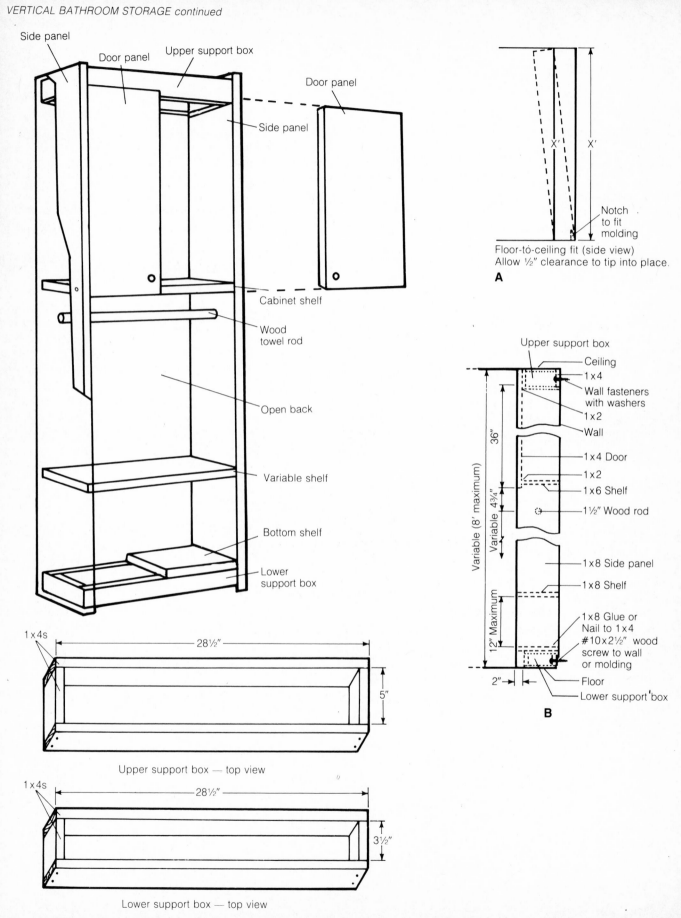

Side panel

Door panel

Upper support box

Door panel

Side panel

Cabinet shelf

Wood
towel rod

Open back

Variable shelf

Bottom shelf

Lower
support box

Notch
to fit
molding

Floor-to-ceiling fit (side view)
Allow ½" clearance to tip into place.

A

Upper support box

Ceiling

1 x 4

Wall fasteners
with washers

1 x 2

Wall

1 x 4 Door

1 x 2

1 x 6 Shelf

1½" Wood rod

1 x 8 Side panel

1 x 8 Shelf

1 x 8 Glue or
Nail to 1 x 4

#10 x 2½" wood
screw to wall
or molding

Floor

Lower support box

B

Variable (8' maximum)

36"

Variable 4¾"

12" Maximum

2"

1 x 4s

28½"

5"

Upper support box — top view

1 x 4s

28½"

3½"

Lower support box — top view

A NOOK FULL OF BOOKS

If you have a nook handy some-where, this is a good idea for that built-in look. The unit consists of boards mounted on standards and brackets (see Chapter 13) secured to the wall. Since the shelves are positioned in the recess, however (in our photo it is a very large one), they have a built-in look, and assume the appearance of a massive bookcase.

Construction

Construction is quite simple. The exact lengths and widths of boards used will depend on what space you have avail-able. For example, if you have a recess six feet wide and eight inches deep, you will use 8-inch wide boards. Be-cause an 8 inch board is actually slightly narrower from finish trimming, the shelves will be recessed a very small distance. You could cut the boards from plywood and face the edges to come out even with the outer flanking surfaces of the recess. In some cases standard size boards can be mounted on brackets to achieve this, but you can also rip trim wider boards to the exact width required. If the recess in your home is not square, then you can cut some boards shorter or wider to correspond to the space available.

Boards used for shelves may be finished in any manner you wish. These were given a light stain and a clear finish.

UTILITY CABINET

The word utility usually connotes drabness. But a utility cabinet need not be drab, and this one — covered with spanking white plastic laminate — attests to that. Nonetheless, the cabinet has plenty of storage space and is very utilitarian indeed.

Construction

Following the sizes given in the drawing and Materials List, cut out all plywood pieces.

Cut the ¾ x ¾ inch dadoes for the bottom shelf in the side pieces, then cut the rabbets in the top and sides. Time spent on a trial assembly with wire brads will insure proper fit. Nail the 1 x 3 bottom facing through the bottom shelf. For final assembly, use flathead screws and white glue.

Bond the laminate to the back of the cabinet; trim with a flush trim bit. Laminate and trim each side. Use a single sheet of laminate to cover the front face; drill a hole to start the router, and trim with a flush trim bit. Laminate and trim the top.

Measure the two drawer openings. Check the drawer pieces for proper fit. Be careful to allow for the installation of the drawer glides you choose. (Follow the manufacturer's instructions for proper clearances and installation.) Assemble drawers with finishing nails and white glue.

The drawers' overlay fronts are cut from ¾ inch stock. Note that although the drawers have overlaid fronts, they fit flush. Fill and sand the edges as required. Apply laminate to the fronts and trim with a flush trim bit.

The edges of the drawer fronts can be enameled or laminated. If you plan to laminate them, cut each dimension of the core stock for the drawers ⅛ inch smaller than the sizes given, to allow for the thickness of the laminate. Use flathead screws and white glue to fasten the overlay pieces to the drawers, driving the screws from the inside of the drawer fronts into the backs of the overlay fronts.

Cut ¼ x ¼ inch dadoes, ½ inch from

bottom, in sides of small drawer, to hold drawer bottom.

Mark the drawer fronts for the location of the pulls. Bore holes and fasten pulls.

Mount drawer glide hardware in the cabinet and on the drawers.

Use bonding adhesive solvent, as recommended by the manufacturer, for final cleanup.

Variations

It would be a simple matter to make a number of these cabinets and combine them into one larger storage unit. There are several ways to do this. For example, you might build three cabinets, and stack one on the other, leaving the tops of the bottom two without laminate. Another variation would be to build a cabinet with high sides which would accommodate four drawers instead of two. You may prefer to make three equal size drawers, or only one deep drawer or, if your storage needs dictate, you could fill the unit with several very shallow drawers and install small, decorative knobs.

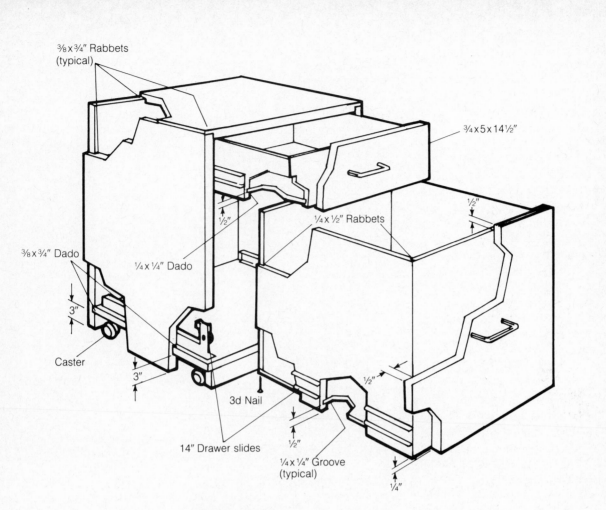

⅜ x ¾" Rabbets (typical)

¾ x 5 x 14½"

⅜ x ¾" Dado

¼ x ¼" Dado

½"

¼ x ½" Rabbets

½"

3"

Caster

3"

3d Nail

14" Drawer slides

½"

½"

¼ x ¼" Groove (typical)

¼"

Materials List

¾" Plywood
1 pc.   16" x 16" for top
2 pcs.   16" x 19⅝" for sides
1 pc.   15¼" x 19⅝" for back
1 pc.   15¼" x 15⅝" for shelf (bottom)
1 pc.   5" x 14½" for small drawer false front
1 pc.   10½" x 14½" for large drawer false front

½" Plywood
1 pc.   9¾" x 13" for front — large drawer
2 pcs.   9¾" x 14½" for sides — large drawer
1 pc.   9" x 13" for back — large drawer
1 pc.   15¼" x 15⅝" for bottom
1 pc.   5" x 14½" for small drawer overlay
1 pc.   10½" x 14½" for large drawer overlay

¼" Plywood
2 pcs.   13" x 14¼" for drawer bottoms

Plastic laminate
1 pc.   1 x 3 x 16" for bottom front facing
Misc. and Hardware
White glue
1¼" ringed nails
1¼" No. 8 flathead screws
1½" finishing nails
Two drawer pulls
Plate casters
4 Drawer slides

BOOKCASE PLUS

This unit features considerable space for books, as well as providing an excellent location for a television set and a large drawer for storage.

Construction
The exact size of the unit will depend on the available wall space in the location you have chosen for it. In essence, you must draw your own plans to your specific space requirements, and you will cut the parts to fit.

Start construction by removing any ceiling and/or base molding, so that the uprights — each of 5/4 x 12 inch pine — can be fitted against the wall. However, you may prefer to notch the pine at top and bottom to fit over the moldings.

Use a plumb line to establish vertical for the uprights, and test for fit against the wall. It will probably be necessary to scribe wall (see Chapter 5). After scribing, remove the uprights and cut 3/4 inch wide x 1/2 inch deep dadoes for fixed shelves and notches to allow for the support braces. Install pilasters for adjustable shelf supports.

You will need to install 3½ inch fillers under the bottom shelves on the left and right to fill the gaps there. To do this, cut four pieces of 1 x 2 or 1 x 3, each 10 inches long, and nail them to the sides of the uprights just below the dadoes of the shelves. When the uprights and shelves are in place, nail the fillers to the ends of these strips using 6d finishing nails.

Next, draw a horizontal line on the wall 40¼ inches above the floor. This will be the guideline for securing a brace which will help support fixed shelves. Locate the brace board so that the top is aligned with your mark, and screw it into studs.

Install the first upright against the wall, using 10d nails to secure it to the top of the wall (the nail should penetrate the plate which sits on top of the studs), and toenail it to the floor.

Put the second upright in place, locking it there by installing the two fixed shelves in the dadoes. Nail it also to the floor and through the side of the upright into a shelf brace screwed to the wall. Install the other fixed shelves and uprights in the same way. Leave the TV shelf for later. Nail the valance in place with 8d nails.

Next, install molding around the top of the unit to match any molding that you may have removed.

Shelf for TV
Add the box that the TV sits on; see the illustration for details. There are two sides to the box. These are secured to the uprights. A short support piece is screwed to the wall. You can use butt joints or half lap joints to connect the sides with the box face. You can finish the edges of the box with molding.

After the box is made, construct an overlay drawer, as detailed in Chapter 8. Install the drawer with high quality hardware. Add the movable shelves, and finish to suit.

Variations
This unit may also be reduced in size, and you may not need the shelf for a television set, or the large drawer. These may be eliminated and be replaced by shelves.

Materials List

1 pc. 1 x 8 for valance — length to your requirements
4 pcs. 5/4 x 12 for uprights — length to your requirements
1 x 12 for fixed shelves
1 x 12 for movable shelves
¾" plywood for TV box shelf
Molding to cover top of unit
Molding to cover gap between unit and wall on side
Drawer stock and hardware to your unit requirements
Pilasters for movable shelves

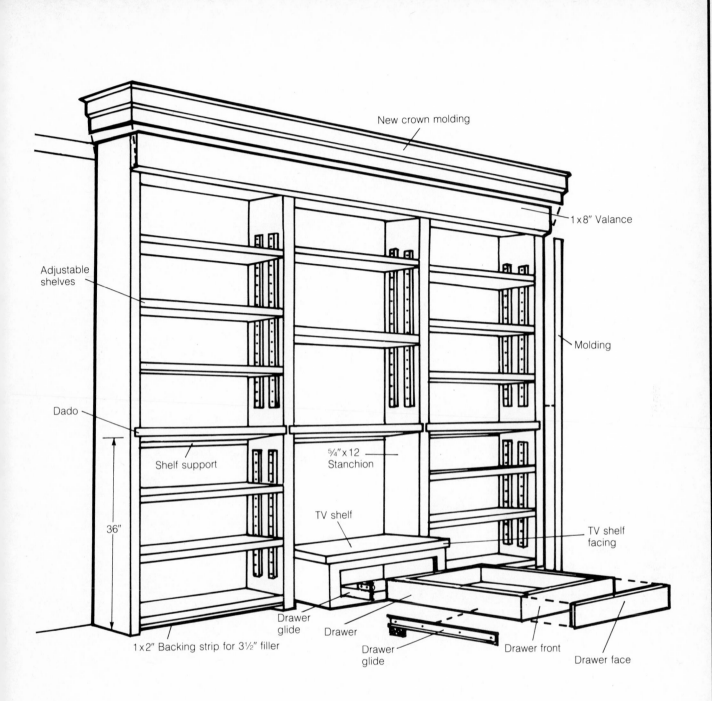

New crown molding

1 x 8" Valance

Adjustable shelves

Molding

Dado

Shelf support

5⁄4" x 12 Stanchion

TV shelf

TV shelf facing

36"

Drawer glide

Drawer

1 x 2" Backing strip for 3½" filler

Drawer glide

Drawer front

Drawer face

This bookcase, with a large shelf for magazines on the bottom, proves that a bookcase need not have a complicated design to be handsome.

The unit, made of redwood, is an assembly of 1 x 10 board framing — two sides, bottom, back, and two pairs of shelves. The top has been ripped down from a 1 x 12 piece to the exact width needed. The addition of 1 x 4 pieces of stock between the shelves helps space, stiffen and support the shelves. Butt joints are used to assemble the boards, but for a finished look, strips of 1 x 2 redwood with mitered corner joints have been used as an edging around the front. Another 1 x 2 serves as a retainer for magazines.

Construction

Cut members to the sizes indicated in the drawing, cutting the pieces square at the ends. Assemble with finishing nails and glue. Nail piece of 1 x 2 stock 39½ inches long to the long back edge of each side piece, nailing through 1 x 2 into edge of each 1 x 10 side piece. Butt join top to side pieces with front edges flush and ¾ inch overhang at back. Measure and mark locations for shelves; nail them in place through the sides. Install shelf supports as indicated in drawing, nailing each support from above and below into shelf. Fit each back piece flush against the next and nail into shelf edges from back. Nail through top into each backboard and into 1 x 2s at corners.

Next, add the retainer along the bottom for the magazines. Then cut and secure the 1 x 2 facing strips around the edge. Set all nailheads, fill with wood putty, and finish the unit with a clear finish to let the beauty of the wood show through.

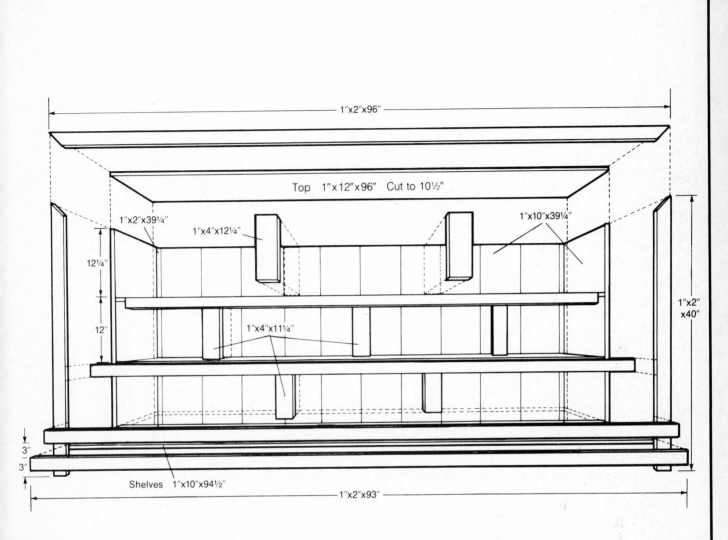

Top   1"x12"x96"   Cut to 10½"

1"x2"x96"

1"x2"x39¼"

1"x4"x12¼"

1"x10"x39¼"

12¼"

12"

1"x4"x11¼"

1"x2"x40"

3"

3"

Shelves   1"x10"x94½"

1"x2"x93"

Materials List

4   1"x10"x10'   Back* and sides for 12 pcs. 39¼"
3   1"x10"x8'   Shelves for 3 pcs. 94½"
1   1"x12"x8'   Top for 1 pc. 96"
7   1"x2"x8'   Facing for 2 pcs. 40"; 4 pcs. 93"; 1 pc. 96"; 2 pcs. 39¼"
1   1"x4"x8'   Shelf supports for 5 pcs. 11¼"; 2 pcs. 12¼"

Saw, hammer, square, white glue, #5 finishing nails.
*For a less expensive, but not quite as attractive result, use a single sheet of ¾" plywood for the back.

ROOM DIVIDER WITH STORAGE

The upper plywood panels of this unit may be painted in bright colors to create a flamboyant room divider. Extensive storage is available in drawers and cabinets below, in addition to two fold-down desk tops.

Construction

Cut parts to sizes indicated on the Materials List. Join tops, sides, bottoms and backs of all cabinets with glue and finishing nails. Use rabbet and butt joints as indicated in the drawings. Square up each assembly as nails are driven and set.

Assemble drawers by fastening sides and backs to bottoms and then nail on drawer fronts using glue blocks. (Refer to Chapter 8 for details on building drawers.) Install drawer guides to fit. Use pin hinges to hang doors on door units. Install metal standards for adjustable shelves in door units.

Fill nail holes and exposed plywood edges of cabinets with wood filler. Sand smooth.

Paint cabinets and plywood panels before assembling into divider. Start with a flat undercoat and follow with one coat of semi-gloss enamel, sanding lightly between coats.

Rout out the slots for the 2 x 4 partition posts with a dado head on a table saw. If you do not have access to a table saw, use a router, guided by a straightedge clamped in place.

Begin partition assembly by nailing a 1 x 4 nine feet long to the ceiling. Then nail the first dadoed post to the wall (at a stud for security). Support the first cabinet at the desired height with a wood block beneath it. Drive screws through the side of the cabinet into the

post. Slip the lower panel (once completely finished) into the slot with the bottom edge resting on the cabinet, then nail dadoed cross-member to post. Insert top panel and the next post into position, attaching through the cabinet side with screws. Repeat this procedure for each section. Install each fold-down desk top with a piano hinge. Note that each panel opposite the desk top is held in place with a ½ inch stop.

Give the posts and cross-members a coat of clear sealer, such as shellac. Fill nail holes with a filler tinted to match your wood and finish with two coats of satin varnish. Install door catches and pulls of your choice.

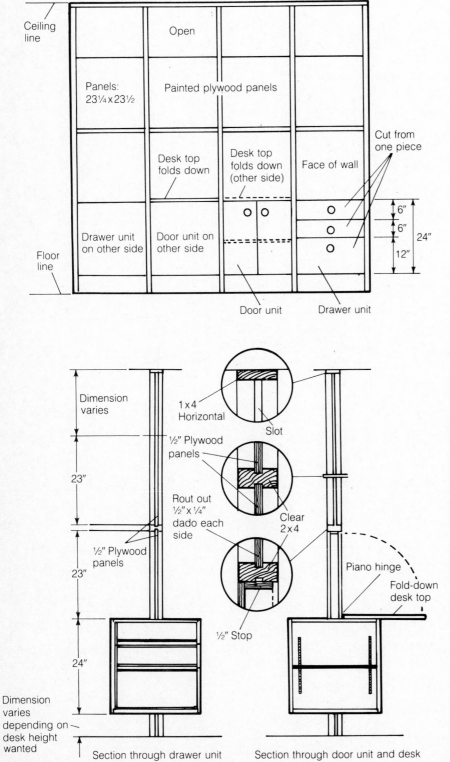

Ceiling line

Open

Panels: 23¼ x 23½

Painted plywood panels

Desk top folds down

Desk top folds down (other side)

Face of wall

Cut from one piece

Drawer unit on other side

Door unit on other side

Floor line

6"
6"
24"
12"

Door unit

Drawer unit

Dimension varies

1 x 4 Horizontal

Slot

½" Plywood panels

23"

Rout out ½" x ¼" dado each side

Clear 2 x 4

½" Plywood panels

23"

Piano hinge

Fold-down desk top

24"

½" Stop

Dimension varies depending on desk height wanted

Section through drawer unit

Section through door unit and desk

Materials List

Plywood—½"
2 pcs. 21½" x 23"   for bottom of drawer units
2 pcs. 22½" x 23"   for top of drawer units
2 pcs. 23" x 24"   for side of drawer units
2 pcs. 23" x 24"   for drawer fronts (to be cut for individual drawer front faces)
8 pcs. 4¾" x 22½"   for drawer sides
4 pcs. 4¾" x 20⅜"   for drawer backs
4 pcs. 10¾" x 22½"   for drawer sides
2 pcs. 10¾" x 20⅜"   for drawer backs
6 pcs. 20⅜" x 22"   for drawer bottoms
2 pcs. 21" x 23"   for bottom of door units
2 pcs. 23" x 24"   for backs of door units
4 pcs. 22½" x 23¼"   for sides of door units
2 pcs. 23" x 24"   for doors (to be cut vertically if desired)
2 pcs. 21¼" x 22½"   for adjustable shelves
8 pcs. 23¼" x 23½"   for panels

1x Stock
48 feet of 2 x 4   for standards and cross members
9 feet of 1 x 4   for nailing strip

Misc. and Hardware
6d and 8d finishing nails and white glue
Hardware: drawer pulls, guides, hinges of your choice; piano hinges
Wood filler

TELEVISION CABINET

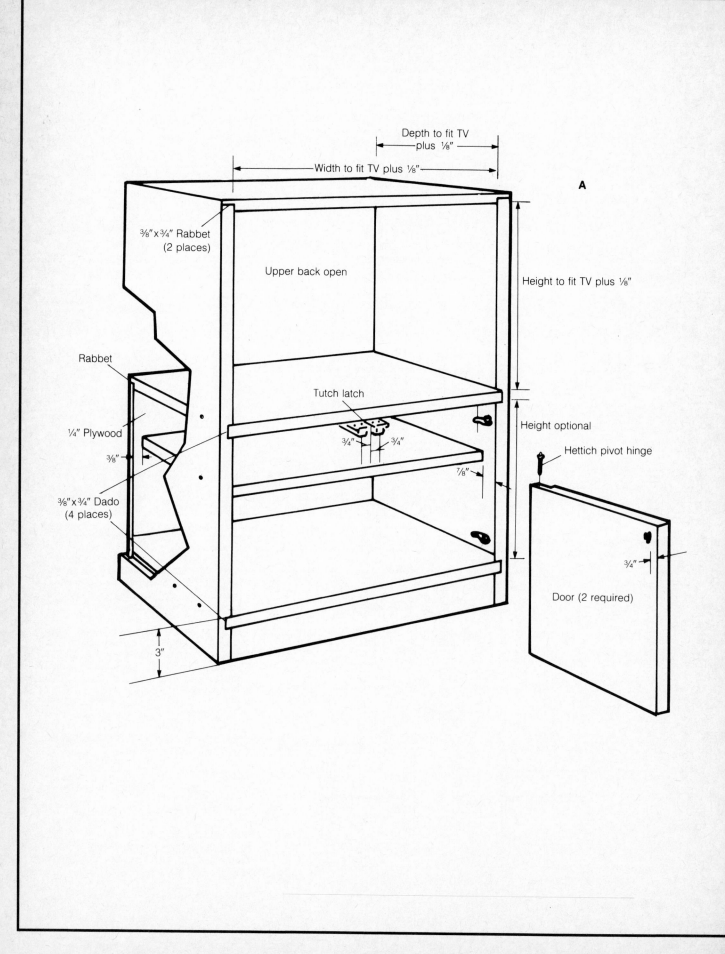

Depth to fit TV plus ⅛"

Width to fit TV plus ⅛"

A

⅜" x ¾" Rabbet
(2 places)

Upper back open

Height to fit TV plus ⅛"

Rabbet

Tutch latch

Height optional

¼" Plywood

Hettich pivot hinge

⅜"

¾"   ¾"

⅜" x ¾" Dado
(4 places)

⅞"

¾"

Door (2 required)

3"

The size of your television set will determine the size of the upper cabinet opening. Measure your set, adding an additional ⅛ inch to each dimension for easy clearance, and write these sizes on the working drawing at left. Decide on the sizes you require for the other optional cabinet dimensions, and mark these on the drawing as well.

Construction

Cut the required plywood pieces to the sizes noted on the drawing. Cut the rabbet for the top and the dadoes indicated for the shelves. Use wood filler on rough edges and sand them.

Before permanently assembling the cabinet, try assembling it using wire brads. This will allow you to make any adjustments easily.

For permanent assembly, use flathead screws and white glue. A damp cloth will clean up any excess glue. Allow an hour for the glue to set.

Now is the time to cut your cabinet doors. When you measure, however, take care to allow sufficient space for the hinges, as shown in drawing A. You will need to allow ⅛ inch at the top of each door, 1/16 inch beneath it, and ⅛ inch behind it to allow the door to pivot.

To complete the cabinet, bond laminate to the sides and trim away the excess. You can laminate the front faces with butted strips of laminate or, for a seamless face, apply a single sheet, drill a hole to start the router, and rout out the interior pieces.

You need to laminate only the fronts and insides of the doors. The door edges and the interior of the cabinet can be enameled. If you plan to laminate the door edges, cut them ⅛ inch smaller than your original measurements, to allow for the thickness of the laminate.

To install the door hinges you need two drill bits. Note the placement of the installation holes in drawings A and B. Drill four holes in the cabinet, 15/32 inch in diameter, ⅜ inches deep. Drill two ¼ inch holes in each door, 1¼ inch deep.

On the inside of each door, mark the position of the upper holes and cut an access slot as shown in drawing B. Set the fixed-pin pivot hinge in the bottom of the door and the spring-loaded pivot into the top. You will be able to press down the spring in the top hinge through the access slot.

Use bonding adhesive solvent, as recommended by the manufacturer, for final cleanup.

Variation

You may choose to build this of veneered plywood for a wood finish rather than a laminate finish. Cover visible edges with veneer tape or molding tape.

Materials List

¾" plywood is used to construct the cabinet, except for the lower back section which is ¼" plywood.

Miscellaneous and Hardware
White glue
Two pair pivot hinges
Two latches
1¼" No. 8 flathead screws
3d common nails
Hettich pivot hinge # PAC 37 or comparable hinges.
Plastic laminate: Here, as with the plywood required, you should determine the amount required. Both sides of doors need to be covered.

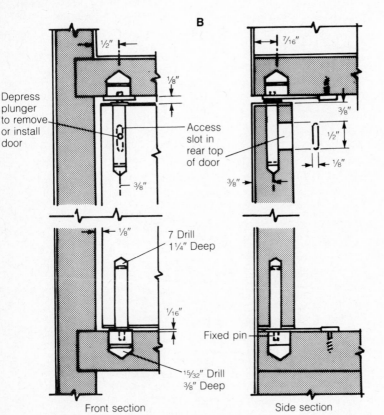

B

Depress plunger to remove or install door

Access slot in rear top of door

½"   7/16"

⅛"

⅜"   ½"   ⅛"

⅜"   ⅜"

⅛"   7 Drill 1¼" Deep

1/16"

Fixed pin

15/32" Drill ⅜" Deep

Front section   Side section

Hinge assembly

BOOKCASE FOR PAPERBACKS AND TAPES

This bookcase is good for the little things in life — paperback books and tapes. The unit can be built in 2- or 4-foot lengths. Short lengths of kiln-dried redwood or clear redwood make a handsome material for the project. The shelves are tilted for easy access to the paperbacks. The storage area at the top hides cassette or 8-track tape recordings and any tape cleaning equipment; or, the hinged top may be left off and the storage bin area used for plant display. In this case, however, a waterproof liner should be added.

Construction

Cut stock to size according to Materials List. Specifications for both the 2 foot and the 4 foot units are provided.

Assemble two shelf units by nailing a 1 x 6 to the back edge of a 2 x 6 with 6d finishing nails, as shown in Side Panel illustration. On the back edge of each 1 x 8 x 27 inch side panel, measure and mark lines 1⅝ inches and 11⅜ inches from the bottom of the panel. On the front edge of each panel, measure and mark lines 2⅝ inches and 12⅜ inches from the bottom of the panel. Draw an angled line on the inside of the panel connecting the marks on the front and back edges.

Align one of the shelf units so that the bottom edge of the 2 x 6 rests on this angled line on the side panel. Be sure the top edge of the 1 x 6 aligns with the back of the 1 x 8 and that the bottom edge of the 2 x 6 aligns with the front of the side panel.

Drill four holes through each side panel to hold the lower shelf, using a ⅛ inch bit. These will accommodate two screws in the shelf bottom and two in the shelf back. Attach shelf pieces with #8-1¼ inch flathead screws. Repeat the procedure for assembling and attaching the middle book shelf. The bookcase will look better if you fill the screw holes with wood or metal plugs or use decorative brass screws.

Tape Storage Bin

Assemble cassette tape storage bin with 1 x 4s and a 1 x 6 using glue and 4d finishing nails, simply securing a 1 x 4 (1 x 6 if you store 8-track tapes) to each long edge of the 1 x 6. Glue and nail the tape bin to the sides of the bookcase, placing the bin ³⁄₁₆ inch below the top of the sides (or else the thickness of your hinges) and flush with the back edge of side pieces. The bin will be indented approximately ¼ inch in front. If you plan plant displays, or think you may have other uses for the bin, attach with screws in the same manner as the book shelves.

A piece of 1 x 8 is used for the lid. Attach cabinet hinges to the 1 x 8 top. For the 4-foot-wide version, you may want to cut the 1 x 8 in half and install a 1 x 4 spacer the width of the storage bin, as shown in the drawing. You can also install a device to hold the top pieces in an upright position.

If you have used redwood, you will probably finish the unit with two coats of polyurethane varnish or other clear finish, so the redwood will show. If you have used other wood, finish as desired.

Variations

You may link two 2-foot shelves and a 4-foot shelf to fit around a short loveseat (48 inches wide or less) if you wish. Use 2½ inch bolts with nuts to attach a 1 x 6 block 3½ inches long to the back of the storage bin of one 2-foot bookcase and the side panel of the adjoining 4-foot shelf, as shown in the Variation Detail. Repeat this procedure for the other 2-foot case.

Materials List (For 2' case)

Clear All Heart or Clear grade redwood or other suitable wood

1 x 4s: 2 pcs. 22½"   bin
    (use 1 x 6s to store 8-track tapes)
1 x 6s: 3 pcs. 22½"   backs & bin
1 x 8s: 2 pcs. 27"   sides
    1 pc. 24"   top
2 x 6s: 2 pcs. 22½"   shelves
Glue (½ pint)
4d finishing nails
6d finishing nails
8 x 1¼" brass screws
Cabinet hinges

Materials List (For 4' case)

Clear All Heart or Clear grade redwood or other suitable wood

1 x 4s: 2 pcs. 46½"
    (use 1 x 6s to store cartridge tapes)
1 x 6s: 3 pcs. 46½"
1 x 8s: 2 pcs. 27"
    1 pc. 48"
2 x 6s: 2 pcs. 46½"
Glue (½ pint)
4d finishing nails
6d finishing nails
8 x 1¼" brass screws
Cabinet hinges

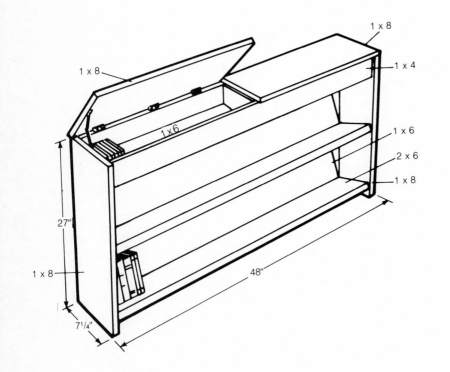

1 x 8

1 x 8

1 x 4

1 x 6

1 x 6

2 x 6

1 x 8

1 x 8

27"

7¼"

48"

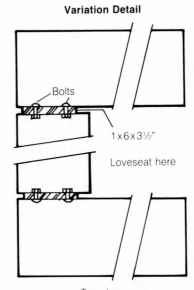

Variation Detail

Bolts

1 x 6 x 3½"

Loveseat here

Top view

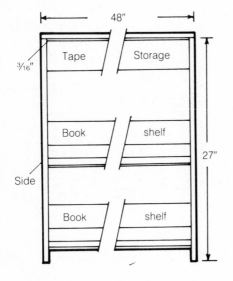

48"

3/16"

Tape

Storage

Book

shelf

Book

shelf

Side

27"

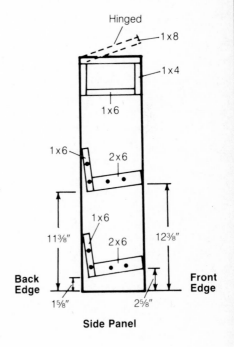

Hinged

1 x 8

1 x 4

1 x 6

1 x 6

2 x 6

1 x 6

2 x 6

11⅜"

12⅜"

Back Edge

Front Edge

1⅝"

2⅝"

Side Panel

ADJUSTABLE DIVIDER

This divider may be built as a single unit two feet deep and two feet wide to give a sense of separation between rooms, or the unit can be duplicated and linked to form a larger divider for privacy.

Construction

Start construction by cutting parts as indicated in the Materials List.

There are twelve shelves — six on one side of the unit and six on the other. Five of these are fixed on each side — two each that form the bottoms and tops of the cabinets, and the one inside the lower cabinet. The shelf in the middle is movable. You may, of course, vary the shelf arrangement to suit your requirements.

After cutting parts to size, groove the centers of both faces of each 23⅝ inch x 78 inch side using a table saw; make the groove 5⁄16 inch wide and ¼ inch deep. This allows for partition section when you add on more sections, as shown on this page.

Cut slots in the fixed shelves for the sliding doors and glue the cleats, for support, to edges of the fixed shelves. Leave gap between cleats as a partition groove. Cover exposed edges with birch veneer tape.

Drill ¾ inch holes in the sliding doors for finger pulls.

Assemble the shelves for one side using clamps, then mark and drill holes for fasteners. Shelf hangers work well for the movable shelves; use 1½ inch No. 10 roundhead screws (these are decorative) to attach the fixed shelves to the sides.

With shelves on one side secured, screw the Masonite partition in place with 1 inch No. 10 flathead screws; then add finger pulls. If you wish, you can use decorative vinyl on the doors and partition as in the narrow unit, or omit the partition, as shown in two sections of the larger divider.

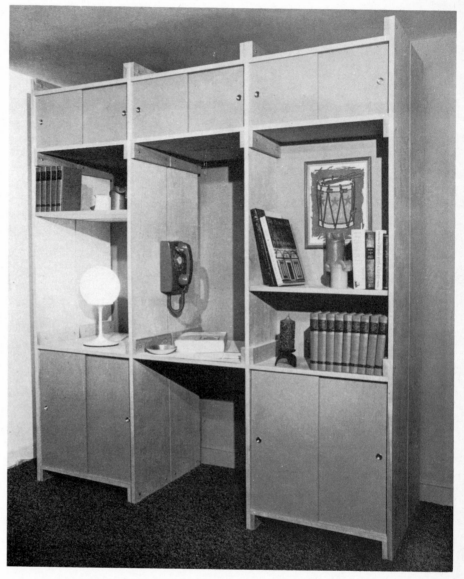

Materials List

¾" Birch plywood
2 pcs.   23⅝"x78" for sides
12 pcs.   22½"x11⅝" for fixed shelves
4 pcs.   11⅝"x22³⁄₁₆" for removable shelves

Stock
16 feet   1"x3" birch
16 pcs.   ¾"x15⅝"x2⁹⁄₁₆" birch or maple
  stock for cleats

¼" Masonite
1 pc.   22¹³⁄₁₆"x75⅜" for partition
4 pcs.   11½"x10⅝" for small sliding doors
4 pcs.   11½"x23³⁄₁₆" for large sliding doors
8   Finger pulls
24   Shelf hangers
1½" No. 10 roundhead screws
1" No. 10 flathead screws
Birch veneer tape

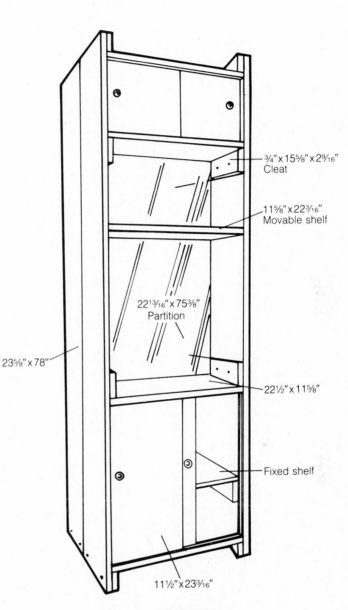

¾"x15⅝"x2⁹⁄₁₆"
Cleat

11⅝"x22³⁄₁₆"
Movable shelf

22¹³⁄₁₆"x75⅜"
Partition

23⅝"x78"

22½"x11⅝"

Fixed shelf

11½"x23³⁄₁₆"

Single Unit with Partition

MODULAR CUBES

These cubes are little more than boxes, although they are elegant boxes. Each is made with lumber core birch plywood and assembled with simple hardware. The more you build, the more storage space you have. Once you have built a few, you should be able to produce them very quickly.

As mentioned, birch plywood is used. Since all sides of the box are finished, you will have to purchase plywood with two good veneer faces. To save money, you could use fir plywood and finish the boxes with paint.

These instructions and the Materials List that follows will produce three cubes with doors.

Construction

Cut the sheet of birch plywood into 15¾ x 15¾ inch squares; one sheet will yield exactly eighteen pieces. Pick three of the pieces for backs, and cut them to a finished size of 15¼ inches square. Select three additional pieces for the doors, and trim them to 14¹¹⁄₁₆ inches square.

Make the sides. To do this, cut six pieces and trim them to 15¼ x 15¾ inches. Cut a ¼ inch deep x ½ inch wide rabbet along one of the 15¼ inch sides of each of the six pieces.

Take the remaining six 15¾ inch square pieces and rabbet each piece ¼ inch x 12 inch on three sides; these parts form the top/bottom portion of the three cubes.

Using white glue and finishing nails, assemble one side to a top or bottom piece and to the back. Then assemble the remaining side and top/bottom for a completed open cube. Set the nailheads and fill the holes with wood putty. Repeat these steps for the remaining two cubes.

Mark the three cubes for the joining holes, as indicated by the sketch. To assure alignment of the holes from cube to cube, lay out the hole pattern on a master drawing and transfer these

hole positions to the units using a sharp instrument. Drill the ¹³⁄₆₄ inch diameter holes required.

Lay out all joining hardware mounting positions. The magnetic catch should be centered, but the exact fastener positions will depend on the particular catch you buy.

Use ½ inch flathead wood screws to mount the hinges to the doors, and ⅜ inch flathead wood screws to join the hinges to the cube. Mount, then remove the hinges before finishing the wood.

The surface of cabinet grade birch plywood is excellent, so your stack cubes will require only light sanding with extra fine sandpaper before ap-

plying your finish, preferably a wood stain that will bring out the pattern and grain of the birch.

Re-attach the hinges and install magnetic catches. Join the cubes with aluminum screw post fasteners; these are available at office supply stores.

Materials List

18 pcs.   ½" lumber core birch plywood (one
   sheet/2 good faces)
⅝"   finishing nails
⅜"   FH wood screws
½"   FH wood screws
White glue
3 pair   1½" x 1" butt hinges
3 magnetic catches
3 brass knobs   ½" diameter
8   1"-long aluminum screw post fasteners

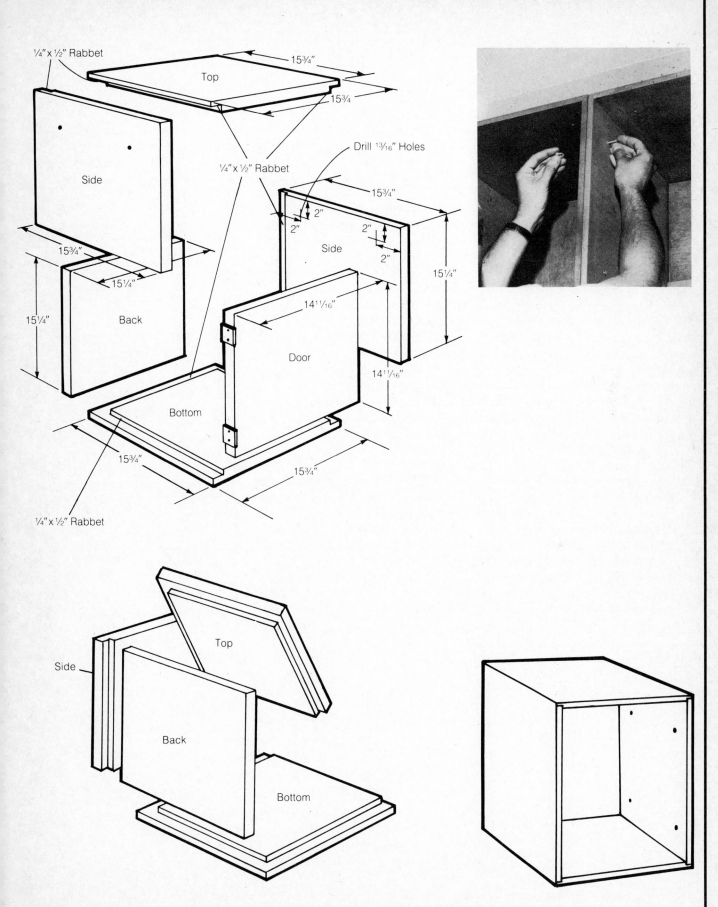

¼" x ½" Rabbet

Top

15¾"

15¾

Side

¼" x ½" Rabbet

Drill ¹³⁄₁₆" Holes

15¾"

2"

2"

2"

2"

Side

15¼"

15¾"

15¼"

Back

14¹¹⁄₁₆"

15¼"

Door

14¹¹⁄₁₆"

Bottom

15¾"

15¾"

¼" x ½" Rabbet

Side

Top

Back

Bottom

BASIC VANITY

There is nothing fancy about this vanity; it is as basic as possible. However, it is neat looking and very durable. The basic material used is ¾ inch plywood, which is very strong.

Construction

Cut out parts following the Materials List and the drawing, notching the sides as indicated 4½ inches by 3½ inches for the kickplate; also notch the back to accept the bracing piece. Note that the back is rabbeted into the sides, while the front framing members butt against the sides and are dadoed to accept the bottom.

Assemble the components (sides, back, bottom, center partition and front framing pieces) using butt joints, except as previously noted, with 6d finishing nails and white glue. Add shelves as you wish inside, using ¾ inch cleats to support the shelves.

Construct the doors, drawer and false drawer front according to the directions given in the chapter on doors and drawers (Chapter 8). The working drawer may be installed with either bottom or side mounted hardware.

Bathroom vanities are commonly covered with plastic laminate because it is impervious to water. If you intend to laminate your vanity, it is best to do it at this point while it is still a basic box. Follow the directions in Chapter 12. Do the sides first, then the front and back, using a bevel trim bit on the edges for a neat appearance. Laminate the drawer and doors before installation.

Cut the sink opening in the 23 x 42 inch plywood top. Instructions for the installation of the sink will come with the unit you buy. The cutout can be made easily with a saber saw.

Laminate the parts of the top section (top and backsplash pieces). Attach top to the base and backsplash pieces to top with No. 8 flathead screws 1¼ inches long. Attach hardware, hinges and pulls that you select, following directions in Chapter 6.

Variations

You may prefer to enamel the base of the vanity and just laminate the top if you need to economize.

In terms of design, this vanity does constitute a basic cabinet that could be used almost anywhere. You can leave the top unfinished and it can serve as a small workbench; the unit is strong enough. The same vanity might serve as a small bar; just add another backsplash piece on the side so bottles or glasses will not be pushed off.

Materials List

¾" Plywood

1 pc.	¾" x 4" x 42" for backsplash
1 pc.	¾" x 4" x 22¼" for backsplash
1 pc.	¾" x 23" x 42" for top
1 pc.	¾" x ¾" x 42" for trim
1 pc.	¾" x ¾" x 22¼" for trim
2 pcs.	¾" x 22" x 30" for sides
1 pc.	¾" x 4" x 12" for back brace
2 pcs.	¾" x 4" x 26⅞" for back braces
1 pc.	¾" x 21¾" x 26" for center partition
3 pcs.	¾" x 1½" x 23⅜" for stiles
2 pcs.	¾" x 1½" x 41¼" for rails
1 pc.	¾" x 1½" x 11¼" for rail
1 pc.	¾" x 1½" x 25½" for rail
1 pc.	¾" x 21¾" x 40½" for bottom
1 pc.	¾" x 4½" x 42" for kick plate

As required, shelf support cleats (2 per shelf) and shelves

½" Plywood
As required for doors, drawer fronts and sides

¼" Plywood
1 pc.   ¼" x 26½" x 40½" for back
As required for drawer bottom

Misc. and Hardware
White glue
1½" long No. 8 flathead screws
6d finishing nails
Plastic laminate
3 magnetic catches
Door and drawer pulls
Hinges
Drawer hardware

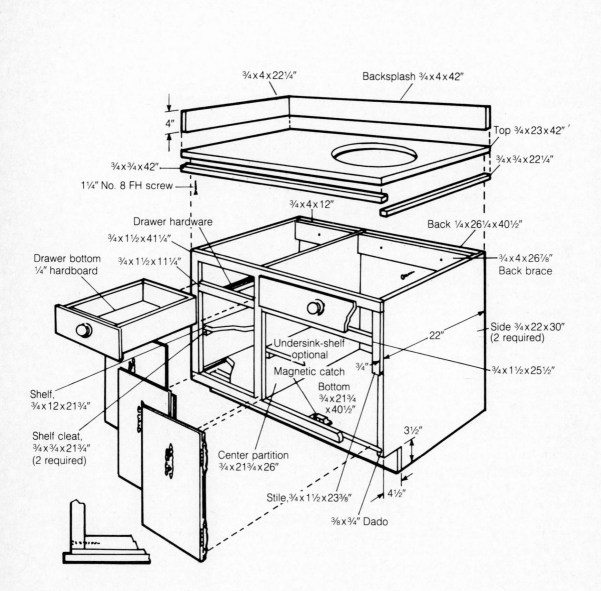

¾ x 4 x 22¼"

Backsplash ¾ x 4 x 42"

4"

Top ¾ x 23 x 42"

¾ x ¾ x 42"

¾ x ¾ x 22¼"

1¼" No. 8 FH screw

¾ x 4 x 12"

Back ¼ x 26¼ x 40½"

Drawer hardware

¾ x 1½ x 41¼"

¾ x 4 x 26⅞"
Back brace

Drawer bottom
¼" hardboard

¾ x 1½ x 11¼"

Side ¾ x 22 x 30"
(2 required)

22"

Undersink-shelf
optional

¾ x 1½ x 25½"

Magnetic catch

¾"

Shelf,
¾ x 12 x 21¾"

Bottom
¾ x 21¾
x 40½"

Shelf cleat,
¾ x ¾ x 21¾"
(2 required)

3½"

Center partition
¾ x 21¾ x 26"

Stile, ¾ x 1½ x 23⅜"

4½"

⅜ x ¾" Dado

CORNER CABINET

In this project nails should be countersunk, and nail holes filled with wood putty. When dry, sand smooth.

Construction

Cut sides for the lower cabinet from ¾ inch hardwood plywood. One side, the panel on the right, will be longer in order to overlap the left panel by ¾ inch. Glue and nail adjoining sides. The front edges of these panels (both top and lower sections) have a 45° miter where they meet.

Cut stock for front from ¾ inch hardwood. Glue and dowel all six joints. Clamp overnight. Nail the front to the side panels.

Glue and nail to the sides the shelf supports of ¾ x 2 inch stock for the bottom shelf and the middle shelf. To create shelves from ¾ inch hardwood plywood, cut a square 35¾ x 35¾ inches, then cut diagonally for two shelves. Nail triangular shelves in place.

Cut lumber for drawer. Drawer bottom is a trapazoid cut from ⅜ inch plywood and set into a ⅜ inch x ⅜ inch rabbet in all sides. Glue and nail.

The drawer slides on metal glides that are supported by the back ¾ x 4 x 21½ inch support brace — which spans the two sides of the unit — and the front ¾ x 2 x 46 inch support brace.

Miter the ends of the back support brace at 45°, insert it until it fits snugly (about 15 inches), glue and nail it. To position the drawer glides, mark the center of the front support brace; mark 9 inches on either side of the center. Fasten the glides to the front and back support braces 18 inches apart.

Cut the countertop into a square 40½ inches on each side. Cut diagonally, and you will have 2 triangles each 28⁷⁄₁₆ inches deep. This gives a front overhang of approximately ¾ inch. Glue and nail to base unit.

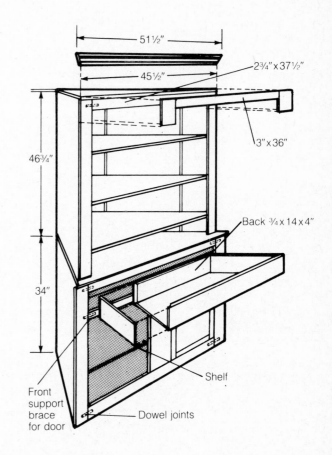

The top unit is assembled the same as the lower unit. Cut sides from ¾ inch hardwood plywood. Cut, dowel, and glue up the front framework.

Cut a square for the top from ¾ inch plywood 34¼ x 34¼ inches. Cut diagonally. The second half can be trimmed to 29½ inches and used for a shelf in the top cabinet.

Cut a square 29⁹⁄₁₆ x 29⁹⁄₁₆ inches (this includes ¹⁄₁₆ inch for the saw cut) from ¾ inch plywood. Cut diagonally for the second and third shelves.

Cut two 5½ x 5½ inch hardwood squares, and one 3 x 36 inch piece for trim which projects from the cabinet top. Glue and nail.

Cut decorative trim for the top 51½ inches, with a 45° miter, making the short edge approximately 45½ inches. Check the cabinet dimensions for exact fit. Glue and nail.

Mount the adjustable shelf brackets. Cut the framework for doors from 2 inch stock, with ⅜ inch rabbet on the inside edges of the horizontal and vertical pieces, and the ends of the horizontal pieces. Glue and clamp.

Cut door panels from ¼ inch plywood and glue in place. Before cutting panels, measure inside dimensions of frames; cut for a snug fit. See page 59, substituting a wood panel for the glass inset.

Mount hardware. The top can just be set onto the lower unit or can be permanently attached. Then sand and finish to suit.

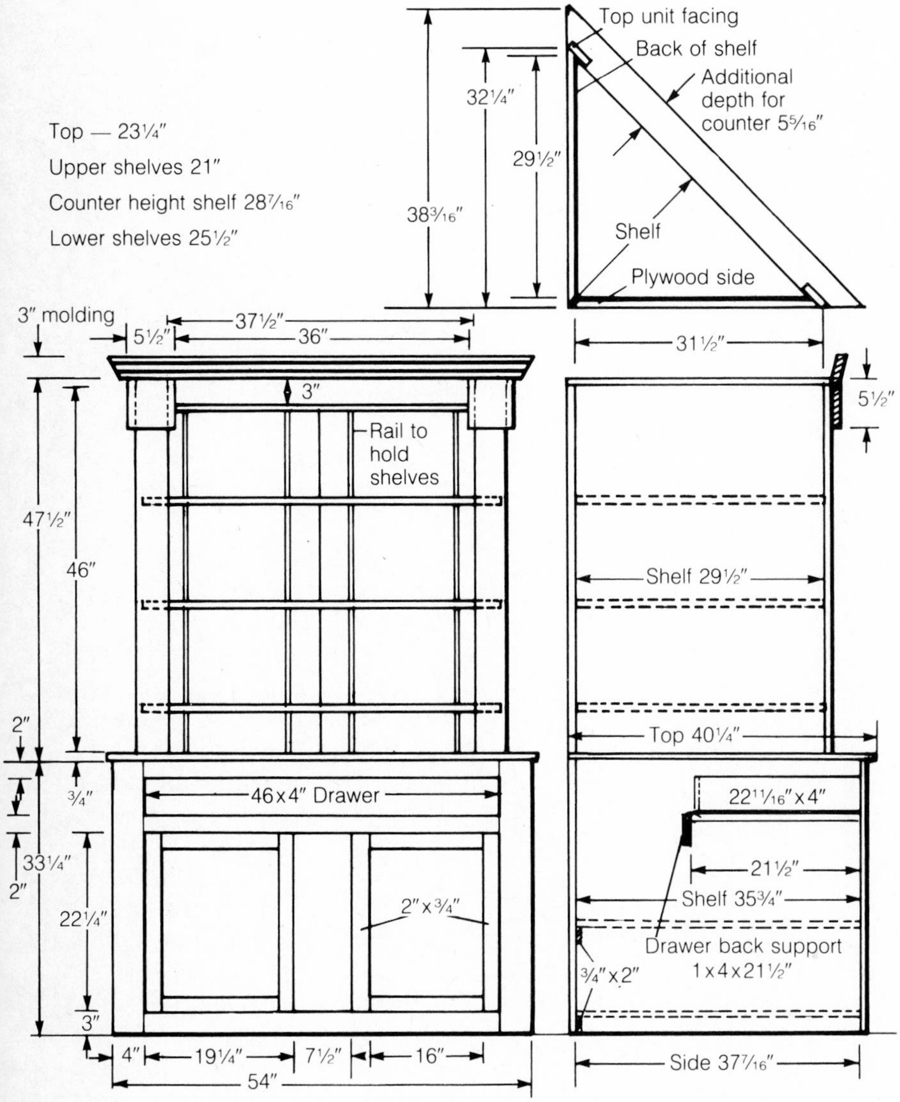
Top — 23¼"
Upper shelves 21"
Counter height shelf 28 7/16"
Lower shelves 25½"
Top unit facing
Back of shelf
Additional depth for counter 5 5/16"
32¼"
29½"
38 3/16"
Shelf
Plywood side
31½"
3" molding
5½"
37½"
36"
3"
Rail to hold shelves
47½"
46"
5½"
Shelf 29½"
Top 40¼"
2"
¾"
46x4" Drawer
22 11/16"x4"
21½"
33¼"
2"
22¼"
2"x¾"
Shelf 35¾"
Drawer back support 1x4x21½"
¾"x2"
3"
4"
19¼"
7½"
16"
54"
Side 37 7/16"

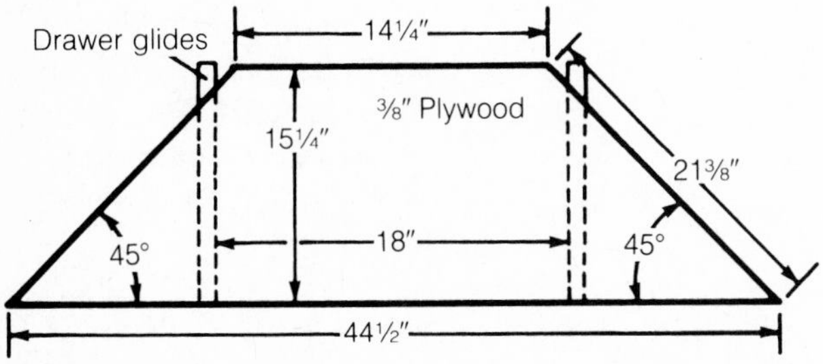
Drawer glides
14¼"
⅜" Plywood
15¼"
21⅜"
45°
18"
45°
44½"

Materials List*

4 Sheets ¾ inch x 4 x 8 foot hardwood plywood (sides and shelves)
22½ feet x ¾ x 4 inch hardwood for front framework, drawer front, sides and back
1 piece ¾x36x3 inch hardwood trim on top of cabinet
1 piece ¾ inch x 4½ feet x approximately 3 inches decorative trim hardwood molding for top
1 piece ¾x2¾x37½ inches trim on top of cabinet
2 pieces 3¼x5½x5½ inches top trim
1 piece ⅜x15¼x44½ inches plywood for drawer bottom
2 pieces plywood ¼x18¾x16 inches (approximately) for door panels
1 piece ¾x4x21½ inches for drawer back support
1 piece ¾x7½x22¼ inches for center framework
2 pieces ¾x2x46 for top trim of lower unit and drawer front support
1 piece ¾x3x46 for bottom trim of lower unit framework
Shelf brackets
4 Rails
12 Clips
2 Sets of hinges
2 Drawer glides
4 Knobs or handles
Nails
Glue
Finishing materials

*Dimensions given are full, final sizes, not nominal.
Buy hardwood in larger sizes and rip to fit.

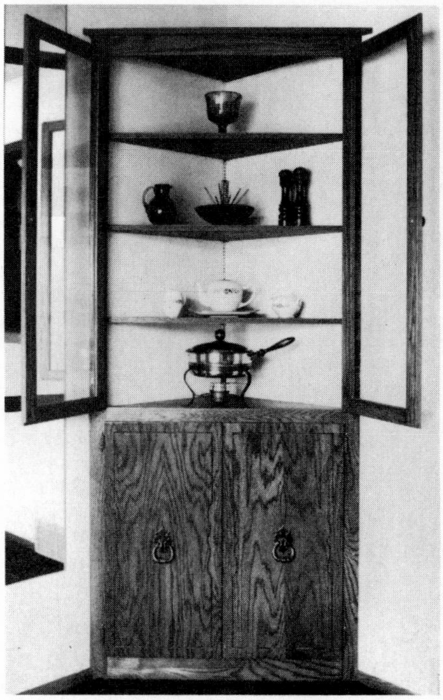

You can use this plan to create your own variations on the basic style. Here, the support rails for the shelves are placed at the three corners of the triangle, and a glass-insert door has been constructed.

DRY SINK

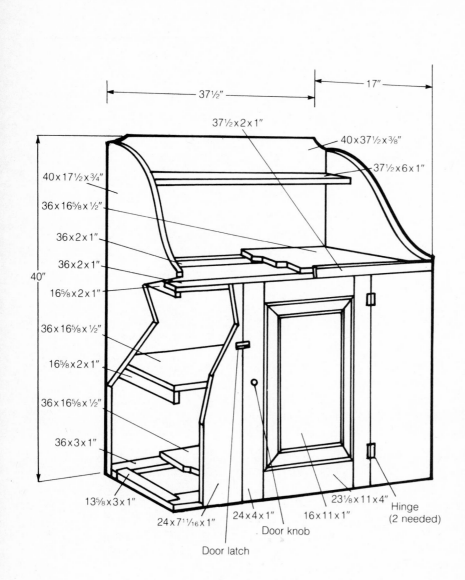

37½"

17"

37½ x 2 x 1"

40 x 37½ x ⅜"

37½ x 6 x 1"

40 x 17½ x ¾"

36 x 16⅝ x ½"

36 x 2 x 1"

36 x 2 x 1"

16⅝ x 2 x 1"

40"

36 x 16⅝ x ½"

16⅝ x 2 x 1"

36 x 16⅝ x ½"

36 x 3 x 1"

13⅝ x 3 x 1"

24 x 7¹¹⁄₁₆ x 1"

24 x 4 x 1"

16 x 11 x 1"

23⅛ x 11 x 4"

Hinge
(2 needed)

Door knob

Door latch

Materials List

1 pc.   plywood 41"x 37½"x ⅜" for back
2 pcs.   plywood (or solid stock) 40'x 17½"x ¾" for sides
2 pcs.   36"x 3"x 1" for long pieces of base frame
3 pcs.   13⅝"x 3"x 1" for crosspiece of frame
2 pcs.   36"x 2"x 1" for long piece of top frame
4 cleats   16⅝"x 2"x 1"
3 pcs.   36"x 6⅝"x ½" for shelves and top

1 pc.   37½"x 2"x 1" for facing strip on top
1 pc.   1"x 6"x 1" for soap and brush shelf
2 pcs.   24"x 7¹¹⁄₁₆"x 1" for front facing pieces

Door Components
2 pcs.   24"x 4"x 1" (sides)
2 pcs.   23⅛"x 1"x 4" (top and bottom)
1 pc.   16"x 11"x 1" frame
Veneer tape

If you have an Early American style home or room, a dry sink will add both atmosphere and utility. This unit is a copy of a piece built by the Shakers, a hardy and handy people who flourished in the northeastern states in the 1800s (a few of the group still survive). This particular piece is adapted from the original in Shaker Sabbathday Lake Community in Maine; it dates from late 1800. Like most Shaker pieces this has a clean, functional design.

Construction

Cut the parts following the Materials List.

You will have to devise a scale plan for the curve of the side pieces and the curve of the back.

Construction is not difficult. Although the sides are connected to the back with rabbet joints, they attach to the front with butt joints. The base framework can be rabbeted at the ends, but a cross brace is dadoed in the middle. The door consists of five parts — four pieces for the framework, with the back piece rabbeted into it. Note that the centerpiece has beveled edges. This can be done carefully with a plane. If you feel this will be difficult, you may use molding to give the desired effect.

The original furniture piece was made with yellow pine, but the widths necessary are no longer available, so it is best to use both pine and plywood.

The original is finished with a light yellow stain, but you can use anything that you feel will look well in your home. Above all, the piece should have a subdued look.

This chapter will concentrate on four basic types of closet possibilities:

(1) Construction of new wall-to-wall or corner closets;
(2) interior arrangements and products for new or existing closets, including built-in dressers and drawers;
(3) built-in closets for difficult areas such as attics or under the stairs;
(4) free-standing units that will serve specialized needs.

ADDING A CLOSET

Although a new closet will look like a built-in architectural feature, actually it is a built-on. Therefore, the framework of the closet requires firm attachment to the room's structural elements — joists, studs, beams. You cannot simply nail into the wall material. If the closet will be located where a portion of its frame cannot be fastened to a beam or stud or joist, then you will have to use expansion anchors or toggle bolts (see Chapter 6). If you have an old, springy floor, always nail into a floor joist. If you have a concrete floor, or only a thin sheet of flooring over concrete, use masonry nails to attach the closet's floor plates. In most cases, where the floor is of wood or has a strong underlayment, you can nail directly into it.

Full-Wall Closet

Because the walls, floors, and ceiling offer support to the new structure, this kind of closet is not hard to build. Once you have determined the depth you will need (usually about two feet) all that is necessary is addition of doors of your choice and the front framework. The doors can be folding doors or sliding doors. In order to make this addition to your room look like an integral part of it, install molding at the closet/ceiling juncture, matching that already in the room. If there is no existing molding around the tops of the walls, add quarter round where the ceiling meets the junctures to help create a unified design. The base of the closet takes baseboard and molding that match the existing room trim.

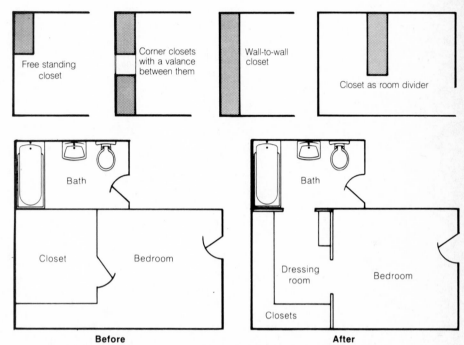

Free standing closet

Corner closets with a valance between them

Wall-to-wall closet

Closet as room divider

Bath

Closet Bedroom

Before

Bath

Dressing room

Bedroom

Closets

After

It was not difficult to improve on this bedroom plan with its space-wasting walk-in closet. Sliding doors give access to a spacious dressing room and the bath. Closets now line the dressing room walls.

Construction Steps. Remove baseboards and gently pry moldings off. Keep these so they can be cut to fit later for the base of the closet. The position of the closet depends upon the depth you have chosen for the closet, and whether or not you will be able to nail into joists and studs. Nailing into joists and studs is always preferred. The first ceiling joist and set of studs may not be near your desired partition location, in which case you will be using expansion anchors or toggle bolts.

Measure exactly from floor to ceiling for the length of vertical members, and then subtract for the thicknesses of the top and bottom plates. Nail the partition together, except for the bottom plate. Remember that walls are often out of square — and ceilings and floors frequently are not level. Use your plumb line and level before fastening to make sure the frame is square and true. Tilt the partition in position and fasten the top plate to the ceiling, spacing nails or anchors every 16 inches. Nail sides of frame to wall studs, spacing every 16 inches. Slide the

bottom plate into position, and toe-nail it to the stiles. If they are too long, you can trim them to fit; if too short, shim as necessary. Fasten the bottom plate to the floor (into a beam if possible) spacing nails every 16 inches.

The size of the opening will be determined by the size of the doors you have chosen. When planning the size of the opening for the doors, leave room not only for the door but also for the 1 x 4 finish framing next to the doors.

Install the hardware for the track underneath the 1 x 4 finish framing, and attach the rollers on the top edge of the door. Test the doors for fit. If there are only minor inaccuracies, they can be handled with the adjustable top and bottom hangers that come with the doors. If necessary, unscrew the track and insert washers as shims between the track and the 1 x 4 finish framing. Remove the doors for later, final installation.

Cut wallboard and install over framework — or use paneling if desired. Finish wallboard seams (as in Chapter 13). If using

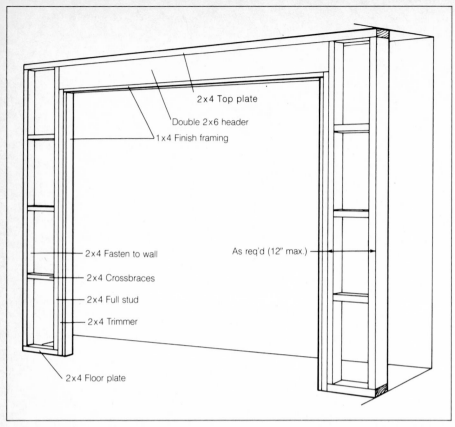

2 x 4 Top plate

Double 2 x 6 header

1 x 4 Finish framing

2 x 4 Fasten to wall

2 x 4 Crossbraces

2 x 4 Full stud

2 x 4 Trimmer

As req'd (12" max.)

2 x 4 Floor plate

A full-wall closet needs framing that fits snugly and provides a sturdy frame for hanging the doors. The height of the door opening can be varied to accommodate either sliding or folding doors. The frame face may be covered with paneling or wallboard.

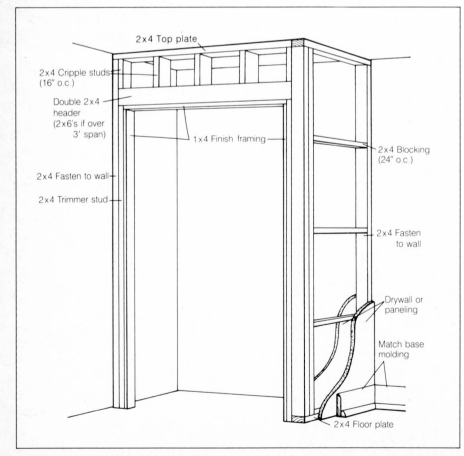

2 x 4 Top plate

2 x 4 Cripple studs (16" o.c.)

Double 2 x 4 header (2 x 6's if over 3' span)

1 x 4 Finish framing

2 x 4 Fasten to wall

2 x 4 Trimmer stud

2 x 4 Blocking (24" o.c.)

2 x 4 Fasten to wall

Drywall or paneling

Match base molding

2 x 4 Floor plate

Framing for a shallow corner closet should provide 20-24 inches of depth for hanging space. Blocking strengthens partitions and provides secure nailing for drywall or paneling.

paneling, add molding strips. Install ceiling trim, countersinking nails for later finishing.

Re-install doors in the previously attached overhead track. Once again, check for level, balance, and smooth movement. Place base trim up against the wall to measure for an exact fit. Cut as needed; nail in position. If necessary, refinish to cover evidence of the re-installation.

FULL-WALL CLOSET

Materials List

2 x 4s for framing and cross braces
1 x 4s for finish framing
4 x 8 gypsumboard sheets to enclose framework
2 x 6 (or larger, to fit height) for header
Sliding or folding doors to suit
Door hardware
Molding to match existing trim ceiling, or quarter-round for entire room baseboard and molding at base of closet

Corner Closet

Building a corner closet is slightly more involved, but follows many of the same procedures used in the full-wall closet.

Opening for Door. Once you have determined the location and size of the closet, checking that the interior dimensions will meet your needs and that the exterior dimensions leave usable space in your room, finalize the location and size of your door.

The door opening must be wide enough to accommodate the door you choose, leaving clearance space on each side (1/8 inch each side) and at the top (1/4 inch). In addition, allow for clearance at the bottom: 1/4 inch minimum; the maximum is that required to clear the carpeting or any threshold.

Construction Steps. Construct the framework entirely from 2 x 4 stock. Lay out the base plate boards on the floor according to the location of the closet. Find the desired position of the door and mark the base plate. Lay the top plate on top of the marked base plate. From the markings on the bottom plate, mark the opening on the top plate. Cut out lengths equal to the width of the door plus the frame and clearances. Now, leaving the gap for the door — including frame and clearances — lay the bottom plate in position. Once again, place the top plate pieces over the bottom plate. Mark the top and base plates for the position of the studs, which will be 16 inches o.c. Nail together the wall section containing the doorway, using 2 3/4 inch long nails through the top and bottom plates into the studs. Add door framing, sides to studs, header across door frame sides (nail into side frames and studs) and

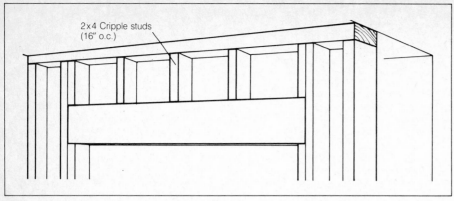

Studs should be placed 16 inches o.c. Since doors are usually 30 to 32 inches wide, you will need cripple studs above the door header to add strength to your closet frame.

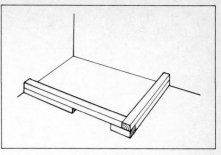

After marking and cutting base plate for door opening, place top and base plate stock in position for finished closet. Transfer markings for door opening onto top plate. Mark stud locations on both pieces for exact vertical lineup.

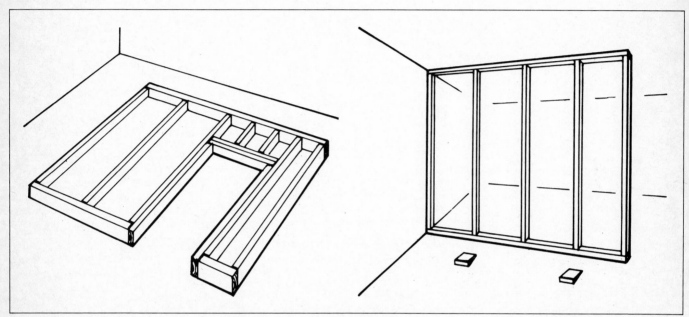

Build the stud wall sections on the floor. Straight-nail the studs through the top and base plates for solid construction. The height must be less than room height so the frame can be tipped into place. Shim the frame tight. Nail to floor and ceiling joists and wall studs.

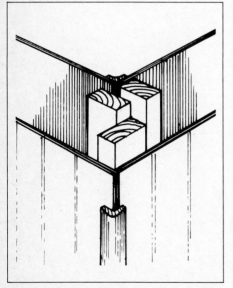

A stud must be provided for edge nailing of all wall panels. Triple studing at corners gives at least a 1½ inch wide area for nailing both inside and outside panels. Use cove molding for inside corners, corner molding for outside corners.

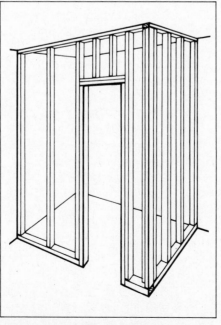

A large, walk-in corner closet requires full-wall stud framing because you are creating a room within a room.

braces between header and top plate.

Raise this section into position. Check plumb. Shim at any point where the floor or ceiling may be uneven. Nail through top and bottom plates into the ceiling and the floor.

Now construct and raise the stud section for the second wall of the closet. The base plate of the shorter section (or side section if both walls are of equal length) should butt against the wall containing the doorway. The top plate of the shorter section should overlap the corner stud of the wall that has the doorway. This means that you will have to provide sufficient clearance to allow positioning and installation. Then shim for a snug fit once in position.

Cover the inside walls of the closet with wallboard taping and spackling joints. The outside walls may be either wallboarded or paneled. Install door and base moldings, and then the corner and top molding.

Add door hardware. Hang the door. The

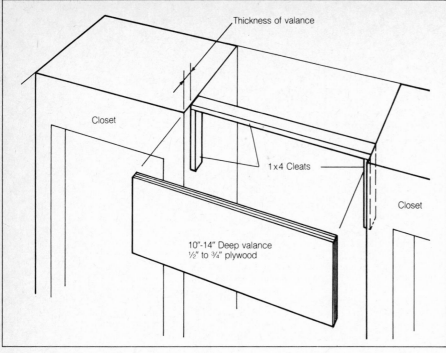

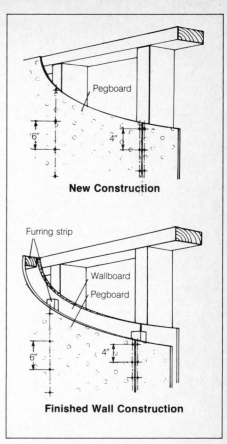

New Construction

Finished Wall Construction

If you have installed two corner closets and left intervening space for a window, desk or dressing table, join the two closets with a valance board. Cut the plywood valance to fit between the closets, and between the top of the closet door openings and the ceiling. Nail 1 x 4 cleats to the ceiling and to closet sides, flush with the front face of the closets.

Pegboard is an excellent wall material for a utility, broom or tool closet. Install directly over studs for new construction, but attach to furring strips if covering a finished wall.

door· installation will be simplified if you purchase a prehung door that comes in a prefabricated frame-and-door unit. The unit includes door and frame moldings, which are removable for easy installation.

CLOSET INTERIORS

In this affluent and acquisitive time, most people need closets, more closets, and special closets. In order to get the most from existing (or newly added) closets, consider special materials, accessories, and arrangements of the closet interior.

Interior Surfacing Materials

It is quick and easy to cover the interior of a closet with paneling or ¼ inch plywood, but this is generally an unnecessary expense. Most closet interiors will be painted to give a bright, light reflective space. Since the interior surface will not be very noticeable in itself it may not need as careful a finishing job as an exposed room wall. While no one recommends sloppy finish work, it is not necessary to tape and spackle and sand the joints of wallboard. You may choose to nail a narrow molding strip over the joints. You do not even have to use wallboard. Other acceptable materials include hardboard, particleboard, cedar chipboard and fiberboard. Except for the cedar chipboard, which is left unpainted so that the aromatic quality of the material is left untouched, all these boards

may be painted. They are also relatively easy to install and have certain useful qualities which may make any one of them a first choice for your particular situation.

Hardboard. This product can be purchased in ⅛ and ¼ inch thickness. The surface is nonporous and will withstand a good deal of abuse, such as might occur in a closet used to store golf clubs, tools, or cleaning equipment. Hardboard is also available in a form generally known as Pegboard. Installed over studs or solid walls with blocking strips as spacers, Pegboard and hangers allow the homeowner to provide a specific storage position for many household items.

Particleboard. A form of pressed sawdust and woodchips, particleboard comes in several thicknesses and can be used as a wall surface. It can be painted; it is durable unless soaked with water repeatedly, and during construction can be handled similar to plywood. It is not as strong as plywood and will require substantial bracing if used for shelves that are both long and will carry heavy loads. It is strong enough without extra support for most closet shelves that will store hats, shoes, purses and other small items of apparel.

Cedar Chipboard. A form of particleboard, this sheet material is a popular choice for closets in which out-of-season clothing or blankets will be stored. While cedar does not prevent infestation by moths, the aroma will

This storage closet is lined with aromatic cedar chipboard. The ventilated shelves allow for excellent air circulation.

give the fabrics stored in the closet a fresh scent. There is an esthetic drawback to cedar chipboard in that it is dark and appears to have an uneven texture. If you paint the board to brighten the closet, your cedar scent will be lost.

Fiberboard. This material is relatively soft, porous and fragile. Fiberboard is sometimes used for bulletin board material, which means you can use tacks, brads or staples to attach a temporary covering. The surface will dent easily and a dent or hole will remain in the surface. However, fiberboard is lightweight, easy to handle, and it can be painted. It absorbs a great deal of moisture and may soften, so it is not a good choice for an area near a bath or laundry room. However, fiberboard can be used in a dry, interior closet, if it will not be used to store objects that might puncture the surface. Because the fiberboard is not strong, any shelves, racks or hooks for the closet must be attached to the studs through the fiberboard.

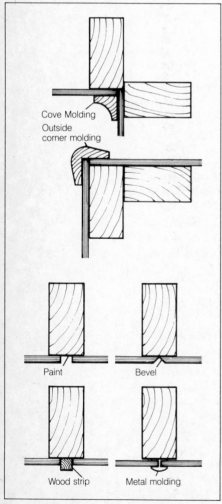

The joints of wallboard at studs may be finished in a variety of ways. Corner-joints may be covered with appropriate moldings. Flat seams may be handled decoratively or simply painted.

Installation. When you are putting up any of these materials, you must provide a stud backing into which you nail the boards. It is imperative that there be a stud at each edge. Assuming that you have provided studs 16 inches o.c., you will have a stud into which you can nail along the edge (at each side) of your panel and at two places between. Studs located at different centers can mean that you will have to add extra studs in order to nail the panels securely. Corner blocking must also be positioned so that there is a stud for each adjoining panel. Use nails designed for the type of board you use. These should be 1 to 1¼ inches long. Nail every 4 to 6 inches at the edges and 6 to 8 inches over inside studs. You may mask the panel joints in several ways. If there is a small gap between panels, you may simply paint the panels, the edges and the exposed side of the stud. You may cover the joint with a strip of lath (available in a standard size of ¼ x ¼ inch by several lengths) nailed over the joint, or fill in the space with a piece of 1 x 1 stock. If the joints nearly touch, you may want to create a "V" bevel with a file. There also are metal molding strips available. Corners can be finished with cove molding for inside corners and corner molding for outside corners.

Interior Accessories

Shelves and Rods. Any closet will need provisions for storage of items. For the ordinary bedroom closet this will mean at least one rod for hanging clothes and one shelf for storing boxes, hats, or other items. You may also require a shoe rack or shelf. If the closet is small (24 inches deep by 36 to 48 inches long) both the shelf and the rod may simply be hung. Install pieces of 2 x 4, 24 inches long, at each end of the closet running from front to back. Position these so your shelf, when laid on top of these cross braces, will be 6 feet above the floor. Installl the cross braces with wood screws driven into the studs. Cut the shelf to fit and lay it across the braces.

The rod should be installed with hardware brackets attached to the cross braces. Locate the brackets so that the rod will be halfway between the front and the back of the closet. Support the center of the rod with another bracket or hook attached to the shelf about midway from each end. If your shelf is 18 inches wide, or wider, you can use a strap support that attaches to the shelf in front and in back of the pole. However, if your shelf is only 12 inches deep, you will have to use a

hook-strap that only attaches behind the rod.

A good guide for planning shelves is to allow for larger spacing at easy access levels. Put narrower spacing up higher. This will prevent your storing large, bulky and possibly heavy items above your head where they will be difficult to handle. The illustration provided shows spacing of 2 feet 8 inches between lower shelves, and one foot between top shelves. This will put smaller items at near eye level for the average person, while allowing ample storage space at floor and hip level.

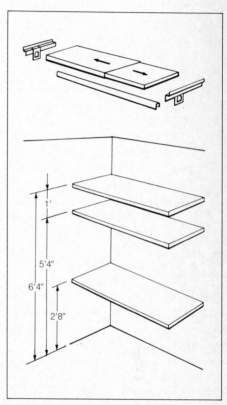

Shelving is available in several prefabricated forms. Some metal shelving telescopes to fit various spaces. Spacing of shelves will vary according to need.

In addition to the usual shelves and poles, there are alternative materials available. The most commonly used pole is a chromeplated pole, which has the advantage of "telescoping" to size, making it adjustable in length. But if your pole is going to carry a significant amount of weight all the time, you may have to consider installing a length of galvanized steel pipe, usually used for plumbing. This metal pipe is serviceable, extremely durable, and not unduly expensive. However, it lacks the attractive sheen of chromeplated hollow tubing sold for closet poles, and is not as smooth. If using pipe, you must measure your pole length precisely and then have the pipe cut to the necessary length at a plumbing supply or hardware store.

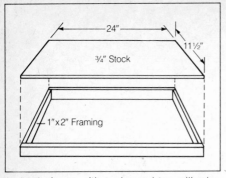

A simple frame with a plywood top will raise shoes off the floor so they will not be kicked or stepped on.

This closet has double poles and extra shelves installed with widely available hardware.

These shelves and racks fill this closet with shelves and hanging space at many levels, while leaving the center open for complete access.

Shoe Shelf. If you do not wish to purchase commercially made shoe racks, you can build a small storage shelf to neet your needs. A slightly raised box, illustrated here, will give you a place for your shoes that is elevated enough so you will not step on them. If you prefer sloped shoe storage, which is not appropriate for sneakers or sandals, build the frame with 1 x 3 or 1 x 4 stock for the back and sides of the frame. Cut the sides at an angle so there is a gentle, even slope from front to back. Add a strip across the upper, back end of the platform to catch the heels of your shoes.

Clothing and Linen Closet. An empty closet space need not be limited to the installation of a long pole and one shelf. Space can be gained in several ways. The most often overlooked is the two-level closet pole. Only a portion of anyone's wardrobe needs a full 5½ feet to hang free of the floor. Install a divider at some near-mid-point of your closet, as shown in the photograph above, and place a second pole high enough off the floor so that you can hang a second level of shirts, blouses, jackets, or skirts. You may be able to find a pole which will simply hang from the higher pole. These are sometimes available at closet shops or notions departments in larger stores.

Clothing, Linen or Office Space. If you need a work or office space in addition to the usual storage, you may be able to combine several standard cabinets in order to achieve the setup you need. This may be especially useful for a student's room or a combination home office/guest room. Depending on the space that you decide to use and fill, you can combine one or more broom closet units with poles added for clothes rods, hanging cupboards and base units. A countertop can be laid across the base units for a smooth work surface. If you leave space under the countertop for a kneehole, you have created a desk. If your countertop height is more

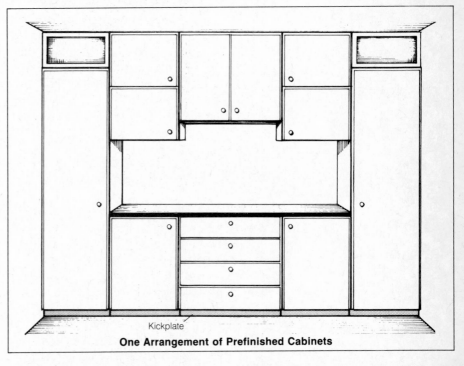

Kickplate

One Arrangement of Prefinished Cabinets

than 30 inches above the floor, you will have to provide an adjustable-height chair for the person using the area as a desk. If you purchase unfinished cabinets, you can paint them to match your room, stain and finish them to match your woodwork, or laminate them (provided they do not have elaborately designed faces) with plastic.

You may want clothing storage to fit into the closet area so that the remainder of your room is open except for the bed and lamp table — especially if the room is very small. In this case, you may purchase ready-made cabinets to be installed into your closet. For custom arrangements, build your own,

adapting the basic plans for cabinets and drawers given in this book.

If you have a "spare" closet, you can sometimes fit a pair of two drawer filing cabinets at either end of the space, and put a piece of plywood or a hollow-core door across the cabinets for a "built-in" desk.

Pantries. When overall floor space is at a premium, the installation of a shallow storage closet may provide the closet you need without consuming too much space in your room. A pantry closet does not need to be deep. Measure the deepest box you have on your shelf and you will probably find that it is approximately 10 inches. Therefore, 10-

inch-deep shelves will suffice for your pantry. The number of shelves you need will be determined by the variety of heights of the boxes, bags and cans you habitually buy. Take an inventory of your usual food stores and, using graph paper, plot the number of shelves you require. Remember to add the thickness of the shelf when you draw your plan. Measure your cans and boxes to avoid mistakes and guesswork.

You may find that you prefer to leave the shelves open. This means that you can see immediately what supplies you have on hand when cooking or planning your shopping list. If you hang plywood doors to cover the pantry, you may wish to have two or three of your interior shelves only 6 or 8 inches deep. Then add very shallow shelves with a retaining strip to the doors to hold very small items such as spices, baby food jars, or small cans of fruit juice. You may also find prefabricated vinyl coated racks that can be attached to your doors, serving the same purposes.

Using Pipes to Your Advantage

Anyone who has ever built or remodeled knows that at some point you have to make adjustments for load-bearing walls that cannot be moved, or for pipes that are not quite where they were expected. Rather than go through the costly process of moving pipes

or ducts which run through your closet space, build a shield around them and use this to your advantage. In our illustration, two corner pipes have been boxed in with plywood. This provides useful corners for built-in shelves.

If heating ducts pass through your closet area, provide insulation between the ducts and the shield. Otherwise, your closet may become needlessly hot while causing the area above, which requires heat, to be needlessly cold.

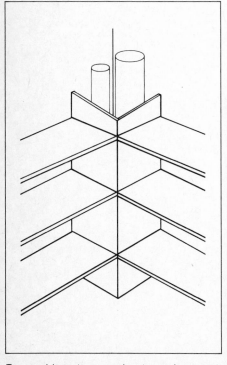

Turn problems to your advantage when creating closet space. Pipes that need to be hidden provide corner support for new shelves. Shelf supports may be 1x stock nailed to corner partition or to slotted pilasters, with hangers for adjustable shelves.

This pantry is immediately off the kitchen of a restored Victorian house. Once converted into a bathroom, the pantry was restored and adapted by the new owners. The refrigerator and shelf space are to the left of the door. The diagonal beam in the back wall supports a stairway. A small powder room is to the right of the door.

A well-organized closet keeps everything handy and neat. This owner-designed closet interior meets the specific requirements of the users.

The same ingenuity has been applied to these closets in the rooms of the owner's children. Each is different and is planned for changes in sizes and needs as the children grow. Storage spaces and pole heights can be quickly adjusted without any rebuilding.

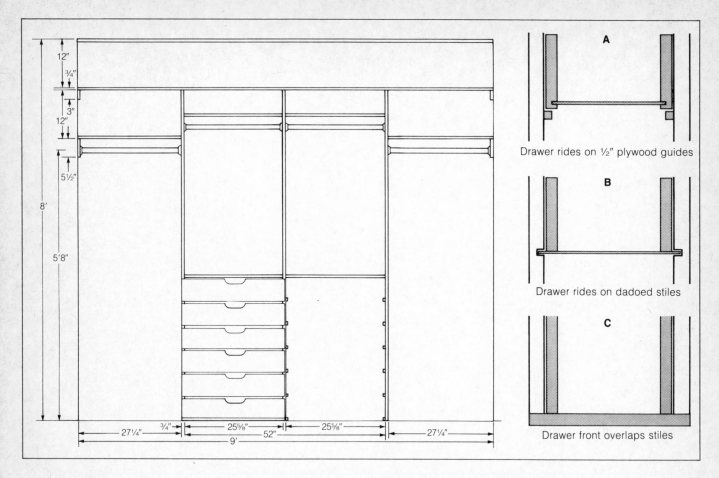

Drawer rides on ½" plywood guides

A

Drawer rides on dadoed stiles

B

Drawer front overlaps stiles

C

Modular Closets

The standard closet consists of an empty space, a closet pole and a shelf. Shown are a variety of standard closets that have been remodeled into more useful, complete storage facilities. The large wardrobe closet (photo opposite and plan above) has been filled with partitions which provide support for four short poles and a series of shelves and drawers.

The carpenter/homeowner who designed and built this storage used the three center partitions as support for cleat drawer guides. A dozen identical drawers were constructed of 1 x 6 stock with hardboard bottoms fitted into dadoes on the front, back and side members of the drawer (Detail A).

It is also possible to construct the drawers with a plywood base, ½ inch wider than the drawer on each side. The excess on the bottom sides fits into dadoes cut in the support partitions. The bottoms of these drawers must be attached with screws for strength (Detail B). In both cases, the fronts of the drawers overlap the partitions (Detail C).

The continuous upper shelf is supported by the partitions in the center and by 1 x 4 cleats nailed to the permanent walls at either end. The smaller shelves are supported by smaller cleats.

The closet poles are held by brackets attached to the walls and partitions. These poles are located so that they are easy to reach and offer adequate hanging space for garments of various styles and lengths.

The shelves immediately above the poles, at either end of the closet, are at the height of the typical full length closet shelf. The top shelf in this closet is the obvious place to store items that are either seasonal or infrequently used. Although the shelf is high enough to require a small stepstool to reach it, the full height opening of the closet permits the owner to see at a glance everything stored there. (The four, track-hung closet doors have been removed to show the full interior).

Another closet in the same home gives a series of open shelves. This unit, in a child's room, has already been adjusted to meet the changing needs of the growing child. The arrangement of the poles can be changed again as the child's needs change.

The third closet is also in a child's room. It offers drawers similar to those in the large wardrobe closet and three sizes of hanging space. Lower shelves provide easy access for frequently needed articles; the upper shelf stores lightweight items.

The shelves on the right side of the closet are easily adjustable because they rest on movable cleats. This means that a pole and shelves can be set at a level a child can reach easily, and adjusted as the child grows.

The adjustable nature of modular closets means that space is fully utilized for maximum storage. The right-sized space is provided for each type of clothing, with better organization of all belongings.

MODULAR CLOSET

Materials List

Drawers

1 x   Stock for fronts, backs and sides
¼" Hardboard for bottoms
                  or
½" Plywood for fronts, backs and sides
¼" Plywood for bottoms

Shelves and Vertical Support Partitions

1 x 12 Boards dowel and glue joined to make
   1 x 24 boards
1 x 3 and 1 x 4 Boards for cleats for permanent
   shelves
                  or
¾" Plywood sheets (two good sides)
4 x 8 Sheets ripped to 2 x 8 or 2 x 8 panels
Doors — Sliding or folding, size to fit, with
   appropriate track hardware.

Hardware

Side mounting drawer hardware, poles and
   hanging brackets, shelf standards or pilasters for adjustable shelf supports.

Owners of this house created a closet by enclosing an open staircase. Coats hang near the door; seasonal items are stored at the back.

CLOSETS IN SPECIALIZED AREAS
Closet Storage under the Stairs

In almost every house there is some unused space that can be turned into a closet — room just sitting empty but unrecognized. The area under basement stairways often offers this bonus. Upper floors also contain stair-runs that are not directly over other stairways, leaving usable area for closet adaptation.

The plan illustrated here may be suitable for any such stair location, although it is shown as a typical basement arrangement. The combination shown is of drawers under the lower stairs and a closet area under the higher steps.

If the stairway is against a solid wall, you will have access from only one side. A stairway which is built as a straight run and is open on both sides — as in some center hall

Colonial style homes — offers greater versatility. Drawers can be built on both sides and the closet area may be split with hanging space on one side and shelf space on the other.

Construction Steps. Build a stud wall using 2 x 4 stock, with the 4-inch side as the face. The wall should extend from the front edge of the bottom stair tread to as far back as the edge of your planned doorway. Sizes will vary according to your understairs area.

If the stair-run has a turn near the top with a landing, you will probably find that your doorway has been determined by the landing area. If the stairs are built on a straight run, you may have a wider range of choice in door placement.

Lay out top plate and baseplate boards at the side of the stairway where you will have the new front wall. Determine the door posi-

tion and cut the base plate to allow for door, frame and clearances. Mark stud locations on both plates. The studs for the wall should be approximately 16 inches o.c. You can adjust slightly to less than 16 inches to fit the space, but set no farther than 16 inches apart. Nail through top and base plates into studs. Lift the wall into position. Nail to ceiling joists and toe-nail to stair stringers or step edges.

If you need to construct a doorway, nail the side frames to the studs and a header to the frames and studs. Use two 2 x 10s as a filler above the header to fill in any space left between the top of the doorway and the bottom of the stairs. Install bracing between the header and the top plate. Nail through the header into the braces and toe-nail braces into the top plate. Cut 2 x 4s to appropriate lengths and fasten to the existing back wall

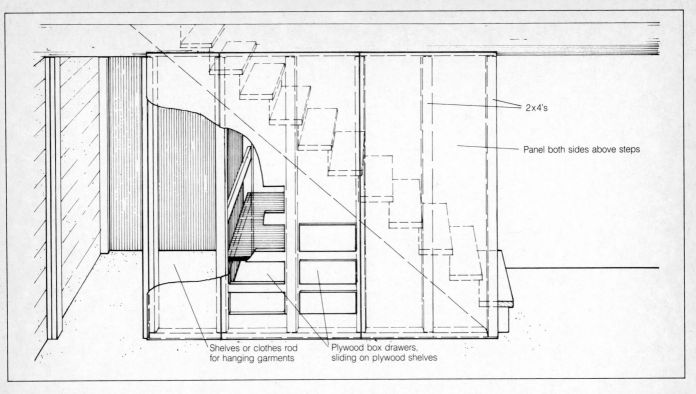

Shelves or clothes rod for hanging garments

Plywood box drawers, sliding on plywood shelves

2 x 4's

Panel both sides above steps

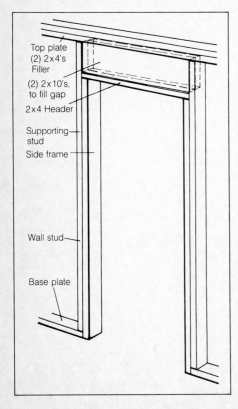

Top plate
(2) 2 x 4's
Filler
(2) 2 x 10's, to fill gap
2 x 4 Header
Supporting stud
Side frame
Wall stud
Base plate

under the stairs. Position the 2 x 4s so each is directly across from a stud in the wall-stud section you have just constructed. If the existing back wall is masonry, use masonry nails, or anchors if the drawers will hold much weight. Decide on the heights of your drawers, and their sizes. Attach 2 x 2 stock spanning between the studs and the 2 x 4s you just fastened to the back wall, using angle irons and screws. These 2 x 2s serve as supports for the plywood shelves on which your drawers will rest. Attach the ½ inch plywood shelves to the 2 x 2 supports with 1½ inch nails.

Construct drawers to your size requirements, allowing for clearances. If you will be using the drawers frequently or be loading the drawers with heavy material, be sure to install hardware and rollers. If you will not be using the drawers frequently, install a guide strip, which has been cut from ¼ inch plywood, on the center of the underside of the drawer, running from front to back. Attach two similar guide strips on the plywood shelf, positioned to hold the drawer guide. At the back of the drawer, nail two short strips perpendicular to the guide. Set these far enough from the guide on the drawer bottom so the guides on the shelf will not touch them. Near the front edge of the support shelf, nail two small blocks, located so they will meet and catch the two perpendicular strips on the drawer bottom. These will serve as drawer stops and prevent your accidentally pulling the drawer all the way.

Sand the exposed sides of the drawer and shelf guides until very smooth and apply wax or soap as a lubricant.

If you will cover the face of the stud wall with paneling, measure for the location of the drawer openings in relation to the wall panel. Mark these and cut them out with a keyhole or saber saw. Nail the paneling into place. The cutouts should line up exactly with the drawer positions. Apply the cutouts to the faces of the drawers so that the drawer faces will match the pattern of the panel. They will be unobtrusive — a good feature if the drawer sizes are varied and the edges of your drawers do not line up horizontally.

The area which has the highest clearance under your stairs can become a closet. The space can be adapted to your needs with shelves and/or closet pole(s), with or without a door. If the space is generous and you plan to hang heavy winter garments or large garment bags, it is advisable to use a length of galvanized plumbing pipe for your closet pole. Set the ends in brackets screwed onto 2 x 4 studs. Support the center with a length of metal strapping fastened to a ceiling joist. As mentioned previously, if your stairs offer access from both sides, you may be able to install the closet with access from one side, and shelves with access from the other side.

CLOSET/CUPBOARD UNDER STAIRS

Materials List

2 x 4s for studs
½" plywood for drawers and shelves (drawer supports and closet shelves)
2 x 2 for shelf supports
¼" plywood or paneling for covering stud wall and frawer faces
¼" plywood for drawer guides and stops
2 x 10s to fill gap above header

Hardware

Drawer hardware and pulls as required
Closet pole and brackets
Metal support strap
Nails, screws
Angle irons (1") for shelf supports

Two uses for the Pegboard cabinet are shown here. The cabinet on the left is used as an ordinary coat closet. The drawer at the bottom provides off-season storage for boots or mittens. The Pegboard also provides a hanging place for the scissors cap rack. The right side has been extensively adapted for athletic equipment. To give more hanging space, an extra vertical partition has been added. It is held securely by a combination of rabbets and dadoes. The Pegboard divider cover extends beyond the frame and fits into the dadoes.

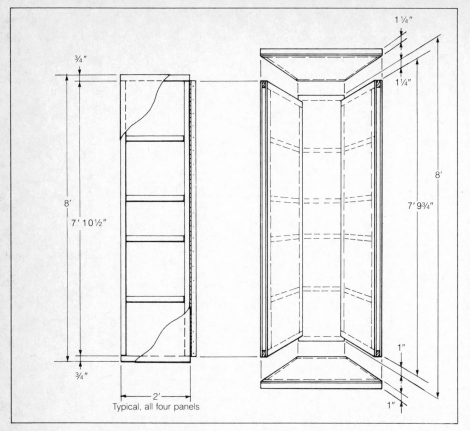

3/4"

1 1/4"

1 1/4"

8'

8'

7' 9 3/4"

7' 10 1/2"

1"

3/4"

2'
Typical, all four panels

1"

Freestanding Pegboard Closet

A free-standing cupboard/closet can be used anywhere in a room — as a divider, in a corner, or in any other open space. The version shown here uses Pegboard to give extra usefulness to the backs and doors. Even the closet pole is supported by the Pegboard.

Pegboard is easy to install. It may be hung with screws and neoprene washers over a solid surface, or, as in this case, glued and nailed to a framework.

This cupboard/closet is constructed of 1 x 1 stock frames that are covered with Pegboard on the inside and with paneling or plywood on the outside. This double unit sits on a base of 2 x 4 faced with paneling. If your space requirements are small, you could build one unit. If you need more storage, you might build several.

Construction Steps. Each unit consists of a series of frames. There is a top, a bottom, a back, two sides and a door. The back and the door frames are identical; the top and bottom frames are identical; the side frames are identical. The total height of the cupboard/closet is 8 feet plus the base, which is a separate unit. When measuring for construction, remember that plywood and paneling are 1/4 inch thick and 1 x 1 stock is actually 3/4 inch by 3/4 inch. The total exterior measurement of the unit shown at left is: height,

8 feet; depth, 27 inches; width, 24 inches.

Top and bottom frames each consist of two pieces of 1 x 1 stock 24 inches long, and two pieces 22 1/2 inches long for the square frame, with one piece 22 1/2 inches long for a center brace. Use butt joints; nail and glue the frames together. Nail the brace in the center of the frame.

Side frames each consist of two pieces of 1 x 1 stock 24 inches long, and two pieces 7 feet 8 1/4 inches long; 22 1/2 inch braces are also required. These should be located approximately every 18 inches to give stability and maintain the square of the frame. Because the braces also serve as support for your shelves, adjust the location to the positions you want for the shelves. Add extra braces if necessary. The braces and frames are glued and nailed together. The top and bottom pieces overlapping the side pieces of 1 x 1 stock.

Back and door frames are each constructed of two pieces 24 inches long and two pieces 7 feet 10 1/2 inches long. These frames also use 22 1/2 inch braces. Glue and nail the frame, with top and bottom 1 x 1 pieces overlapping the long side pieces. Add bracing. The location of the braces in the back must align with the location of the bracing on the sides for shelf support. The bracing in the door may be spaced approximately 18 inches apart, for stability.

Measure the Pegboard and cut to sizes to fit the frames. Glue and nail in place. Cover the inside faces of the frames with Pegboard.

Assemble the cupboard/closet with wood screws. Attach top and bottoms to the sides. The sides butt against, and are overlapped by, the top and bottom sections. Turn the unit over and attach the back. All pieces fasten flush to the back edges.

Now measure the inside dimensions to determine the exact size for your shelves. The interior width should be approximately 22 inches, with a depth of 24 inches. Cut 1 x 1 stock as required for your shelves, including one cross brace per shelf. Cover the shelves with Pegboard or plywood as you wish. Paint or finish the shelves and the Pegboard interior before installation.

To install shelves, drill pilot holes through braces in the back and sides of the cupboard, starting the pilot holes through the Pegboard holes. Drive wood screws through the pilot holes into the braces, until tips of screws are visible from the inside. Now have a helper hold the shelf in place, or brace it in position. Drive the screws all the way into the 1 x 1 frame of the shelf. Repeat for all shelves.

Cover the exterior as desired. Hang the door using a piano hinge. Install the magnetic catches and door pull.

Drawers are constructed of 1/2 inch plywood to your size and style requirements. Mount with side hardware.

The base is a framework of 2 x 4s. To provide a base for a pair of cupboard closets, the frame should be 8 feet long and 24 inches deep. Locate cross bracing so that wood screws can be driven through the cross bracing in the bottom of the cupboard/closet, into the cross bracing of the base. Face the base with paneling to match the cupboard/closet, or paint.

Place the units of the base; secure with wood screws as directed above. At two or more places, join the cupboards with nut and bolt sets pushed through the Pegboard of adjoining faces.

PEGBOARD CLOSET

Materials List

1 x 1 Stock for frames
4 x 8 Sheets Pegboard for interior
1/4" Plywood or paneling for exterior and
    shelves
2 x 4 Stock for base

Hardware

Piano hinges for doors
Magnetic catches
Nails and screws

Attic Closets

These built-in closets were added when the attic as a whole was finished off. Before any other work was carried out, however, the walls and the ceiling were insulated.

Construction Steps. The closets were created by building and installing partitions following the steps and the procedures discussed earlier under "Building a Corner Closet." The major difference is that each closet unit is open to the room rather than being closed off against the wall. The stud framing was covered with gypsumboard on the side facing the interior of the closets. The side of the partition facing the sloping edge of the ceiling, (behind the closets) was left unfinished. This back area was left for extra storage.

As shown, short divider partitions were constructed and then attached at right angles to the back partition. The ends of these shorter walls, facing into the room, served as members to which the shuttered doors could be attached. The partition ends were first covered with narrow door casing — the casing was fastened with finishing nails. Then the casing was finished, and the hardware and the doors were installed. The series of doors forms an entire wall of floor-to-ceiling closets.

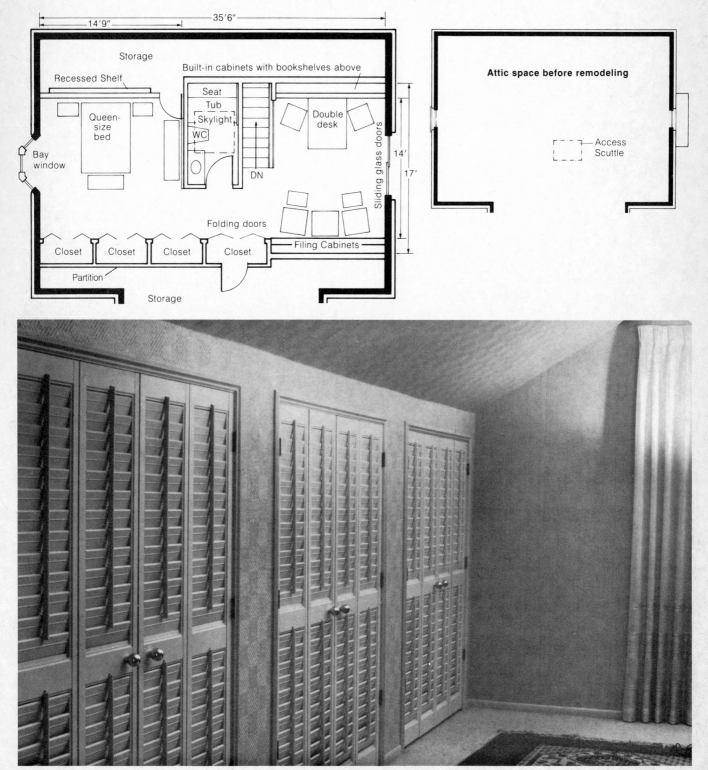

Wasted space was transformed when this attic was finished off. Louvered doors provide ventilation for stored articles in this set of closets.

SPECIALTY CLOSETS

Most of the time we think of closets as spaces behind doors where we hang clothes. This is not an immutable law. Just as one may put more than brooms in a broom closet, other things can be put into "clothes closets." The next few pages offer pictures of closets that have been put to different uses or designed in different styles, but are within the capabilities of most homeowners.

Dust-free Closet

This unit was designed and built specifically in order to store materials in a dust-free environment. The construction is that of an ordinary, built-to-fit cabinet. However, some small adjustments have been made to keep the interior as free of airborne dust as possible without installing special air filters.

The sides and center vertical support are made of smooth particleboard, routed so that support pilasters are set flush with the surface. 1 x 8 stock is ripped down and glued and nailed to exposed edges of particleboard to provide strong anchoring surfaces for hinges. These also protect the edges from wear and abrasion. The shelves are ¾ inch plywood, sanded and sealed.

The plywood doors are mounted so that their horizontal edges are even with the outside edges of the top and bottom shelves. The insides of the doors touch the edges of the shelves. The doors close tightly and are held in place by friction catches. The center edges of the doors are spaced to allow clearance, and the narrow, open gap is covered with a piece of lath. Foam weatherstripping has been applied to the cabinet walls where they meet the doors so that when the doors are closed they press against the foam. This weatherstripping is available at most hardware stores. It is usually ¼ inch thick, in widths of ¼ inch to 2 inches, or more. It is self-adhesive and comes in white, black or grey.

DUST/FREE CLOSET

Materials List

1 pc.   lath at door joint
Foam weatherstripping, cut to height
2 pcs.   4 x 8 — ¾" Particleboard
5 pcs.   4 x 8 — ¾" Plywood good 1 side
1 pc.   1 x 8 Pine, few knots (must be tight)
2 pcs.   1 x 2 x 8' hinge filler strips, rip to fit at sides and center
2 x 4s for base

Hardware

8   3" Steel T hinges (no screws)
4   Friction catches (not magnetic)
12   6' KV Standards with 84 clips

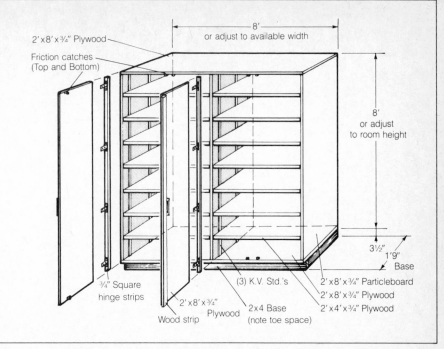

Half of this open shelf storage unit was adaped to provide a dust-free closet by adding a set of doors fitted with weatherstripping and a lath strip to overlap the center gap.

A well-equipped wet bar is built into this closet. There is room for glasses, ice bucket and blender as well as work space. Doors conceal the bar.

Thoughtfully designed closets can be too beautiful to hide behind doors. This closet provides a decorative accent as well as storage.

A laundry room was created in this narrow area by stacking the washer and dryer in a closet. Open shelves are used for laundry and cleaning supplies and towels.

A shallow area is all that is needed for a small pantry closet in or near a kitchen.

Index

LUMBER

Sizes: Metric cross-sections are so close to their nearest Imperial sizes, as noted below, that for most purposes they may be considered equivalents.
Lengths: Metric lengths are based on a 300mm module which is slightly shorter in length than an Imperial foot. It will therefore be important to check your requirements accurately to the nearest inch and consult the table below to find the metric length required.
Areas: The metric area is a square metre. Use the following conversion factors when converting from Imperial data: 100 sq. feet = 9.290 sq. metres.

METRIC SIZES SHOWN BESIDE NEAREST IMPERIAL EQUIVALENT

mm	Inches	mm	Inches
16 x 75	5/8 x 3	44 x 150	1¾ x 6
16 x 100	5/8 x 4	44 x 175	1¾ x 7
16 x 125	5/8 x 5	44 x 200	1¾ x 8
16 x 150	5/8 x 6	44 x 225	1¾ x 9
19 x 75	¾ x 3	44 x 250	1¾ x 10
19 x 100	¾ x 4	44 x 300	1¾ x 12
19 x 125	¾ x 5	50 x 75	2 x 3
19 x 150	¾ x 6	50 x 100	2 x 4
22 x 75	7/8 x 3	50 x 125	2 x 5
22 x 100	7/8 x 4	50 x 150	2 x 6
22 x 125	7/8 x 5	50 x 175	2 x 7
22 x 150	7/8 x 6	50 x 200	2 x 8
25 x 75	1 x 3	50 x 225	2 x 9
25 x 100	1 x 4	50 x 250	2 x 10
25 x 125	1 x 5	50 x 300	2 x 12
25 x 150	1 x 6	63 x 100	2½ x 4
25 x 175	1 x 7	63 x 125	2½ x 5
25 x 200	1 x 8	63 x 150	2½ x 6
25 x 225	1 x 9	63 x 175	2½ x 7
25 x 250	1 x 10	63 x 200	2½ x 8
25 x 300	1 x 12	63 x 225	2½ x 9
32 x 75	1¼ x 3	75 x 100	3 x 4
32 x 100	1¼ x 4	75 x 125	3 x 5
32 x 125	1¼ x 5	75 x 150	3 x 6
32 x 150	1¼ x 6	75 x 175	3 x 7
32 x 175	1¼ x 7	75 x 200	3 x 8
32 x 200	1¼ x 8	75 x 225	3 x 9
32 x 225	1¼ x 9	75 x 250	3 x 10
32 x 250	1¼ x 10	75 x 300	3 x 12
32 x 300	1¼ x 12	100 x 100	4 x 4
38 x 75	1½ x 3	100 x 150	4 x 6
38 x 100	1½ x 4	100 x 200	4 x 8
38 x 125	1½ x 5	100 x 250	4 x 10
38 x 150	1½ x 6	100 x 300	4 x 12
38 x 175	1½ x 7	150 x 150	6 x 6
38 x 200	1½ x 8	150 x 200	6 x 8
38 x 225	1½ x 9	150 x 300	6 x 12
44 x 75	1¾ x 3	200 x 200	8 x 8
44 x 100	1¾ x 4	250 x 250	10 x 10
44 x 125	1¾ x 5	300 x 300	12 x 12

METRIC LENGTHS

Lengths Metres	Equiv. Ft. & Inches
1.8m	5′ 10⅞″
2.1m	6′ 10⅝″
2.4m	7′ 10½″
2.7m	8′ 10¼″
3.0m	9′ 10⅛″
3.3m	10′ 9⅞″
3.6m	11′ 9¾″
3.9m	12′ 9½″
4.2m	13′ 9⅜″
4.5m	14′ 9⅓″
4.8m	15′ 9″
5.1m	16′ 8¾″
5.4m	17′ 8⅝″
5.7m	18′ 8⅜″
6.0m	19′ 8¼″
6.3m	20′ 8″
6.6m	21′ 7⅞″
6.9m	22′ 7⅝″
7.2m	23′ 7½″
7.5m	24′ 7¼″
7.8m	25′ 7⅛″

All the dimensions are based on 1 inch = 25 mm.

NOMINAL SIZE	ACTUAL SIZE
(This is what you order.)	(This is what you get.)
Inches	**Inches**
1 x 1	¾ x ¾
1 x 2	¾ x 1½
1 x 3	¾ x 2½
1 x 4	¾ x 3½
1 x 6	¾ x 5½
1 x 8	¾ x 7¼
1 x 10	¾ x 9¼
1 x 12	¾ x 11¼
2 x 2	1¾ x 1¾
2 x 3	1½ x 2½
2 x 4	1½ x 3½
2 x 6	1½ x 5½
2 x 8	1½ x 7¼
2 x 10	1½ x 9¼
2 x 12	1½ x 11¼

NAILS

NUMBER PER POUND OR KILO / **LENGTH AND DIAMETER IN INCHES AND CENTIMETERS**

Size	Weight Unit	Common	Casing	Box	Finishing	Size	Length Inches	Length Centimeters	Diameter Inches	Diameter Centimeters*
2d	Pound	876	1010	1010	1351	2d	1	2.5	.068	.17
	Kilo	1927	2222	2222	2972					
3d	Pound	586	635	635	807	3d	1/2	3.2	.102	.26
	Kilo	1289	1397	1397	1775					
4d	Pound	316	473	473	548	4d	1/4	3.8	.102	.26
	Kilo	695	1041	1041	1206					
5d	Pound	271	406	406	500	5d	1/6	4.4	.102	.26
	Kilo	596	893	893	1100					
6d	Pound	181	236	236	309	6d	2	5.1	.115	.29
	Kilo	398	591	519	680					
7d	Pound	161	210	210	238	7d	2/2	5.7	.115	.29
	Kilo	354	462	462	524					
8d	Pound	106	145	145	189	8d	2/4	6.4	.131	.33
	Kilo	233	319	319	416					
9d	Pound	96	132	132	172	9d	2/6	7.0	.131	.33
	Kilo	211	290	290	398					
10d	Pound	69	94	94	121	10d	3	7.6	.148	.38
	Kilo	152	207	207	266					
12d	Pound	64	88	88	113	12d	3/2	8.3	.148	.38
	Kilo	141	194	194	249					
16d	Pound	49	71	71	90	16d	3/4	8.9	.148	.38
	Kilo	108	156	156	198					
20d	Pound	31	52	52	62	20d	4	10.2	.203	.51
	Kilo	68	114	114	136					
30d	Pound	24	46	46		30d	4/4	11.4	.220	.58
	Kilo	53	101	101						
40d	Pound	18	35	35		40d	5	12.7	.238	.60
	Kilo	37	77	77						
50d	Pound	14				50d	5/4	14.0	.257	.66
	Kilo	31								
60d	Pound	11				60d	6	15.2	.277	.70
	Kilo	24								

*Exact conversion

WOOD SCREWS

SCREW GAUGE NO.	NOMINAL DIAMETER Inch	NOMINAL DIAMETER mm	LENGTH Inch	LENGTH mm
0	0.060	1.52	3/16	4.8
1	0.070	1.78	1/4	6.4
2	0.082	2.08	5/16	7.9
3	0.094	2.39	3/8	9.5
4	0.0108	2.74	7/16	11.1
5	0.122	3.10	1/2	12.7
6	0.136	3.45	5/8	15.9
7	0.150	3.81	3/4	19.1
8	0.164	4.17	7/8	22.2
9	0.178	4.52	1	25.4
10	0.192	4.88	1 1/4	31.8
12	0.220	5.59	1 1/2	38.1
14	0.248	6.30	1 3/4	44.5
16	0.276	7.01	2	50.8
18	0.304	7.72	2 1/4	57.2
20	0.332	8.43	2 1/2	63.5
24	0.388	9.86	2 3/4	69.9
28	0.444	11.28	3	76.2
32	0.5	12.7	3 1/4	82.6
			3 1/2	88.9
			4	101.6
			4 1/2	114.3
			5	127.0
			6	152.4

Dimensions taken from BS1210; metric conversions are approximate.

BRICKS AND BLOCKS

Bricks

Standard metric brick measures 215 mm x 65 mm x 112.5. Metric brick can be used with older, standard brick by increasing the mortaring in the joints. The sizes are substantially the same, the metric brick being slightly smaller (3.6 mm less in length, 1.8 mm in width, and 1.2 mm in depth).

Concrete Block

Standard sizes

390 x 90 mm
390 x 190 mm
440 x 190 mm
440 x 215 mm
440 x 290 mm

Repair block for replacement of block in old installations is available in these sizes:
448 x 219 (including mortar joints)
397 x 194 (including mortar joints)

PIPE FITTINGS

Only fittings for use with copper pipe are affected by metrication: metric compression fittings are interchangeable with Imperial in some sizes, but require adaptors in others.

INTERCHANGEABLE SIZES mm	INTERCHANGEABLE SIZES Inches	SIZES REQUIRING ADAPTORS mm	SIZES REQUIRING ADAPTORS Inches
12	⅜	22	¾
15	½	35	1¼
28	1	42	1½
54	2		

Metric capillary (soldered) fittings are not directly interchangeable with imperial sizes but adaptors are available. Pipe fittings which use screwed threads to make the joint remain unchanged. The British Standard Pipe (BSP) thread form has now been accepted internationally and its dimensions will not physically change. These screwed fittings are commonly used for joining iron or steel pipes, for connections on taps, basin and bath waste outlets and on boilers, radiators, pumps etc. Fittings for use with lead pipe are joined by soldering and for this purpose the metric and inch sizes are interchangeable.

(Information courtesy Metrication Board, Millbank Tower, Millbank, London SW1P 4QU)

Acknowledgments

We wish to extend our thanks to the individuals, associations and manufacturers who generously provided information, photographs, line art, and project ideas for this book. Specific credit for individual photos, art and projects is given below with the names and addresses of the contributors.

Allmilmo Corporation c/o Hayes-Williams, Incorporated, 261 Madison Avenue, New York, New York 10016 *cover, 16 upper.*

American Olean Tile 2583 Cannon Avenue, Lansdale, Pennsylvania 19446 *2, 9 lower, 11 lower, 12 lower left, 81, 82.*

American Plywood Association Box 119 A, Tacoma, Washington 98401 *8 top, 27, 29 upper, 34 lower left and right, 37 upper right and center right, 38 center, 39 upper and center right, 41, 42 right, 47 center right, 52, 53, 54, 58, 60, 61, 62, 63, 64, 104-106, 115, 112-114, 126-127, 136-137.*

Charles Auer EGO Productions, 1849 North 72nd Street, Wauwatosa, Wisconsin 53213 *66 lower right, 75.*

Azrock Floor Products P.O. Box 531, San Antonio, Texas 78292 *18 top.*

Bell System Yellow Pages c/o Cunningham and Walsh, 260 Madison Avenue, New York, New York 10016 *90-91, 115, 132-133, 134-135.*

Bendix Molding Incorporated 235 Pegasus, Northwall, New Jersey 07647 *22 lower left.*

Black & Decker Manufacturing Company East Joppa Road, Towson, Maryland 21204 *23.*

California Redwood Association 1 Lombard Street, San Francisco, California 94111 *12 upper left, 19, 25, 100-101, 102-103, 116-117 (as seen in* Popular Mechanics© *1979 by the Hearst Corporation), 119, 130-131.*

Formica Corporation Wayne, New Jersey 07470 *22 lower, 107, 120-121, 124-125, 128-129.*

Marlite Division/Masonite Corporation Dover, Ohio 44622 *96-97.*

Georgia-Pacific Corporation 900 South West 5th Street, Portland, Oregon 97204 *14.*

Maytag Company Newton, Iowa 50208 *10 right, 17.*

Minwax 72 Oak, Clifton, New Jersey 07014 *68-69.*

Richard V. Nunn Media Mark Productions Falls Church Inn, 6633 Arlington Boulevard, Falls Church, Virginia 22045 *26 lower, 28 upper, 29 lower right, 30 lower right, 31 upper left, 32 left, 42 lower left, 85.*

Nutone Division Madison and Red Bank Roads, Cincinnati, Ohio 45227 *16 lower right.*

Poggenpohl U.S.A. Corporation P.O. Box 10-F, Teaneck, New Jersey 07666 *13 right.*

Strahan c/o Lis King; P.O. Box 503, Mahwah, New Jersey 07430 *12 upper right.*

Summitville Tile c/o Belden Franz Lahman, 1400 Keith Building, Cleveland, Ohio 44115 *11 upper right.*

Tile Council of America c/o Lis King, P.O. Box 503, Mahwah, New York 07435 *11 upper left.*

U.S. Forest Products Laboratory Madison, Wisconsin 53706 *72-73.*

James Eaton Weeks Interior Designs, Inc. 223 East Silver Spring Drive, Milwaukee, Wisconsin 53217 *71.*

Wood-Mode Cabinets c/o Faltz-Wessinger, Inc, 800 New Holland Avenue, Lancaster, Pennsylvania 17604 *16 lower left.*

Wood Moulding and Millwork Producers P.O. Box 2578, Portland, Oregon 97225 *13 lower left, 20.*

Western Wood Products Association Yeon Building, Portland, Oregon 97204 *5, 8 lower, 10 top, 15, 18 lower, 108-110 (as seen in* Popular Mechanics© *1979 The Hearst Corporation).*

CLOSETS SUPPLEMENT CONTRIBUTORS

Allmilmo Corporation *156.*
American Olean Tile *155 lower.*
American Plywood Association *152.*

Craig Buchanan Photographer, 490 2nd Street, San Francisco, California 94107 *147.*

William Manley Interior Design, 6062 North Port Washington Road, Milwaukee, Wisconsin 53217 *154.*

Laura Odell Kitchen Design, 130 East 75th Street, New York, New York 10021 *156.*

John Ward Carpentry, 8419 West Hillview Drive 114N, Mequon, Wisconsin 53092 *148-149.*